BEYOND

Northwestern University
Studies in Phenomenology
and
Existential Philosophy

BEYOND

The Philosophy of Emmanuel Levinas

Adriaan Theodoor Peperzak

Northwestern University Press
Evanston, Illinois

Northwestern University Press
Evanston, Illinois 60208-4210

Copyright © 1997 by Northwestern University Press.
Published 1997.

Second paperback printing 1999

Printed in the United States of America

ISBN 0-8101-1481-X

Library of Congress Cataloging-in-Publication Data

Peperzak, Adriaan Theodoor, 1929–
    Beyond : the philosophy of Emmanuel Levinas / Adriaan Theodoor
Peperzak.
        p. cm. — (Northwestern University studies in phenomenology &
existential philosophy)
    Includes bibliographical references and index.
    ISBN 0-8101-1481-X (pbk. : alk. paper)
    1. Lévinas, Emmanuel. I. Title. II. Series.
B2430.L484P44 1997
194—dc21   97-17519
                                                                        CIP

The paper used in this publication meets the minimum requirements of the
American National Standard for Information Sciences—Permanence of Paper
for Printed Library Materials, ANSI Z39.48-1984.

In Memory of

Hannie Lenglet-Peperzak

† 8 July 1996

Contents

Preface

Although Emmanuel Levinas is now widely respected as one of the classic thinkers of our century, the debate about his relevance is still going on. Studies on his philosophy should help readers to understand the originality of his method and show how his transformation of philosophy contains promises for further developments.

This book presents Levinas's thought as a persistent attempt to point beyond the borders of an economy where orderly interests and ways of reasoning make us feel at home—beyond the world of needs, beyond the self, beyond politics and administration, beyond logic and ontology, even beyond freedom and autonomy. Desire drives the self out of its circularity into an exodus, an extraordinary but humble kind of transcendence that follows the trace of an immemorial past. Obsessed by the Other, historical through and through and yet transcendent, religious without betraying the earth—such is the existence reflected in Levinas's surprising search for a truth that resists our wish for conceptual domination. Few adventures in philosophy are more exciting than taking part in such an exploration of the radical intrigues that constitute a human life.

The first six chapters of this book concentrate on explanation and commentary. I refrain from criticism here, trying instead to act as an interpreter and friend.

Chapter 1 gives a general overview of Levinas' life and thought. The text was originally written as an entry for the *Encyclopedia of Phenomenology* (Boston: Kluwer, 1996).

Chapters 2 and 3 situate Levinas's thought by sketching his Jewish background and the way he interprets the Talmudic tradition he draws on when he does not limit himself to strictly philosophical work. The second chapter ("Jewish Existence and Philosophy") is the thoroughly revised text of a lecture given at Yale University on 18 October 1982 and published in *Philosophy Today* 27 (1983), while chapter 3 ("Judaism According to Levinas") grew out of a talk on Levinas's attitude toward Judaism and Christianity which I gave in 1990 at Brigham Young University at the invitation of the philosophy department.

Chapter 4 ("From Phenomenology through Ontology to Meta-physics") summarizes the development of Levinas's relations to Husserl and Heidegger from the time of his dissertation until 1950, when he published his most explicit farewell to Heidegger, "Is Ontology Funda-mental?" The first version of this chapter was presented in September 1981 at Duquesne University, under the title "Phenomenology-Ontology-Metaphysics: Levinas's Perspective on Husserl and Heidegger." It was published in *Man and World* 16 (1983).

In chapter 5 ("From Intentionality to Responsibility") I show more thematically how Levinas transforms phenomenology by rooting its basic principle, intentionality, in the more radical quasiprinciple of responsi-bility. The first version of this chapter was presented in October 1987 as a plenary address to the annual conference of the Society for Phenomenol-ogy and Existential Philosophy at the University of Notre Dame, and was published in *The Question of the Other: Essays in Contemporary Continental Philosophy* (Albany: SUNY Press, 1989).

As the source of responsibility, "substitution" is the central topic of Levinas's second *opus magnum, Otherwise than Being or Beyond the Essence* (1974). In its first chapter Levinas gives a summary of this difficult book. "Through Being to the Anarchy of Transcendence" (my sixth chapter) offers an interpretation of that summary. Some parts of this text were submitted for discussion at the "Sophia" Conference of 23–25 October 1992 at Penn State University.

Chapters 7–11 treat some topics on which Levinas has taken a clear but controversial position. Although here, too, I try to explain Levinas's position as fairly as possible, I do not refrain entirely from taking a critical perspective, and some passages point in the direction of non-Levinasian thoughts that are or will be developed elsewhere.

Chapter 7 ("The Other, Society, People of God") draws on Levinas's work for a reflection on the difficult but urgent question of how inter-subjectivity, sociality, and community (and consequently ethics, politics, and religion) are intertwined. This chapter is the English translation of a paper in French ("Autrui, Société, Peuple de Dieu") which was discussed at the 1986 Colloquium "Castelli" in Rome and published in *Intersoggettività Socialità Religione* (*Archivio di Filosofia* 54 [1986]. The English version was first published in *Man and World* 29 (1996).

"Technology and Nature" (chapter 8) is a discussion of Levinas's anti-Heideggerian view of technology and his critical attitude with regard to any enthusiasm about nature. The text was first published in *Man and World* 25 (1992).

Chapters 9–12 belong together. In "Presentation" (chapter 9) I analyze Levinas's interpretation of skepticism as an expression of the impossibility of reducing speaking (or writing) to spoken (or written) texts. The first version of "Presentation" was a contribution to the Levinas conference held at the University of Essex on 27–29 May 1987, and was published in *Re-Reading Levinas* (Bloomington: Indiana University Press, 1991). God or the Good is the topic of the next two chapters. "Transcendence" (chapter 10) was presented at the international Levinas conference held at Loyola University Chicago, 20–24 May 1993, and published in *Ethics as First Philosophy* (New York: Routledge, 1995). "Passages" (chapter 11) is the English translation of a French text ("Passages") which appeared in the volume *Emmanuel Levinas*, as part of the series *Les Cahiers de l'Herne* (Paris: L'Herne, 1991).

In chapter 12, "Becoming Other," I respond to Levinas's conception of the relations between morality and religion by defending the purity of authentic mysticism. This chapter is the English version of "Devenir autre," which was written for a *liber amicorum* that was to have been offered to Levinas on the occasion of his seventieth birthday (1976) but appeared only in 1980, *Textes pour Emmanuel Levinas* (Paris: Place, 1980).

"Becoming Other" also belongs to a group of chapters in which I confront Levinas with other thinkers: Eckhart (chapter 12), Kant and Hegel (chapter 13), Heidegger (chapters 4, 8, and 14) and Wyschogrod (chapter 15).

"*Il y a* and the Other" (chapter 13) shows a certain similarity between Levinas's "there is" and Hegel's concept of nature, and compares Levinas's description of the ethical relation with Kant's conception of respect. I offer here a thoroughly reworked version of a paper presented at the Levinas symposium organized in April 1982 by the philosophy department of the State University of New York at Stony Brook. That paper was published as "Some Remarks on Hegel, Kant and Levinas" in *Face to Face with Levinas* (Albany: SUNY Press, 1986).

Levinas's relations to Heidegger demand special attention because of their characteristic mixture of proximity and separation. There are several reasons why a clarification of these relations is particularly difficult. Few Heidegger scholars are satisfied with Levinas's interpretations of his former master. The keywords both authors use (such as "being," "ontology," "metaphysics," "nature," "God," "technique," "philosophy," "conscience," etc.) do not have the same meaning; they evoke profoundly different contexts and traditions of life and thought, but it is not easy to point out what exactly goes awry in Levinas's unilateral discussion of Heidegger. It is relatively easy to show how Levinas understands and criticizes Heidegger, but it is extremely difficult to do justice to both authors and still bring them together from the perspective of a judge or a mediator who has a perfect insight into the problematic that is at stake in their oeuvres. I have not included in this book my own attempts at doing justice to both authors by overcoming their biases, because that would require me to present a more personal (neither Heideggerian nor Levinasian) way of thinking which would break the unity of this book. The essays that focus on Levinas's anti-Heideggerian polemics (chapters 8 and 14, and to a certain extent also chapter 4) remain Levinasian rather than trying to judge or reconcile both philosophers from a higher or more profound perspective. In chapter 8 I analyze Levinas's fiercest attack on Heidegger, and in chapter 14 I try to detect the core of their disagreement. The latter chapter ("On Levinas's Criticism of Heidegger") is the translation of "Einige Thesen zur Heidegger-Kritik von Emmanuel Levinas," which appeared in *Heidegger und die praktische Philosophie* (Frankfurt: Suhrkamp, 1987).

The closing chapter is a homage to Edith Wyschogrod, who introduced Levinas's work to North American readers through her book *Emmanuel Levinas: The Problem of Ethical Metaphysics* (The Hague: Martinus Nijhoff, 1974) and many other publications that testify to the fecundity of Levinas's inspiration. The text of this chapter was presented at a session on Wyschogrod's work at the SPEP meeting held in Boston 8–11 October 1992.

Since most chapters of this book grew out of separate papers given over the last fifteen years, some repetitions and overlaps are almost inevitable, though I tried to eliminate the unnecessary ones as much as I could. I do not want to base my apology for the remaining repetitions on the fact that Levinas's own work, like that of Heidegger, Hegel, Kant, and other discoverers, is full of repetitions, for their groundbreaking work was much more original than my explanations. However, I hope that the shift of thematic perspectives presented in the different chapters compensates for the advantages of a more linear and "(re)constructive" book that could have been written, although I am not sure that it would adequately fit Levinas's style of thought.

Many friends were involved in the production of this book, too many to be named here. My special thanks go to Catriona Hanley, who translated the first, French versions of chapters 7, 11, and 12, and revised the English of several others; to Aron Reppmann, who translated chapter 14 from German and ameliorated the English of other chapters; to Beth Spina and Katrine Poe, who, together with Aron Reppmann, rectified my English and inscribed the entire manuscript on disk with great patience and accomplished skill.

Acknowledgments

For permission to print new versions of formerly published parts of this book, I thank the following journals and presses: *Philosophy Today* (chapter 2), Kluwer (chapters 3, 4, 7, and 8), SUNY Press (chapters 5 and 13), *Archivio di Filosofia* (chapter 8), Indiana University Press (chapter 9), Routledge (chapter 10), L'Herne (chapter 11), Jean-Michel Place (chapter 12), and Suhrkamp (chapter 14).

Abbreviations of Works by Levinas

AE *Autrement qu'être ou au-delà de l'essence.* Phaenomenologica, vol. 54. The Hague: Martinus Nijhoff, 1974; 8th edition, Dordrecht: Kluwer, 1988.

AV *L'au-delà du verset: Lectures et discours talmudiques.* Paris: Minuit, 1982.

CP *Collected Philosophical Papers.* Translated by Alphonso Lingis. The Hague: Martinus Nijhoff, 1987.

DEE *De l'existence à l'existant.* Paris: Vrin; 1st edition, 1947, 2d edition, 1978.

DL *Difficile liberté: Essais sur le Judaisme.* 2d ed. Paris: Albin Michel, 1976.

DMT *Dieu, la mort et le temps.* Paris: Grasset, 1993.

DVI *De Dieu qui vient à l'idée.* Paris: Vrin, 1982.

EDHH *En découvrant l'existence avec Husserl et Heidegger.* 3d ed. Paris: Vrin, 1974.

EE *Existence and Existents.* Translated by Alphonso Lingis. The Hague: Martinus Nijhoff, 1978.

EI *Ethique et infini.* Paris: Librairie Arthème Fayard, 1982.

EN *Entre nous: Essais sur le penser-à-l'autre.* Paris: Grasset, 1991.

EV *De l'évasion.* Paris: Vrin, 1981. 1st ed., 1935.

HAH *Humanisme de l'autre homme.* Montpellier: Fata Morgana, 1976.

HN *A l'heure des nations.* Paris: Minuit, 1988.

HS *Hors sujet.* Montpellier: Fata Morgana, 1987.

IH *Les imprévus de l'histoire.* Montpellier: Fata Morgana, 1994.

NP   *Noms propres.* Montpellier: Fata Morgana, 1976.

OB   *Otherwise than Being or Beyond Essence.* Translated by Alphonso Lingis. The Hague: Martinus Nijhoff, 1981.

PP   "Paix et proximité." In *Les Cahiers de la Nuit Surveillée,* vol. 3: *Emmanuel Levinas.* Lagrasse: Verdier. 339–46.

QLT   *Quatre lectures talmudiques.* Paris: Minuit, 1968.

SF   "Sécularisation et faim." In *Herméneutique de la sécularisation.* Paris: Aubier-Montaigne, 1976. 101–9.

SS   *Du sacré au saint.* Paris: Minuit, 1977.

TA   *Le temps et l'autre.* Montpellier: Fata Morgana, 1979.

TaI   *Totality and Infinity: An Essay on Exteriority.* Translated by Alphonso Lingis. The Hague: Martinus Nijhoff, 1969.

TeI   *Totalité et infini: Essai sur l'extériorité.* The Hague: Martinus Nijhoff, 1961.

TIH   *Théorie de l'intuition dans la phénoménologie de Husserl.* Paris: Félix Alcan, 1930.

TrO   "The Trace of the Other." Translated by Alphonso Lingis. In *Deconstruction in Context.* Edited by M. Taylor. Chicago: University of Chicago Press, 1986. 345–49.

Tra   "La trace de l'autre." EDHH, 187–202.

Other Abbreviations

GA   Martin Heidegger. *Gesamtausgabe.* Frankfurt: Klostermann.

HU   Edmund Husserl. *Husserliana: Gesammelte Werke.* The Hague: Martinus Nijhoff, 1950–.

SZ   Martin Heidegger. *Sein und Zeit.* 7th ed. Tübingen: Niemeyer, 1953.

Since I published a commentary on *Totality and the Infinite* in *To the Other: An Introduction to the Philosophy of Emmanuel Levinas* (Lafayette: Purdue University Press, 1993), I will sometimes refer to this work as *To the Other,* in order to prevent repetitions.

Emmanuel Levinas

E mmanuel Levinas was born in Kaunas (Lithuania) on 12 January 1906 (or, according to the Julian calendar, which was used then, on 30 December 1905).[1] His parents were practicing Jews and members of an important Jewish community where the study of the Talmud was practiced at a high level. As a child, Emmanuel learned to read the Bible in Hebrew, while Russian was the language in which he was educated. This enabled him to read the great novelists and poets Pushkin, Gogol, Dostoyevsky, Tolstoy, etc., writers who, together with Shakespeare, remained important to his thinking. In 1916, during the First World War, the family moved to Charkow in Ukraine, where Emmanuel attended the high school and experienced the upheaval of the Revolutions of February and October 1917.

In 1920, the family returned to Lithuania. In 1923, Emmanuel traveled to Strasbourg, where he matriculated at the University, after having studied Latin for one year. In his autobiographic "Signature" (1963 and 1966), as well as in the interview *Ethique et Infini* (1982), he mentions Charles Blondel, Henri Carteron, Maurice Halbwachs, and Maurice Pradines as the four professors who for him embodied all the virtues of the French University. These years also mark the beginning of his lifelong friendship with Maurice Blanchot.

Having obtained his *license* in philosophy, on the advice of Gabrielle Peiffer, with whom he later translated the *Cartesian Meditations* (1931), Levinas began his study of Husserl's *Logical Investigations*. Phenomenology, and especially the analysis of intentionality and its horizons, revealed entirely new ways of thinking, different from intuition, induction, deduction or dialectics. Levinas decided to write a dissertation on Husserl's theory of intuition and spent the academic year 1928–29 in Freiburg-in-Breisgau, where he gave a presentation in one of Husserl's last seminars. It was Heidegger, however, who, through his *Sein und Zeit* and his teaching, impressed Levinas as the greatest innovator and one of the very great thinkers in the ranks of Plato and Kant. In 1929, Levinas attended the famous encounter between Cassirer and Heidegger in Davos, where he explained parts of *Being and Time* to some French scholars. After returning to Strasbourg, he defended his dissertation entitled *La théorie de l'intuition dans la phénoménologie de Husserl* (1930), which received a prize from *l'Institut*. This book had been preceded by a long review article on Husserl's *Ideas* I in the *Revue Philosophique de la France et de l'Etranger* (1929). Through these and later publications on Husserl and Heidegger, Levinas introduced phenomenology to Sartre and other key figures of postwar French philosophy.

In 1930, Levinas became a French citizen; he married, performed his military service in Paris, and got a job in the school of the Alliance Israélite Universelle in Paris. This institution was a center which strived to emancipate Jews from countries around the Mediterranean such as Morocco, Tunisia, Algeria, Turkey, Syria, etc., through education. At the Sorbonne, Levinas attended the courses of Léon Brunschvicg and—though irregularly—the famous lessons of Alexandre Kojève on Hegel's *Phenomenology of Spirit* at the *Ecole des Hautes Etudes*. There he also met Sartre, Hyppolite, and other future celebrities and participated in the monthly soirées of Gabriel Marcel.

In his early Parisian years, Levinas started writing a book on Heidegger, but abandoned this project when Heidegger became involved with the Nazis. A fragment of the book entitled "Martin Heidegger et l'ontologie," which was perhaps the first essay on Heidegger in French, was published in 1932. His next essay on Heidegger did not follow until 1948 and was the Spanish translation of a paper which Levinas had given in 1940 to the students of Jean Wahl at the Sorbonne. The French text appeared in 1949 in a collection of Levinas's articles on phenomenology, *En découvrant l'existence avec Husserl et Heidegger* (1949; augmented edition 1967).

Levinas's first thematic essay, "De l'évasion," was published in 1935. In retrospect, the central question of his later work can be recognized in it: Is it possible to transcend, in thinking, the horizon of Being? Although the question was not expressed in a polemical way, this essay was a first attempt by Levinas to wrestle free from Heidegger's "ontology" (as Levinas consistently calls Heidegger's "thought of Being").

In 1939, Levinas was called to serve in the war, where he functioned as an interpreter of Russian and German, and in 1940 he became a prisoner of war. As a French officer, he was not sent to a concentration camp but rather to a military prisoners' camp, where he did forced labor in the forest. During his captivity he also read and discussed Hegel, Proust, Diderot, Rousseau, and others, while most members of his family in Lithuania were murdered by the Nazis. According to his own words, the forebodings, the reality, and the memory of the Holocaust have always accompanied Levinas's thinking.

His first personal book, most of which had been written during his captivity, appeared in 1947, shortly after the war had ended. Its title, *From Existence to Existents* (*De l'existence à l'existant*), clearly proclaims the need for a thought beyond ontology; it reverses the orientation of Heidegger's thought, which aims to transcend the "metaphysics" of beings (*Seiendes l'étant, l'existant*) to Being (*Sein, être, existence*). Levinas points to another transcendence: the Good commands an exodus beyond the limits of Being. This book had been preceded in 1946 by the publication of a fragment of it under the title *Il y a*. The expression "*il y a*" translates the German *es gibt* (there is), but it receives an interpretation which is very different from Heidegger's: rather than the generosity of a radical Giving, *il y a* is the name of a dark and chaotic indeterminacy that precedes all creativity and goodness. It was not until 1951, however, in the article *L'ontologie est-elle fondamentale?*, that Levinas presented an explicit critique of Heidegger's enterprise.

In the context of postwar existentialism, where Marcel, Sartre, Camus, and others determined the philosophical scene, Levinas's first thematic publications went almost unnoticed, due perhaps to their originality and extreme difficulty. Another publication of 1947 drew more attention however. On invitation of Jean Wahl, professor of philosophy at the Sorbonne and director of the para-universitarian *Collège Philosophique*, Levinas gave a series of four lectures on "Time and the Other" ("Le temps et l'autre") during the academic year 1946–47. The text of these lectures was published in the same year as part of a collective book entitled *Choice-World-Existence*. Despite its still partially experimental character, it already expressed the core of all of Levinas's later work: the Other is the center, and time, as ultimate horizon, determines the relations between the Other and me.

Until 1961, Levinas was known as a specialist of Husserlian and Heideggerian phenomenology, but his modest number of publications in the field of philosophy was no reflection of the fact that one of the most important thinkers of the century was preparing an impressive oeuvre. His contributions to philosophy seemed far outweighed by his numerous essays on questions related to Jewish spirituality. Given his involvement in the education of foreigners at the Alliance's school, of which he had become the director in 1947, and the fact that he did not hold an academic position at the French University, his influence in philosophy was limited, as compared to his growing impact in the field of Jewish studies. After the war, he studied the Talmud under some of the best scholars and, in 1957, began giving a personal kind of talmudic lessons at the annual Colloquium of Jewish Intellectuals of French expression. His philosophical fame was, however, established when he published *Totalité et Infini: Essai sur l'extériorité* (1961). This book was the main thesis which he presented for his *doctorat d'Etat,* while the collection of his already published philosophical works was accepted as the complementary thesis. Soon his international fame led to many invitations, prompting the production of an overwhelming number of papers in philosophy. In 1961, Levinas became professor of philosophy at the University of Poitiers, and in 1967 he was appointed to the University of Paris-Nanterre. From there he moved to the Sorbonne (Paris IV) in 1973, where he became an honorary professor in 1976.

Totality and the Infinite[2] proposes a revolution, not only in phenomenology, but with regard to the entire history of European philosophy, from Parmenides to Heidegger. It even contains a critique of the whole of Western civilization, marked by the spirit of Greek philosophy. Western thought and practice are ruled by a desire for totalization; an attempt is made to reduce the universe to an originary and ultimate unity by way of panoramic overviews and dialectical syntheses. This monism must be criticized in the name of a thought that starts from the phenomena as they present themselves. Such a critique meets old traditions of thought that reach back to Biblical and Talmudic sources, but it is also perceptible in Plato and Descartes. Against Western totalitarianism, Levinas maintains that the human and the divine Other cannot be reduced to a totality of which they would only be elements. A truthful thought respects the nonsynthesizable "separation" that characterizes the relations between the Other and me, or—to borrow the terminology of Plato's *Sophistes*—it respects the irreducible nonidentity of the Same (*tauton*) and the Other (*to heteron*). The Same is clearly connected to the traditional subject, the ego or the Consciousness of modern philosophy, a subject for whom the totality of beings is spread out as a panoramic universe, but the Other is associated with the Infinite. Whereas the category of *totality* summarizes the way in which the ego inhabits the world—its worldly economy—*the Infinite* names the Other's ungraspable or incomprehensible character. "The Other" is in the first place the other human being I encounter; in a later development it also stands for God. Levinas refers to Descartes's third *Metaphysical Meditation* for a formal analysis of the relation that simultaneously links and separates the infinite and the ego, whose consciousness originarily contains "the idea of the infinite," and thus thinks more than it can fathom. His own, more concrete approach, is given through a phenomenology (or "transphenomenology") of the modes in which the human Other is revealed to me. The Other's face or speech (or any other typically human aspect that reveals the Other) is revealed as a refutation of any totalitarian or absolutistic form of economy. Thus, the Other presents him- or herself neither as a phenomenon in the normal sense of phenomenology, for which all phenomena belong to wider horizons, nor as a being within the totality of beings. "The Face" transcends all phenomenality and beingness and is, in this sense, "invisible," other than being, "ab-solved" and "absolute." Ego's contact with the Other's face or speech is incomprehensible but not unreal. It cannot be expressed in an ontological framework; the description must also use ethical terminology. To encounter another is to discover that I am under a basic obligation: the human Other's infinity reveals itself as a command: the fact of the Other's "epiphany" reveals that I am his or her servant.

The intentional (or rather quasi-intentional) analysis of the relation between the Other and me reveals an asymmetrical relationship which precedes every possibility of choice or decision. The tension between this asymmetry and the economy of ego's enjoyment of the world is unfolded in analyses of all the topics of twentieth-century philosophy, such as freedom, language, corporeality, sensibility, affectivity, work, history, love, death, etc., and many consequences for a radical transformation of phenomenology are made explicit. In constant discussion with Heidegger, Levinas struggles to develop a nonontological language in order to express the beyond of Being, but, in doing so, he uses that very same language to overcome it. This struggle continues to lead in a direction which can already be perceived in those parts of the book that were written last.

After 1961, Levinas produced a considerable number of texts in which his second *opus magnum* was prepared. This was published in 1974 under the title *Autrement qu'être ou au-delà de l'essence.* Clearer than *From Existence to Existents* and *Totality and the Infinite,* this title, a double translation of Plato's characterization of the Good as "beyond the *ousia,"* declares its intention to overcome ontology. Surprisingly new descriptions of Being, interest, sensibility, language, ethics, etc., are given. The asymmetrical relation between the Other and me is further analyzed as contact, being touched, proximity, vulnerability, responsibility, substitution, being a hostage, obsession, and persecution. Time is analyzed as radical diachrony. The unchosen character of responsibility is unfolded as a passivity more passive than the passivity that is opposed to activity. *"Me voici"* (see me here; here I am) is shown to precede any self-consciousness, and God is referred to as having passed into an immemorial past, a passing which has left a trace from which the human Other rises up as primary command.

The difficulty with any attempt to think beyond Being lies in the philosophical unavoidability of a thematizing language. In thematizing the asymmetry of substitution, Levinas's text betrays the nonobjective, nonthematic, and nonontological nature of that asymmetry. The resulting incongruency is made explicit in the distinction between the Saying (*le Dire*) and the Said (*le Dit*). Philosophy produces instances of the Said, but every Said is preceded and transcended by a Saying, to which the Said must be brought back. This reduction refers all philosophical texts to the proximity of "the-one-for-the-other." If philosophy is love of wisdom, it is also, and primarily, the wisdom of love.

The fact that Levinas not only published a great deal on topics related to Judaism, but writes on God and religion in his philosophical work too, has induced some interpreters to think that Levinas offers a masked theology instead of a phenomenologically rooted philosophy. *Difficile liberté* (1963, 1976), *Quatre lectures talmudiques* (1968), *Du sacré au saint* (1977) and *L'au-delà du verset* (1982) show his attachment to the Talmudic tradition; *De Dieu qui vient à l'idée* (1982) is an example of his philosophical concern about the question of God. Levinas, however, without ever denying his roots, always insists on the philosophical character of his work assigned as such. In his philosophical studies he operates in a manner similar to Descartes, Hegel, or Heidegger; even when he quotes from the Bible, his argumentation does not appeal to extraphilosophical authorities. All people able to read his texts are invited to validate the truth of his arguments on the basis of their own experiences and thought. However, as a language that strives for universality, philosophy does not exclude the explicit and implicit thoughts of particular traditions and spiritualities.

Jewish Existence and Philosophy

L evinas's thought has at least two main sources of inspiration: the experience of Jewish life in intimate contact with the Hebrew Bible, and the European tradition of philosophy and literature. However, according to his autobiographical note, "Signature," his life has also been "dominated by the premonition and the remembrance of the nazi horror" (DL, 374). *Otherwise than Being or Beyond Essence* is dedicated "to the memory of those who are closest among the six million murdered by the National Socialists besides the millions and millions of human beings of all confessions and all nations, victims of the same hatred of the other humans, of the same antisemitism." This dedication shows—and this will be one of the topics on which this chapter concentrates—that anti-Semitism is for Levinas the equivalent of antihumanism, and that to be a Jew is identical with being authentically human.

The reading of the great Russian novelists, who continually asked questions about the meaning of human life, and an early love of Shakespeare's *Hamlet, Macbeth,* and *King Lear* prepared Levinas for the study of Plato, Descartes, Kant, Bergson, and Heidegger, all of whom asked similar questions in different ways. In a series of radio talks broadcast in February and March of 1981, Levinas calls philosophy "thought that directs itself to all humans" (*penser en s'adressant à tous les hommes*), (EI, 19), and not only to those who share the particular convictions of the thinker. Isn't philosophy, as the activity by which universal reason—as universal as humanity—produces universally valid discourses, opposed to the particularism of discourses appealing to specific traditions or experiences? Before we can answer this question we should find out whether the Western way of philosophical thinking is as universal as it claims. Hasn't Heidegger shown that Western philosophy, from Plato to Nietzsche, speaks a particular, objectifying and manipulative, language, and that it relies on certain unquestioned presuppositions? And isn't it commonly said that *the* language of philosophy is Greek, although it has been translated, with more or less success, into Latin, from the sixteenth century on into French and English, from the eighteenth century on into German, and since a century or so ago also into American? The desire and the claim of every philosopher is to speak in the name and at the service of *all* people. But is anyone able to speak a universal language? Can thought wrestle free from the particular experiences, traditions, readings, and instructions in which it is rooted?

One of Levinas's achievements is his diagnosis of Western philosophy as a way of thought in which specific attitudes and perspectives reveal themselves. Though his criticism of the occidental way of life and thought would probably have been impossible if he had not been educated as Jew, the means through which he justifies his diagnosis and his own perspective are emphatically philosophical. More precisely stated, his method is a personalized version of the phenomenological techniques inaugurated by Edmund Husserl and transformed by Martin Heidegger.

Before discussing the relations between Jewish experience and philosophy in the work of Emmanuel Levinas, we must clearly identify his message and the way in which he claims to have shown its truth. I will begin with his critique of Western thought, a critique that includes not only the classical texts of philosophy, but also the ideology expressed in the occidental lifestyle, practice, planning, and technology.

The expression "Western philosophy," as it is used by Levinas and other French philosophers since Heidegger, describes the average knowledge of a French university professor concerning European traditions. It stresses the modern characteristics of our culture, ignores for the most part Medieval philosophy, and identifies the Greek heritage mainly with selected texts of Parmenides, Heraclitus, Plato, Aristotle, and Plotinus. A more precise study of the spiritual and attitudinal history of the Western world would certainly reveal the inadequacy of the way in which we have been accustomed to discussing our past, but the central issue here is not a historical one. Rather, we wish to understand what motives and choices dominate our own habitual understanding of the world, God, society, ourselves, and our past—an understanding that seems to be natural and to be supported by the best representatives of our culture.

According to Levinas, Western philosophy from Parmenides to Heidegger, is an *egology*. The discourses in which it has expressed itself display a universe centered around an ego that not only functions as subject of the "*cogito*," but also as the center and end of the world and the source of all its meaning. Egology is the theoretical side of a more fundamental attitude: the egocentrism of Western civilization realizes itself in a peculiar way of life, of which philosophy is the theoretical counterpart. Objectification, material enjoyment, and the privilege accorded to seeing, manipulation, planning, and exploitation form a pattern which could be characterized by the word "egonomy": the world of Western culture is ruled by ego's law. To characterize the Western project, Levinas himself uses the word "economy," in the etymological sense of a life-pattern subordinating everything to the establishment and maintenance of a house or home. The "law" (*nomos*) of ego's "home" (*oikos*) rules the universe.

The second part of *Totality and the Infinite*, titled "Interiority and Economy," is dedicated to a series of refined phenomenological analyses in which Levinas takes up and partially refutes, partially corrects, Heidegger's famous description of "being-in-the-world" (SZ, secs. 14–24). Instead of beginning with *Befindlichkeit*, Levinas starts with enjoyment (*jouissance*) (TeI, 82–125; TaI, 110–42). I "live on" (*je vis de*) or I feast on the elements: I breathe the air, and feel the warmth of the sun on my skin; I walk on the earth and rest on its solid support; I enjoy swimming in the surrounding water. As a humanly living being, the ego is primarily characterized by a spontaneous egoism: love of life, happiness, and self-centered affectivity are the central concerns. This ego-centered dimension of human existence constitutes an individual's independence separating him or her from all other individuals. The elementary affectivity of enjoyment explains the fact that each ego is unique and radically solitary.

Levinas continues his discussion with Heidegger's *Sein und Zeit* by showing that human existence is not primarily thrown into a world of things that are ready-at-hand (*Zuhandenes*), but rather a way of being at home in the world (TeI, 125–31; TaI, 152–56). A human dwelling (*la demeure*) is not a tool or utensil, but my private domain, the concrete form of my intimacy presupposed by all possibilities of using and discovering things in the worldly network of utilitarian relationships. Being at home in the world has neither the structure of a subjective activity or passivity in the face of objects, nor the meaningful coherence of a hammer, nails, a wall, and a painting, as described by Heidegger (SZ, secs. 16ff.). The home precedes the world of the useful. It is the elementary center of the human condition. More than once, Levinas observed that hunger and food are absent from Heidegger's world. The same could be said of the intimacy of a home, although the later Heidegger has written in a beautiful—too beautiful—way about "the real plight of dwelling" and our task of "bringing dwelling to the fullness of its essence."[1] As the vital basis of material satisfactions the house has been ignored in his work, however.

Being somewhere at home, I am able to go out into the world, to discover and exploit its possibilities. Only by having a place of my own can I bring other beings into my presence, represent them and make them into objects that I can observe, handle, and transform by labor and study within the framework of scientific theories (TeI, 131–49; TaI, 158–

74). The existence of objects, objectifying theories, industry, planning, technology, administration, and politics presupposes rulers who believe themselves to be centers of the universe and who transform that universe into a domain for their power and sovereignty. On the level of philosophy, such a world expresses itself in a systematic vision according to which the universe appears as a totality of beings unfolding their features, essences, and relationships before a panoramic *cogito* as wide as the horizon of that totality. The presence of all beings in one whole, experienced by one encompassing consciousness, is the egological world of Western philosophy. This world can also be characterized by the word "ontology," insofar as the intentional correlate of the central ego coincides with the totality of all beings seen as grounded in or given by Being itself. God then becomes either the ground, as first, highest, and most fundamental of all beings, or He coincides with the totality insofar as it originates and gathers the parts or "moments" of which it is composed. Heidegger's description of Western metaphysics as onto-theo-logy is reinterpreted by Levinas as a manifestation of the natural egoism which constitutes the elementary level of human life. This reinterpretation places Heidegger's "thought of Being" under the same verdict, however. According to Levinas, Heidegger's attempt to overcome onto-theo-logy by asking the forgotten question of Being itself—as essentially different from the collectivity of beings—fails for the following reason. If Being is considered to be the first and ultimate, then it is inevitably conceived of as a totality and, therefore, as excluding the possibility of real infinitude. The gods (*die Götter*) and "the God" (*der Gott*), of whom Heidegger sometimes speaks, cannot be infinite since they appear within the horizon of a more radical, though still finite, horizon: Being. Although Levinas regards Heidegger as one of the greatest philosophers of the entire history, he claims Heidegger's thought is still dominated by the traditional tendency to totalization. This might also explain why Heidegger could collaborate—though briefly— with the most horrible expression of that tendency: Nazism.

Heidegger would certainly reject the thesis that the way in which he himself questions Being implies a sort of holism. Levinas, however, would maintain that Being itself, as distinguished from single beings, cannot mean anything other than either (1) something common to all beings (rejected by Heidegger in the beginning of *Sein und Zeit*), (2) their encompassing horizon, e.g., the light in which, or the openness thanks to which, all beings appear; (3) the totality of beings in which their differences are immersed and drown; or (4) the oceanic fund from which all beings emerge. In this chapter, I will not dwell on this most difficult question. Together with the question of the relations between Heidegger and Levinas, it will occupy us in chapters 4, 6, and 15. For now it is sufficient that we have an idea of Western philosophy and of the word "totality" as understood by Levinas.

The most adequate example of philosophical totalitarianism, fitting perfectly into Levinas's descriptions, is Hegel's system, which, in this respect, can be considered to be the completion of our philosophical history. In what is perhaps too Hegelian of a conception of philosophy's history, Levinas extends his diagnosis to all the heroes of Western thought:

> Everywhere in Western philosophy, where the spiritual and the meaningful are always located in knowledge, one can see this nostalgia for totality. As if the totality were lost and this loss were the sin of the spirit. Truth and spiritual satisfaction are only reached by a panoramic vision of reality. (EI 80–81)

Levinas's criticism, as well as his orientation, are summarized by the title of *Totality and the Infinite*. The idea of the Infinite (*l'idée de l'Infini*) cannot be reduced to or developed from the idea of totality.[2] The universe of egocentrism is separated by an abyss from the manifestations of the Infinite. In order to distinguish between the "manifestation" or "monstration" of the phenomena which are all finite, and the infinity of the Infinite, Levinas uses the words "revelation" and "epiphany" to describe the latter. These words do not refer to anything thaumaturgic or "supernatural" or theological; rather, they indicate *the* wonder: the wonder that distinguishes humans from self-centered forms of life. This wonder is revealed in the epiphany of the Other: another man or woman or child that emerges "in" (or over against) my world. When I encounter another human, I become aware that "economy" is not an appropriate response to this event. The Other condemns my monopoly of the world and imposes an infinite number of demands on me by simply appearing. The Other's face, the fact that he or she looks at me, makes me responsible for the Other's existence, life, and behavior.

In order to avoid misunderstandings, I would like to state, as clearly as possible, that Levinas explicitly recognizes the positive and necessary aspects of the practical and theoretical totalizations produced by all people in every civilization. More than once he insisted that a systematic totality is indispensable for human practice and theory; what he fights against is not totality as such, but rather its absolutization: totality cannot be the ultimate. Science and technology, economy, law and justice, administration and politics would be impossible if we were not allowed to see and treat the facts and beings of our world as factors within possible networks and as elements of planning and organization. A just world demands institutions by which human beings are *also* treated as elements of larger wholes, numbered, weighed, used and seen, as parts that do not live for themselves alone. A society would die if it were not held together by collective regulations. As Kant put it, respect for humans as "ends" does not exclude that they are *also* treated as means.[3]

This cannot be the whole of social truth, however. If collective organization and politics were the highest perspective, individual life would not have an absolute worth in itself. Kant would say that such a view denies humans their dignity (*Würde*) which is incomparable to, and not exchangeable with, any value (*Wert*).[4] All totalities must be subordinated to a higher criterion which maintains the dignity of the individual.

The radical originality of Levinas's philosophy lies in the formulation of this highest criterion. It is not the "human essence" (*die Menschheit*) common to all human beings, myself included, as Kant claims; it is the epiphany of the Other's face and speech rupturing the homogeneity of my universe and breaking its totality. The mere fact of another's existence dethrones me and makes me into a subject in the strong sense of someone who supports the Other's life and is responsible for it. Such a subject is rather a servant than a sovereign (AE, 125–66; OB, 99–129).

The force of economy and egology is condemned and broken by the asymmetry of the interpersonal relationship, not by a fundamental equality of subjects having the same human rights. Indeed, the idea of a human essence that makes us equals presupposes a perspective transcending the community of all individuals. Who looks from that perspective? Who is capable of taking a place above the collectivity of all humans? Doesn't such a perspective presuppose an egological and totalitarian point of view? Speech presupposes another standpoint. When I speak, I address myself to another person who reveals that my monopoly has come to an end. She robs me of my sovereignty, but thereby frees me from solitude. The first social relationship is characterized by a radical dissymmetry. The mere existence of another human—not his decisions or choices—commands me. I look up to another as to someone who imposes respect and devotion. The Other is characterized by "height" or "highness" (*hauteur*). The absoluteness with which the Other's existence transcends the claims of my self-centered universe by more radical demands, is what Levinas calls its infinity. The Other (*to heteron*) comes from beyond all appearances and transcends the horizon of Being itself. This explains the title of *Otherwise than Being or Beyond Essence*. Adopting Plato's characterization of the Good as "not an *ousia*" but "beyond the *ousia*" (*Republic* 509b), while simultaneously hinting at Heidegger's ontology, Levinas points to the Infinite by stating that it "is" in another way than beings. Its way is not "essence" (*Anwesen* or "*essence*") but otherness (AE, 3–25; OB, 3–20).

The asymmetry of the basic social relation can easily be misunderstood as a simple reversal of the inequal relationship implied by the monopolistic attitude of a solitary ego. The latter functions as the starting point of various social theories in the style of Hobbes, according to whom the "wolfish" nature of humans must convert itself into a more "divine" one by means of a fundamental revolution. Some hasty readers of Levinas's work have misunderstood him to be a moralist or even a preacher who protests against the widespread treatment of other humans as slaves or servants. His oeuvre would tell us for the nth time: You must be the servant of your neighbor! I don't think that anyone should be ashamed of proclaiming or repeating this biblical admonition if it can be done in a nonmoralistic and nonpaternalistic way. Levinas's philosophical message is different, however. He does not write an ethics, but shows, by means of subtle descriptions and analyses, that the ethical perspective must be the starting point of every philosophy that hopes to be true to the *facts*. The discovery that I am a subject who is infinitely responsible for the Other's life—a discovery immediately "given" in any encounter—answers questions like "what is there?" and "how and why are there beings?" by transforming their meaning and status: "is," "Being," "essence," etc., reveal themselves subordinate to my responsibility for others. This discovery is the beginning of all self-knowledge and all knowledge in general. The search for knowledge is redeemed from its natural tendency to egocentrism by a unique revelation of the absolute.

To ease the understanding of his analyses, Levinas sometimes refers to our experience of being more obliged toward others than justified to impose demands on them. I may dedicate and even sacrifice my own life for you, but when I oblige you to sacrifice your life for me, I am a murderer. The basic asymmetry of the social relation is also expressed in a phrase of Dostoyevsky often quoted by Levinas: "We are all responsible before all for everything and everybody, and I more than others."[5] Ethics, taken radically, is not a discipline to be developed on the basis of a theoretical foundation given by epistemology and/or ontology. The epistemological question as to how we know "other minds" and, more generally, how knowledge relates to objects, presupposes a precise description of the peculiar mode in which another appears and an analysis of speech as revealing a speaking existence that cannot be reduced to a moment of my consciousness. The most radical forgetfulness in philosophy is not its neglecting the question of Being, but rather its insensitivity to face and speech, for it is there that the Infinite reveals itself to me.

Devotion is not primarily a nice attitude to be preached, but the most intimate structure that constitutes me as *subject*. I am *sub-jectus*, "sub-ject-ed" to the Other, bearer of an endless responsibility for the

Other's existence. The structure of "the-one-for-the-Other" constitutes me as a unique individual, because nobody can replace me for the task it implies. To have a conscience means that I am conscious of being infinitely responsible for others. I am a hostage (*otage*) for the Other. My life is "substituted" for the Other's. I am responsible not only for the satisfaction of your hunger, but also for your behavior and guilt, even for your discriminating against or persecuting others, including myself (AE, 148–51; OB, 116–18).

If Levinas's description of the Infinite is faithful to the facts, human existence is the contrary of a force that ruthlessly conquers a realm of its own against similar attempts made by others. The subtle violence of our behavior is detected by Levinas, as it was by prophetic authors from Amos and Ezekiel to Pascal, Dostoyevsky, and Claudel. At the opening of *Otherwise than Being* a word of Pascal is quoted: "This is my place under the sun.' That is the beginning and the image of the usurpation of the entire world" (AE, vi). Against the tendency of the "Nietzscheans" who cultivate violence because it seems a primordial and irrepressible force, the moral experience reveals that I have not the right to live if my life means robbing or oppressing others (EI, 128–32). Proclaiming human rights is hypocritical and ridiculous if it covers a machinery of money-making and power-gathering paid for by its victims. Are we capable of inventing forms of behavior which correspond to the asymmetrical structure of intersubjectivity, or is our incapacity a reason for declaring Levinas's descriptions exaggerated and unreal?

Levinas's discovery of the Infinite, as the epiphany to which all other phenomena owe their ultimate meaning, has important consequences.

The epiphany of the Other subordinates the world of phenomena and experiences to responsibility. Insofar as we have learned the meaning of the words "phenomenon," "experience," "manifestation," "truth," etc., within the context of Western egology, they are all marked by the "egonomic" mode of being described above. As an intruder into this world, the Other, or the Infinite, can neither be described as an object of our knowledge, nor as a phenomenon in the proper sense of the word. The supreme demand is not "experienced" as a "presence" and, in its complete difference from any observable figure, the face is *invisible*. The invisible is, however, the closest and most intimate reality of our lives, because it commands and constitutes the innermore interiority of our selves. The absolute presents itself without being a phenomenon. Its presence is our awareness of a demanding obedience and humility.

In the name of this law, devoted to whomever we meet, we must establish a world of institutional justice, fair politics, and humane economy. Indeed, besides and behind this human Other, present here and now, who is the absolute for me, other human others present themselves. The absoluteness of their claim forbids me to concentrate on one to the exclusion of others. An unlimited extension, and therewith a limitation, of devotion is inevitable, but this does not lead back to egoism. The multiplicity of others constitutes a universal fraternity which must secure itself through the construction of a just society. Here lies the necessity of collective and totalizing views, planning, administration, and political strategy. All social institutions receive their inspiration from the asymmetrical relationship which has made me infinitely more responsible than any other.

The acceptance of this responsibility here and now is the heart of religion. "I am not afraid of the word 'God,' " says Levinas in the interview quoted above,

> The Face signifies . . . the Infinite. This never appears as a theme [i.e., as an object that we could posit, observe, study or discuss], but [only] in the ethical signification [i.e., in the signifying character of the asymmetrical relation] itself. The more I am just, the more I become responsible. One is never without debt with regard to another. (EI, 111)
>
> When I say before another "Here I am," this "Here I am" is the place where the Infinite enters into language, without, however, permitting me to see it (EI, 114).[6]

The fact of such a "Here I am" reverses the natural tendency of life's self-preference and of Being's *conatus* to persevere in existence. The possibility of *me voici* testifies that there is something higher than Being and life. The "otherwise than Being" is the glory of God (EI, 116 and AE, 187; OB, 146–47).

Who would not recognize this God as the God of Moses and the prophets? It is the God of human justice; not a mythical, mystical or sacramental God, insofar as such might imply a fusion of the finite with the Infinite. Levinas is following the sober and severe tradition of the Talmud when he refuses all forms of religious enthusiasm and participation, because he thinks that they endanger the purity of the prophetical inspiration. The austere figure of the pharisee—so slandered by the Christians—is the best example of loyalty to that spirit. But this spirit is not altogether different from the spirit that can be discovered by a philosophical analysis of human existence as such.

This brings us back to the question from which we began: How does Levinas's philosophy relate to the Jewish traditions and experiences by which his life has been determined? Let us first discard the idea that any philosophy is possible on the basis of purely formal procedures applied to experiences so trivial that a discussion about their evidence is superfluous. If we want to call such an enterprise "philosophical," we must add that it has little to do with the meditations to which the classics of Western thinking were devoted.

The ideal of *modern* philosophy is a theory that begins with universally evident elements, in order to build a generally acceptable, and in that sense objectively valid, system. But such an ideal expresses exactly what Levinas rejects: the idea that we could reach some Archimedean point from which we could overlook and conceptually master all beings, theories, cultures and ways of life. A thought which "addresses itself to all people" is hardly a thought if it has not addressed the most radical questions. This presupposes, however, that it has gone into the depths of the traditions from which it stems, integrating the heritage by which it has been nourished. Only by becoming a thoughtful exponent of my own history can I become a valuable participant in the discussion with other, equally particularized ways of seeking the universal and the One.

The reproach of some readers that Levinas contaminates philosophy with religious reminiscences can be responded to by quoting the following affirmations:

> I have never explicitly intended to "accord" or to "reconcile" the two [viz., the biblical and the philosophical] traditions. If they are in fact in agreement, this is probably due to the fact that all philosophical thought rests on pre-philosophical experiences and that the readings of the Bible belonged in my case to these fundamental experiences. The Bible has therefore played an essential role in my philosophical way of thought—for the most part, however, without my being conscious of it. (EI, 9)

This quote could be interpreted as a concession. Unconsciously Levinas would have been led more by his faith than by his "way of thinking philosophically." However, the agreement between his faith and his philosophy does not constitute an agreement against the authenticity of either philosophy or faith—unless we would accept a priori that philosophy and religion cannot agree. The only way to answer our question is of course by carefully studying the actual way in which Levinas's texts were written; however, the difficulty with which we have to struggle is that we cannot compare those texts with a ready-made rule or method on which we could agree in advance. For, Levinas, who learned the *métier* from Husserl and Heidegger, shows, in his descriptions, that the realities of human life—"*die Sache selbst*" and "the facts"—urge us to transform their phenomenological method into an approach more truthful to the singular kind of events and appearances we encounter in everyday life. Some interpreters think that Levinas's work only translates old convictions into

a phenomenological or quasi-phenomenological jargon, without adding
anything important to the actual practice of philosophy. I am afraid that
they do not see how radical a level is reached by Levinas's long meditation on the various Hebrew, Greek, Russian, Roman, and Germanic
components of history. Every human conscience can recognize, in one
way or another, the demands described in his works. "The ethical truth
is common." But

> that which is said to be written in the souls was first written in the
> books. I think that the human face speaks—or stammers or gives itself
> airs or fights with its caricatures—[not only in the Bible, but] in all
> literature. Notwithstanding the end of Eurocentrism disqualified by so
> many horrors—I believe in the eminence of the human face expressed
> in Greek literature and in our literature which owes everything to it.
> It is due to that literature that we are ashamed of our history. The
> national literatures, Homer and Plato, Racine and Victor Hugo [etc.]
> partake in Holy Scripture, just as Pushkin, Dostoyevsky or Goethe, and of
> course, Tolstoy and Agnon. But I am sure of the incomparable prophetic
> excellence of the Book of Books expected or commented on by all texts
> of the world. The Holy Scriptures do not signify through the dogmatic
> story of their supernatural or sacred origin, but through the expression
> and illumination of the other's face before he gives himself a countenance
> or takes a pose. This expression is as irrefutable as the concern for the
> everyday life of our historical world is imperious. (EI, 124–26)

To this convergence of philosophy and biblical religion, we must
first add that religion promises certain consolations which can neither
be denied nor affirmed by philosophy (EI, 121–22, 127), and, second,
that—contrary to an idea held by many philosophers from Parmenides
to Hegel—knowledge does not constitute the supreme perfection of
spiritual life. Ultimately, philosophy is no more than a commentary on
that which reveals itself as the absolute from beyond the essence: the
Good. The Good commands a turn toward the Other who does not leave
me enough time for a monopolistic universe. It urges me, like Moses,
to live for those who continue to live after my death. If philosophy is
inspired by this desire, it is not a desire for absolute wisdom, but a *sophia*
of *philia*, a "*sagesse du désir*" (AE, 195ff.; OB, 153ff.), a wisdom of desire
and proximity.

3

Judaism According to Levinas

Philosophy and Religion

The idea that philosophy could justify fully its own roots is as dead as modernity, of which it was a clear expression. Although it still has adherents among the academic population, none of the classical authors after Hegel has defended that idea or tried to show the possibility of its realization. In questioning incessantly its own emergence from the generations and corruptions of its past, contemporary philosophy analyzes the many prephilosophical—linguistic and literary, mythical and religious, political and economical, aesthetical, ethical and material—elements that have left their traces in thought or even determined its essence.

In reading Emmanuel Levinas, we are struck by many allusions to the Bible and the Talmud. The acquaintance with his "Talmudic lectures" and his nonphilosophical, more "parochial" essays gathered in *Difficile liberté* confirms the impression that the theses of his philosophy converge, or even coincide, with the convictions of his Jewish tradition. Hence, the suspicion might arise that Levinas's philosophical work, too, is the exposition of a belief or "faith" that cannot be proved to be true by philosophical means alone, especially when the difficulty of that work makes the reader believe that it is caused by a nonconclusive obscurity. Of course, the coincidence of philosophical truths with certain affirmations of a positive religion is neither an argument against such truths, nor against their philosophical character, but the defense of "typically Jewish" (or, for that matter, "Christian") theses in a book that claims to be philosophical intensifies the reader's vigilance and quest for proofs.

Here is not the place to treat the old and intricate problem of the relations between philosophy, on the one hand, and opinion, ethos, faith, and other beliefs, on the other, but let me at least state, in a rather dogmatic way, from which perspective I will treat the relations between

Levinas's Judaism and his philosophy. If we could agree on a definition or description that determines the task and the limits of philosophy in our time, the only way to check the philosophical character of Levinas's works would consist in their careful analysis and interpretation in light of the given definition. In no way, however, can we neglect the most fundamental ones amongst the existential experiences echoed in all serious philosophy. To what extent these experiences support the formulated thought and logic, to what extent they are fully integrated, translated into an argumentative or analytic language—such questions must be decided on the basis of standards and methods that are commonly applied to other texts claiming to be philosophical, metaphilosophical, or postphilosophical, like those of Hegel's *Philosophy of Religion*, Nietzsche's *Beyond Good and Evil*, or Heidegger's *On the Way to Language*. If philosophy is not an isolated compartment of human existence, it is necessarily intermingled with life's entire struggle for meaning and "wisdom"—a struggle that involves emotional and doxastic attachments to particular traditions. It will, therefore, hardly be possible to separate the strictly philosophical elements of a work from the existential and traditional elements by which it is generated, and vice versa.

It is my conviction that Levinas's philosophical work does not differ, in this respect, from that of other classical and contemporary philosophers. But in this chapter I will not try to prove that Levinas's basic beliefs are justified in a "purely" philosophical way. I rather will start from the other end of the relationships between philosophy and nonphilosophy, by giving a sketch of Levinas's Judaism, after which I will indicate briefly how important parts of his Jewish convictions can be recognized in the arguments developed in his philosophy. In other chapters of this book I stress the authenticity of Levinas's philosophical procedures, but for now I will concentrate on the fact that this thought is rooted in a specific mode of existence whose authenticity expresses itself also, but not only, in philosophy.

I. Judaism According to Levinas

Being myself a Christian, I cannot speak in the name of Jews about the meaning of their mode of existence and thought. Although I, too, hope to be a son of Abraham, I am aware of the great differences in religious practice and interpretation caused by two thousand years of separation in which Christianity betrayed so often its fidelity to Moses and the Gospel in treating Jews as scapegoats of the Christians' incapability of establishing a just and peaceful world. Not being a specialist of Jewish literature throughout the ages, I cannot offer either a balanced picture of all the varieties of Judaism that have marked our history or the actual situation. Most of my knowledge stems from biblical exegesis studied under the guidance of Christian specialists and from Levinas's writings on Judaism. In view of the purpose of this chapter I will limit myself, therefore, to a portrait of Judaism as described by Levinas, a description that appeals especially to the Talmud, but maintains a big distance toward kabbalistic and chassidic versions of Judaism. In drawing the portrait that follows, I am, thus, well aware that there are other respectable ways of belonging to Israel.

One more proviso is necessary. Levinas's description of authentic Judaism not only carries accents of a specific tradition, but is also characterized by an extreme modesty with regard to the most intimate elements of religion, as, for instance, prayer and emotions of hope, consolation or inner peace. His strong aversion against sentimentality and his hate of all exhibitionism forbids a complete exposition of the most consoling and mystical aspects of spiritual life.

God

Since religion seems always to imply a relation of human beings to God (or gods or some reality structurally akin to them), we might begin by asking how Levinas describes the Jewish way of relating to God. Now, one thing is clear, and throughout all his publications Levinas does not get tired of insisting on it: intimacy with God is primarily and basically obedience to his commandments; not knowledge about God's nature, thoughts, or deeds.[1] Even prayer does not mean anything if it is not accompanied by the practice of the Law of the Torah or if it is cut off from the solidarity with Israel and humanity as a whole (DL, 317, 319, 346–47). However, religious adherence expresses itself also in the invocation of God's name.

Among the many names of God the invocation "the Saint (blessed-be-He)" expresses the abyss that separates God from the universe (AV, 144; "Nom de Dieu"). "The saint" is beyond the essence of beings that can be gathered by a unifying intellect or will. It names a relation instead of an essence, like other names as, for instance, "Master of the world" or "Chekhina" (God's sojourn in the world, in the midst of Israel). God is not named as a principle of cosmology; he is neither found through an analogy between his nature and the nature of other beings, nor by a reduction of the world to an unconditional Ground or Absolute. God is "known" and glorified by obedience to his percepts. All God's names are gathered by "the Name," which functions as their genus. However, "the Name" or

"God" are no genera in the sense of universals that would encompass other possible instances of the same, as if God—as only one among many gods—were the highest or the only surviving god. The Unique and the gods do not belong to one family; they do not inhabit the same dimension and cannot be discovered by a final distinction within the dimension of the saint or the sacred.[2] God is absolutely unique and separate from anything else. He has no place in the space between heaven and earth; on the contrary, these belong to him, "with the entire firmament."

The invocation of God's name expresses an attitude that is radically different from any form of contemplation. Even theology is not an adequate attitude because it approaches God as a topic or theme of consciousness and reflection. Prayer is a more adequate response to his revelation, but the most adequate answer is the practice of his Law.

This conviction is expressed, for instance, in the old question of why the Bible begins with the story of creation, instead of giving the commandments of the alliance between God and Israel. Rachi (eleventh century) gives the following answer: If man did not know that the earth has been created by God, he would be a usurper. The promised land is received; what we possess is entrusted to us in order to be used for establishing justice (DL, 32–33; cf. AV, 170 [Révélation]). Without excluding completely the possibility of thematization, it must be stated firmly that religion is not in the first place acceptance of certain truths as "articles of faith" (cf. AV, 165–69 [Révélation]). Being not a dogmatic religion, Judaism does not have a highest magisterium or an official catechism in which its faith is summarized. Religion should not either be equated with a theology or a *Weltanschauung*.

The Jewish religion is also very different from all sorts of *enthusiasm* for the sacred, however. By trying to overwhelm and inebriate the human spirit, mythical gods and demons invite us to participate in their mysteries, but this seduction is a subtle and sublime form of violence. It will be followed by the human sacrifices that are demanded by all idols (DL, 29–31, 44, 72). The biblical God is not the heir or master of the gods; he demands full human responsibility and human proximity. God is not a survivor of the mythical tradition, for none of the idols can destroy another one (DL, 29–30). All idols must be destroyed, not sublimized. The religious relation to the Infinite does not resemble ecstatic or oceanic feelings of absorption in the One-and-All of romantic pantheism; it remains at a distance from the raptures by which the sacred overwhelms the longing mind.

> The numinous or the sacred wraps and transports humans beyond their power and will. But true freedom takes offence at these uncontrollable

excesses. The numinous annuls the relationships between persons by making beings participate—albeit in ecstasis—in a drama that is not wanted by these beings, in an order in which they dissolve. This somehow sacramental power of the divine is seen in Judaism as an insult to human freedom and as contradicting human education, which remains an action with regard to a free being. . . . The sacred that wraps me up and transports me is violence.[3]

As a religion of the spirit Judaism is an atheism with regard to all gods; it understands all human experiences as relations between free intelligence in the clear light of consciousness and language. Atheism with regard to the one and only God is better than mythical piety, because monotheism presupposes that one has become adult by traversing the doubts, the rebellion and the solitude engendered by the "all too human" images of God that are the "normal" ones.

It is a great glory for the Creator to have put into existence a being that affirms him after having contested and denied him by involvement in myths and enthusiasm. It is a great glory for God to have created a being capable to search for him or to hear him from afar, starting from separation, from atheism. (DL, 31)

Ethics

As free obedience, religion is an ethical relationship. The personal rela-
tion to a personal God coincides with the ethical relationship to other human persons. Religious intimacy is the welcoming of the stranger, the clothing of the naked, the protection of the orphan.

A host of texts from the Bible and the Talmud can be quoted for this coincidence of authentic religion and ethical goodness with regard to the human Other. It dominates the entire Jewish life, as well as the talmudic interpretation of the Bible. For Levinas's philosophy it is the background for his analyses of transcendence, ethics, metaphysics, and all other topics to which his attention is drawn.

For Christians the coincidence of love and obedience toward God and love for other humans should not be a foreign idea, since for them, as heirs of Moses, too, the coincidence of the first two commandments belongs to the core of their faith. From their sources Levinas sometimes quotes Matthew: "Lord, when did we see you hungry or thirsty or a stranger or naked or sick or in prison? . . . Truly, I say to you, as you did it (not) to one of the least of these, you did it (not) to me." One could also quote the letter of James: "Religion that is pure and undefiled before

God, the Father, is this: to visit orphans and widows in their affliction, and to keep oneself unstained from the world."[4]

If the aversion to violence is a distinctive feature of a truly spiritual religion, Judaism must fight the arbitrary and irrational forces of the mythical and magical. Instead of Dionysian rapture it venerates the naked face and the speech of the human person appealing to me in the clarity of obligations (DL, 21, 23, 70–73). If the opposite of this ethical spiritualism can be called "materialism," we understand why Levinas can write: "The adherence of the sacred is infinitely more materialistic than the proclamation of the—undeniable—value of bread and steak in people's life," and "the material needs of my neighbor are spiritual needs for me." Jewish spirituality is intimately bound to the earth and far from a "Platonic" contempt for the body and its pleasures. "Great is eating! The other's hunger—a carnal one, a hunger of bread—is sacred" (DL, 20, 12; cf. 216). To enjoy life is a necessity; but to obey the law is to give, and this implies a very concrete donation of food and shelter. Justice includes a rearrangement of the economy of earthly goods. The ethical relationship cannot be limited to a practice that is based on the conviction that all humans are equal in having basic rights, being citizens of democratic institutions, members of one human race. This conviction of all honest people since the French Revolution is not alien to the Judeo-Christian roots of the Western civilization, but the Thora is more profound and more demanding. The Other comes from "on high," is superior to me, not necessarily, of course, in the sense of superior intelligence, skills, talents, virtues or holiness, but as a human existence that, in its poverty and needs, surprises and inevitably obligates me. The relation revealed in any encounter is a relation of *in*equality and height, a relation of asymmetry. The appearance of another in the world, which is also mine, reveals to me that I am a servant, responsible for this Other's life and destiny.

> The fundamental intuition of morality is perhaps the discovery that I am not equal to the other, namely in this very rigorous sense: I know that I am obligated with regard to the other, and consequently I demand infinitely more from myself than from others. "The more I am just, the more severely I will be judged" says a talmudic text. (DL, 39)

This "teaching," too, cannot be foreign to a Christian conscience aware of sentences like these: "Whoever would be great among you must be your servant, and whoever would be first among you must be slave of all" (Mark 10, 43–44), or: "Do nothing from selfishness or conceit, but in humility count others better than yourselves" (Phil. 2, 3).

Thus, the law that is the revelation of God, makes Israel responsible for all human beings, the servant of the entire humanity for establishing justice and preparing true peace (DL, 289–91).

Justice and peace demand, however, more than good intentions and individual deeds. Although the face-to-face of unique individuals is the indispensable source of all true justice, it cannot be realized without objective institutions based on the universality of human reason. For freedom and right remain abstract as long as the factual situation does not permit people to liberate themselves from all participation in unjust structures and customs. The state is necessary to establish and maintain the conditions of concrete morality, but the demands of ethics have set the standard by which all politics must be judged, and the spirit of revelation is indispensable to remind the state of its purpose, which lies in universal justice only (DL, 277, 279).

Against the neo-Hegelian and neo-Marxist slogans of the 1960s Levinas often repeats that it is not history that judges and, by its happy end, will justify the moral and immoral means used to hasten that end; on the contrary, "morality judges history" (*la morale juge l'histoire*) (cf. DL, 217, 266, 293). This conviction, consistent with Israel's distance with regard to politics and world history, shows "the eternity of Israel." Not Greece, in the false eternity of which Europe has sought refuge in all its crises, but rather a people "as old as the world" represents the perspective of eschatological hope and eternity (DL, 274–75; cf. PP, 339).

The Jewish conception of the state is described by Levinas in several commentaries on talmudic texts about the Messiah and in a paper on "The State of Caesar and the State of David" (DL, 83–129; AV, 209–20). Not having the space to render all the subtleties of these texts, I summarize here their main lines.

Notwithstanding Israel's being a people separated from the history of nations and capable of survival in the diaspora, it does not despise the state or politics in general, but emphasizes that its goal—universal justice—lies beyond politics. Even Rome, this monument of idolatrous imperialism, is praised in the Talmud because of its protecting the just from total anarchy by the maintenance of a certain order (AV, 215–16). However, there is a great danger that the state, left to its own *raison d'Etat*, will transform itself into an organization of injustice and persecution (AV, 211–12). Even its inevitable use of violence, like the punishment of criminals, is problematic (AV, 209–13). To commit an unavoidable killing—like, for instance, in defending a child against its murderer—is at the same time to tremble under the weight of this very act (DL, 41, 296). And certainly, the appeal to the happy ending of history does not justify the victimization of innocent persons or generations

(DL, 109–15). According to a passage from the Talmud, as explained by Levinas, even God's punishment of the evil ones causes a double hesitation: God hesitates because He will cause suffering ("His just deed still contains a violence that makes suffer") but, on the other hand, angels and reasonable humans, who see God's hesitation, are afraid that God will refrain from the perfectly just justice that punishes evil and recompenses the Good (DL, 108–9, 41, 204–5; cf. PP, 341–43). In light of the Thora all violence is bad; moral goodness is the absolute criterion by which all politics must be judged. There is, thus, a certain margin or marginality that puts the state at a distance, although it is, at the same time, recognized as necessary.

> This is also the reason why the necessary involvement [in the political] is so difficult for a Jew,—why a Jew cannot engage himself without immediately disengaging himself,—why he has always that aftertaste of violence, even when he engages in a just cause. Never a Jew will be able to depart for war with deployed flags under the triumphant sound of military music and with the blessings of a Church. (DL, 109; cf. 39, 274–76, 312)

The relationship between ethics and politics, as reflected upon in the Bible and the Talmud, centers on the king in his relation to the prophet who is the purest representative of God's revelation. The king must be elected by God; he expresses his loyalty in copying by his own hand the entire Thora, in studying continually and heeding its commandments. While David fought by day, he studied the Law by night (AV, 209, 211–13).

The Messiah announced by the prophets still is a king, but his politics is entirely penetrated by the exigencies of the Thora; ethics and politics no longer conflict in his realm. Until his coming, politics is a long way of patience; the provisional abdication of complete moral purity for the sake of objective justice is the reverse side of a steady education by which the eternal penetrates the world, not in an overwhelming or dramatic way, but humbly and almost imperceptibly (AV, 211–12).

The Talmud mentions many interpretations of the messianic times, but all of them stress the overcoming of all violence and most of them see the Messiah as the arrival of a morally pure politics. Some Rabbis, however, maintain that the Messiah will not abolish the social and economic inequalities—the presence of the poor will *always* necessitate the gifts of generosity—and at least one Rabbi sees him as a nonpolitical figure who brings the consolation of God's own direct intimacy (DL, 83–95, 109–15, 117). This Rabbi seems to identify the Messiah with "the coming world," which is sharply distinguished from the messianic times by the other teachers of Israel. As salvation by God himself in total peace of conscience, this consolation is beyond all politics and history. It is even beyond the announcements of the prophets, known as it is to God alone and to whom God wants to reveal it (AV, 214, 216–19; DL, 83–95).

Who is the Messiah and how will he come? (DL, 95–106). Does he come from the outside, for instance as a radical revolution of the political reality, or am I myself the Messiah insofar as I am the suffering servant for the whole of humanity? (DL, 118).

One of the questions on which the talmudic discussions concentrate is the question as to how necessary human endeavors are for the coming of the Messiah. Sinners must convert themselves and hasten the advent by lawful practice. But how can they, after having isolated and cut themselves off, convert themselves? They must first be taught and freed from idolatry, which is the source of all sins. Will God deliver the world if we do not obey? We are capable of disobedience, but are we free enough to cut the ties that connect us with God? Are we able to undo the alliance through which God married Israel? Even if we do not convert to God in freedom and a clear consciousness of our situation, God comes anyway. To believe in the possibility of evil's ultimate victory would be equivalent to disbelief with regard to God's final glory. But that would be equivalent to atheism and despair. Goodness and suffering are indispensable, as well as political action, but thanks to God there will be a time of peace and justice beyond politics (DL, 95–106).

Israel and the Nations

Levinas's description of the Jewish religion seems to privilege Israel, but this privilege is rather a burden than a honor: it is an election that puts the responsibility for the entire humanity on the shoulders of Israel. This election does not justify contempt for non-Jews, for "Israel" is also the name for all people who accept and practice the law of a justice that precedes and goes beyond politics. Israel is a particular people with its own language, its books and its laws, but it is also the spiritual society of all the just: "Traditional Jewish thought procures . . . the framework for conceiving of a universal human society encompassing the just of all nations and of all beliefs with which the ultimate intimacy is possible."[5] Conversely, "anti-Semitism" has a narrow as well as a universal meaning: it embraces all the forms of racial hatred, all persecutions of the weak and all sorts of exploitation.[6]

Israel's universalism is radically different from a philosophical universality. The latter has a political character, since philosophy tries to confront and surpass a multiplicity of conceptions and discourses by gathering them as particular expressions of one complete truth. Israel's universality, however, is the essential feature of its particularity; its essence consists in its being the servant of the whole universe for an ethical service beyond politics. Its messianism is not the attempt to prepare a dialectical synthesis of all the differences separating human ideologies or states; its reserve with regard to politics and philosophy—and, in general, to the culture of arts and sciences—is the expression of its prophetic vision of the truth. Israel supports the universe by loving all humans rather than caring about the differences of their opinions. Its fraternity does not demand one synthetic truth (DL, 74, 122–29, 289, 309–11).

The Individual

What is the meaning of individual existence in light of the position hitherto explained? As elected to responsibility for the Others, every individual is irreplaceable and unique. Nobody can take my responsibility from my shoulders. I cannot give my conscience away. This responsibility constitutes my unicity: nobody can replace me; I am not just an instance of a class; I am *unique* (eg., AV, 172, 178 [Révélation]).

The spiritual vocation of human individuals is not primarily a concern for one's own salvation or eternal happiness (DL, 44). That would still be a sublime form of egoism: "The soul is not a demand of immortality, but a [moral] impossibility of murdering . . . ; the spirit is the very concern for a just society" (DL, 136–37).

Redemption coincides with the practice of this spirituality, and universal justice is more important than isolated intimacy with God. Hence the nonblasphemous title of one of Levinas's short pieces: "To love the Thora more than God"

> The spiritual does not manifest itself as a sensible substance, but as an absence; God is concrete, not through incarnation, but through the Law; and his grandeur does not provoke fear and trembling, but it fills us with higher thoughts. To veil his face in order to demand everything from man—in a superhuman way—to create a human being capable of a response, capable of contacting his God as a creditor, and not always as a debtor—this is truly a divine grandeur. . . . Here we are as far from the warm and almost sensible communion with God, as from the desperate pride of the atheist. Integral and austere humanism, bound to a difficult adoration. (DL, 192–93)

The unicity of each human individual means that everybody is needed, not only for the practical realization of God's purpose of *salvation*,

but equally for the understanding of his revelation (DL, 44; AV, 162–
63 [Révélation]). That is why the Talmud conserves all its exemplary
teachers' voices and conflicting explanations. A Jewish hermeneutic is
essentially pluralistic. No final synthesis or dogma stops the ongoing
concretization of God's concern with humanity (AV, 163–64, 167–68,
175 [Révélation]). The history of its interpretations is a constitutive part
of the revelation itself and the reader participates in the prophetic task
of proclaiming the law. In all this, the human subject is never seen or
treated as a will-less instrument, the oracular voice of a god, or a bundle of
emotions called to ecstasis. Responsibility entails freedom; God's revelation excludes violence, rapture, and "mysticism." God cannot overpower
man's refusal to obey his law. Since human freedom is necessary to
establish justice, God is powerless when humanity submits to princes of
evil like Hitler or Stalin. God cannot even pardon in the name of those
who do not want to pardon or are unable to do so because they are dead.
Human responsibility is too serious and God is at the same time too full
of respect and too vulnerable (DL, 37; AV, 210–11).

> Jews don't want to be possessed, but to be responsible. Their God is the
> master of justice. . . . . This God can not charge himself with all the sins of
> man; the sin that is committed against man cannot be pardoned except
> by the person who has suffered from it. God cannot. His glory, the glory
> of a moral God, and the glory of man, an adult being, demand that God
> be powerless. (DL, 79)

As soon as an individual hears the voice of the law, he discovers the
contradiction between his spontaneous egoism and the infinity of his
obligations toward other humans, that is, he discovers his guilt.

> What is an individual, a solitary individual, if not a growing tree without
> regard for all that it cuts off and destroys, absorbing the nourishment, the
> air and the sun, a being which is fully justified in its nature and its being?
> What is an individual if not a usurper? What does the advent of conscience
> mean . . . if not the discovery of cadavers at my side and my horror of
> existing as a murderer? As attention to others, and, consequently, as
> possibility of counting myself among them, of judging myself, conscience
> is justice. Existence without murder. One can break away from this
> responsibility, denying the point at which it holds me down, seeking the
> salvation of a hermit. One can choose utopia. But one can also choose, in
> the name of the spirit, not to flee the conditions to which one's work owes
> its import. And that means to choose ethical action. (DL, 134–35)

We saw already how concrete and "materialistic" this spirituality wants us to be; the spirit needs hands and bread to realize its dedication. We must, however, add that generosity inevitably implies also suffering. Nothing in Judaism despises or condemns the joys of life: eating, drinking, bathing, etc. Enjoyment as such is not only innocent, but constitutive for the human life of a free individual. What makes me guilty, however, is my taking away light, food, and water from others by monopolizing them. To become hospitable or a servant means, thus, to restrict my satisfaction to the extent necessary for the satisfaction of others' needs. The discontentment that follows from this restriction can grow and take the dimension of real suffering or even death. As long as my pains can be understood as connected with my fidelity to the law—i.e., as belonging to my being the servant of humanity—they are meaningful. It is much worse to kill than to be killed; it is worse to make others suffer than to be sacrificed for the sake of others.

Summary

The fundamental message of Jewish thought in Levinas's version can be summarized by the following quote:

> It ties the meaning of all experiences to the ethical relation among humans; it appears to the personal responsibility of man, who, thereby, knows himself irreplaceable to realize a human society in which humans treat one another as humans. This realization of the just society is *ipso facto* an elevation of man to the society with God. This society is human happiness itself and the meaning of life. Therefore, to say that the meaning of the real must be understood in function of ethics, is to say that the universe is sacred. But it is sacred in an ethical sense. Ethics is an optics of the divine. No relation to God is more right or more immediate. The Divine cannot manifest itself except through the neighbor. For a Jew, incarnation is neither possible, nor necessary. After all, Jeremiah himself said it: "To judge the case of the poor and the miserable, is not that to know me? says the Eternal."[7]

The One who is revealed in this ethical religion differs greatly from the almighty and triumphant God whose image dominates any thought in which politics procures the highest perspective. The "Master of the world" is powerless against human violence and sin, vulnerable and persecuted. His passing by is not in the thunderstorm, not in the earthquake, and not in the fire either, but "after the fire there was a voice of subtle silence"

(1 Kings 19, 11–12). God penetrates the world almost imperceptibly, in extreme humility.[8]

Ritualism

A sketch of Judaism cannot be silent about the ritualism that seems to be an essential element of its orthodoxy. As an orthodox Jew, Levinas testifies to his adherence by fulfilling the ritual precepts and he explains the meaning of this practice by referring to the ethical responsibility as the center of Jewish existence. In order to be free for obedience and service one has to be free with regard to the forces through which nature steers our actions and to one's own spontaneous and "natural" egoism. Without discipline we are not able to be entirely dedicated to God and justice. The élan of passion and pathos must be simultaneously broken and maintained to concentrate conscientiously on the main task. This discipline is procured by the ritual structuring of daily life (DL, 18, 34–35, 45, 368; AV, 173–75 [Révélation]). As realization of the independence and "an-archic" marginality of those who belong to the God of justice, this "yoke" is a joy rather than a burden.

II. A Jewish Philosophy?

In a short but dense article on "Peace and Proximity" Levinas characterizes the European civilization as a preference for the Greek way of wisdom: philosophically as well as politically it has desired to establish peace by harmonizing all human divergences in the synthetic unity of their togetherness. Its fight against violence would need a history of confrontations and reconciliations, but this would ultimately be crowned by the peace of a universal compromise. The reality of European history has been in flagrant contradiction to this ideal: its slow decadence during the last hundred years, its systematic mass murders, its social and nuclear explosions testify against the wisdom of its choices (PP, 339–41). Europe's bad conscience about these facts manifests that—notwithstanding its Hellenic character—it lives also from another tradition, for which "You shall not kill!" is the nucleus of wisdom. Levinas's thought can be summarized as an attempt to develop this wisdom and its peace in a philosophy that, as philosophy, speaks the language of "the Greeks," without, however, accepting their assumptions about the meaning of life, the good, synthesis, and reason. As a philosopher, Levinas is of course bound to a discourse that can be understood and checked by his fellow philosophers; instead of offering opinions, views or visions, he must analyze and argue, deduce and prove his proposals. This he does as an accomplished phenomenologist who learned his skills from Husserl and Heidegger. But still, we can look at his philosophical work from two sides: in the light of the Jewish convictions described above it looks like the transcription of a Jewish thought in a "Greek," more conceptual language, while, as a discussion with ancient, modern, and contemporary philosophers, its claims must be judged by the normal standards of philosophy. In order to do justice to Levinas's claim of being a philosopher, the other chapters of this book concentrate on the philosophical aspects of his work, but the following pages want to show its unity by giving some indications about the connections that link his philosophy to the religious convictions described above. Since it is not possible to separate one's innermost convictions from the foundations of one's philosophy, however, it was inevitable that Levinas's portrait of Judaism was already influenced by his philosophical skills and knowledge, just as his philosophical thought is penetrated by the perspectives of his Jewishness. The question is thus not so much that of a bridge between two different dimensions, as that of a unique mode of existence of which that portrait and Levinas's philosophy are two closely related and not altogether separable expressions.

Otherness, Transcendence

The separation of "the Saint-blessed-be-He," his incomprehensible and unfathomable, invisible and untouchable escaping from any human experience is translated in *Totality and the Infinite* as the ab-soluteness or ab-solution of the Other who ab-solves or separates himself from all sorts of union with anything else. God does not inhabit the universe; neither earth nor heaven, nor the space between or embracing them can contain him. God is not attached to any place or space; the Eternal is neither now nor then; He is not present in the form of specific forces or elements and is certainly not confined to the dimension of the sacred. Nietzsche's atheism and the contemporary disbelief in miracles and interventions from out of a *Hinterwelt* are much closer to the truth than the image of a God who blessed the law and order of a bourgeois culture with its armies and capitals.

And yet, the Saint, in all his otherness, is nearby and offers his intimacy: the intimacy of the ethical. This vicinity of the invisible Infinite is shown in Levinas's discussion of the philosophical concept of transcendence. If "God" is not a word without meaning, transcendence—a separation that does not exclude relation—must be possible. But where and how can we show this by philosophical means?

Levinas prepares his answer by a reflection on some classical attempts to think the transcendence from the finite to the Infinite. He could have quoted theologians, but preferred to appeal to less suspected authorities, such as Plato and Descartes, whom even philosophers cannot dismiss without ado. The "good beyond being" of Plato's *Republic* is repeatedly mentioned, but its context is not extensively analyzed. Descartes's third *Meditation*, however, is analyzed very often in order to show that the relation that links human consciousness to the Infinite by which it is preceded is contemporary or even anterior to consciousness. Having recognized in Descartes's text the structure of the transcendence he was looking for, Levinas must, then, show where and how such a transcendence realizes itself concretely as a phenomenon or quasiphenomenon "in the world." That is, a phenomenological (or—as I would call it—a "transphenomenological") analysis must "show" how the Infinite reveals itself for the finite consciousness of a desiring ego.

Starting from a phenomenological perspective, I perceive (without perceiving) one phenomenon (which is not a phenomenon) that manifests (without manifesting) a visible invisibility: the face of another man, woman, or child presents me with a reality that is not a possible moment of the totality constituted by the world and its parts. The Other, in the sense of *Autrui*, does not fit into my consciousness; it breaks through my circular or elliptic horizon, thus revealing his/her transcendence. As transcendent, the Other responds to the desire that opens my interiority to an absolute exteriority. The Other is, thus, the epiphany of a transcendent otherness or absoluteness.

But how does my relationship to God relate to my relationship to *Autrui*? Do they coincide? Are they two sides of one and the same transcendence? Are God and *Autrui* transcendent, invisible, absolute, and infinite in exactly the same sense? This question is not answered clearly in Levinas's publications until after *Totality and the Infinite*. On one of the first pages of this book he writes that the meaning of the desired Otherness "is understood as otherness of *Autrui and* as otherness of the Most-High" (TeI, 4; TaI, 34; my emphasis), but the "and" in this sentence is not explained. Later works, like "The Trace of the Other," "Enigma and Phenomenon," "God and Philosophy," and parts of *Otherwise than Being* are dedicated to a clarification of that connection, but they always maintain the basic coincidence of the relation to God with the transcendence to the human infinitude and absoluteness of other persons. The guiding formula, which emerges for the first time shortly after *Totality and the Infinite*, is then that *Autrui* "is in the trace of" the divine Other.[9]

Transcendence and the Ethical

The only way in which transcendence, as relation to the Other, is possible, is an ethical relationship. Metaphysics and a radical analysis of the ethical (also called "ethics") are identical. The human Other "appears" as separated: an "ab-solute" surprise from above. The first "given" is here the difference between the Other and me—a difference that opens a dimension of superiority. The Other and I are related through a nonsymmetric relationship; transcendence is trans*as*cendence.

This thesis is not only in perfect agreement with Levinas's portrait of religion as given before; it is also perfectly correct from a phenomenological point of view. Against Husserl, Scheler, Heidegger, and most theoreticians of the "other minds" problematic, we must state that, between a human Other whom I encounter and myself, I do *not* experience in the first place a similarity or equality, but rather a "fundamental" or "essential" difference; that this difference includes a normative and ethical moment which cannot be separated from it; and that this ethical moment manifests an asymmetry that calls for metaphors like "height" or "superiority." Levinas's descriptions of the (Other's) face, of language as speech and conversation (which is always a "teaching"), and so on, can therefore be read as skillful discussions with other researchers of intersubjectivity, but also as philosophical translations of a religious attitude. That the distinction between these two readings is factitious has already been said. Their unity expresses itself, for example, in the transformation of the "tone" and the sense which Plato's "Good" and Descartes's "infinite" undergo in Levinas's retrieval: instead of a primarily ontological principle, Levinas's Infinite is, first of all, the Lord whose precepts I must obey, whereas the affinity of Plato's "Good" with the beauty of *kalokagathia* has been sacrificed to a more prosaic but seriously radical generosity.

Ethics and Ontology

If the epiphany of the face reveals that the absolute is inseparable from an ethical demand, we cannot deny that the roots of metaphysics and "ethics" (in the sense of a "foundational" ethics, like Kant's second *Critique*) are the same. This thesis involves Levinas in a discussion with other philosophies of our age, and especially with the most influential ones of the situation in which he writes, to wit, with Heidegger and some currents of Neo-Hegelian and Neo-Marxist philosophy. For them, ethics is secondary or dependent on ontology or a philosophy of history. Again and again Levinas tries to convince their adherents that the primacy of the ethical perspective—so clearly suggested in the experience of the Other, but so much neglected by the Western tradition of philosophy— cannot be denied, and that the question as to "what there is" (and how and why) cannot be answered if we decide to exclude all normative connotations.

From the analysis of transcendence as the ethically determined relation to the Other it follows that the entire project of Western ontology must be revised and relativized. Indeed, the objectifying thematization inherent to the Western logos as onto-logy does not do justice to the way in which the Other exists. The only adequate response to the face is my being devoted to the Other. If I reduce the Other to an interesting topic for my observation or reflection, I am blind to the claim that is constitutive of the Other's coming to the fore. Hence Levinas's relentless polemics against all forms of ontology that submit the Other to the overview of an objectifying and panoramic reason. Just as a theoretical analysis of God borders on blasphemy, so an ontological thematization of the Other distorts this Other's very epiphany.

If the only adequate response to the Other's existence is the acceptance of one's being elected for the realization of justice—an election from which I cannot free myself—philosophy has lost its place at the top. Its desire for an overall and absolute knowledge expresses its desire of possessing and mastering conceptually the universe from an absolute standpoint: the standpoint of an unshaken and unconquerable ego. In writing an "essay on exteriority,"[10] Levinas not only pleads for a religious and ethical wisdom beyond egology, but also retrieves a philosophical tradition that oriented thinking to the *Agathon*, the *Hen* or *Deus* beyond the totality of all essences and ideas. This retrieval necessarily is a discussion with contemporary thought about speech and discourse, vision, the grasping hand, being in the form of *Vorhandenes* and *Zuhandenes*, the universality of reason, the truth of Being, and so on. Ontology is made secondary and transformed in subordination to a metaphysics of transcendence, starting from the insuperable but ordinary relation of facing and speaking in which all thematic thought is caught. The central argument from which all changes follow is here not an appeal to the Jewish tradition, but the (trans)phenomenological analysis of intersubjectivity.

The Saint and the Sacred

The foundational role of "the ethical" in Levinas's "metaphysics" not only colors all his analyses, but changes the whole structure and meaning of traditional philosophy. Besides a consideration of the ethical and anthropological aspects of nature and the human body, Levinas did not offer a philosophy of nature, nor do we find much of an independent consideration of art and the aesthetical in general. He did, however, deliver a critique of those philosophies which subordinated the ethical to theoretical, aesthetic, or "religious" perspectives. Most clearly in this respect is his often repeated criticism of Heidegger's celebration of Being's anonymous "phosphorence" and the neglect of morality in the name of "more originary questions." The opposition between Levinas and Heidegger is perhaps clearest in those passages in which the former attacks what he sees as restoration of a world dominated by the mysterious powers of the sacred. Heidegger's "fourfold" is too small to contain God, and when Heidegger, in his "Letter on Humanism," declares that Being itself must take the initiative to open for us the dimensions of the holy or the sacred (*das Heilige*) as a space in which the essence of the divine can unfold,[11] he places "the God and the gods" within a horizon that prevents authentic transcendence. Within the dimension thus indicated only pantheism and polytheism are possible, a divinization of Being and beings, followed by all the violences that belong to idolatry. It seems clear to me that Levinas's insistence on transcendence and the separation of the Infinite from the universe of beings is motivated primarily by the scandal of God being contaminated by the finiteness of "Being" (cf. AE, x; OB, viii). He tries to show by philosophical means that the quasireligious and poetic restorations of a half-Hellenic, half-Hölderlinian cosmos do not do justice to one of the most "obvious" and central "experiences" of everyday life: the prosaic, sober, and demanding fact of our being obliged before we can contemplate or think.

In a universe created by the Unique (who is not a God alongside or greater than other gods, like, for instance, Zeus or Kronos) there are no sacred places or times; the only "place" where you can meet him is the powerless destitution of the human Other, and this can be found in the desert as well as in a town, but not in sacred woods, holy temples, or gathering works of art.

The rationalist prose of the Enlightenment and the atheism of post-Nietzschean philosophy come closer to a sound understanding of transcendence, especially when they are accompanied or motivated by a desire for moral purity. Using the word "materialism" in the sense of a thought without ethical breath or spirit, Levinas calls Heidegger's amoral meditation on the gods "a shameless materialism."[12] The fundamental assumptions of this philosophical "enthusiasm" must be wrong: Heidegger's Being cannot embrace the Transcendent. This must therefore command Being and "exist" beyond.

Ethics and Politics

Levinas's thematization of the relation between originary "ethics" and the realm of politics is certainly a philosophical expression of many talmudic reflections on this problem; but it can also defend itself on the battle-ground of ancient and modern philosophy. The necessity of political institutions is deduced from the demands of the ethical, notwithstanding the part of violence inevitable in any state. A thorough analysis of the basic principles of modern political theory—involving Hobbes, Locke and Rousseau, Kant, Hegel and Marx—would show that their theory is based on fundamentally unsolved contradictions between a powerless desire of peace and the inevitable conflicts of egoistic attempts to oppress others.[13] The universality of modern reason has not found a solution for these contradictions, because it has not seen the necessity of a prepolitical, marginal, or "an-archic" relation of transcendence. This philosophical parallel of prophetic justice points to a dimension beyond world history. The "history" (or "fecundity") of transcendence is lived by an incessant dedication to the cause of justice, not captured within the limits of the state, but practiced in a tradition of spirituality at a distance from world politics.

How the people of Israel, the family and various spiritual "families," function in the "history" of responsibility and justice, and how their contributions relate to one another has not become altogether clear in the philosophical analysis of erotic love and the family contained in the fourth section of *Totality and the Infinite*. Its argumentation neither seems to be constrained to the Jewish people, nor to the biological family alone. The spiritualization of Israel that is thus performed translates Israel's messianic expectations into a universal but an-archic "history" of all individuals who love true justice and peace.

Individuals

The autonomy of the human individual is not denied but shown to be demanded by the heteronomy of the metaphysical (or "ethical") relationship. This constitutes the ego as a responsible subject, obsessed and taken hostage for the Other. This responsibility makes me unique and irreplaceable. And therewith Levinas has answered the old question of how we can distinguish human individuality from being particular or only an instance of universalities.

As a philosopher of responsibility (and not primarily of freedom), Levinas still must explain how freedom is possible. He does this in an antidualist and anti-Kantian way in section 2 of *Totality and the Infinite* by showing that a corporeal and vitalistic enjoyment of elements and earthly goods makes it possible to establish oneself as an independent center of the world. The appearance of another—the fact of my being caught in heteronomy—puts restrictions on the extent of my hedonism, but it should not diminish my freedom.

Here a problem emerges that is not treated extensively by Levinas: If freedom is the process of appropriation and enjoyment, how then can its limitations—or rather its conversion into service and donation—avoid being a lessening of my freedom? Repeatedly, Levinas affirms that the ethical demands of transcendence do *not* "limit" my freedom—and this is understandable if only an ethical orientation can procure freedom with an ultimate meaning—but his affirmation seems to presuppose that freedom (or autonomy or independence) is open to a generous or morally good, as well as to an egoistic existence. But then autonomy cannot be connected preferably to an economy of egocentric hedonism. Levinas's discussion of other conceptions of freedom, like those of Kant, Hegel, Sartre, and Merleau-Ponty, seems to be open to further development and correction.

Levinas's analysis of human subjectivity clearly echoes the Jewish interpretation of the Thora as law of life. The nondualistic mode of existence as inspired body, the memory of paradisiac innocence and the shame about my insufficiency in justice, the ethical necessity of giving away my own earthly and cultural goods, the impossibility of an escape from my being a hostage, the marginality and the suffering that follow from election to a nonchosen but universal responsibility—all these features characterize Israel in its most spiritual form of life, but at the same time they can be shown phenomenologically to be constitutive of human existence as such. Not an endeavor for personal immortality, but an inspiration that mobilizes a human body—with hands, head, mouth, and feet—for justice and peace beyond the state—that is me thanks to the passing of the Infinite.

4

From Phenomenology through Ontology to Metaphysics: Levinas's Perspective on Husserl and Heidegger from 1927 to 1950

evinas's works refer to Plato, Descartes, Berkeley, Kant, Hegel, Nietzsche, Bergson, Rosenzweig, Buber, Marcel, Sartre, Merleau-Ponty,
and others, but Husserl and Heidegger are the only twentieth-
century philosophers who are almost continually present in his thought.
They are the respected masters and adversaries with whom he is in discussion.[1] Husserl started the revolution in philosophy called "phenomenology"; Heidegger exploited hidden possibilities of phenomenology and
transformed it into a new ontology; Levinas developed and tried to overcome phenomenological ontology by a radical renewal of "metaphysics,"
rehabilitating the existent (*das Seiende, l'étant* or *l'existant*) by a thought
"beyond being" (*au delà de l'être, jenseits des Seins*).

This chapter focuses on the first period of Levinas's discussion
with Husserl and Heidegger, a period beginning in 1927, when Levinas
started his study of phenomenology at the University of Strasbourg,
and ending in 1950, when he published the article "L'ontologie est-elle
fondamentale?" ("Is Ontology Fundamental?"), in which the main lines
of his later more elaborated criticism of Heidegger's thought, and the
central theme of his first *opus magnum, Totality and the Infinite,* are clearly
expressed. The texts on which I will base my exposition are the following.

Besides an important review article on Husserl's *Ideen* (1929) and
his dissertation *La théorie de l'intuition dans la phénoménologie de Husserl*

(1930), Levinas published a second article on Husserl in 1940, in which he reaffirmed and deepened the criticisms he already had expressed in his publications of 1929–30.[2] Heidegger's philosophy is the subject of a series of articles between 1932 and 1950, of which the first one does not contain any criticism, whereas the last one is a sharp polemic against Heidegger's central thought. The titles of these articles are: "Martin Heidegger and Ontology" (1932), "Ontology in the Temporal" (1940), "From Description to Existence" (1949), and "Is Ontology Fundamental?" (1951).[3]

I will here concentrate upon the articles in which Levinas treats the philosophy of Husserl and Heidegger explicitly, and I will not go into all of the implicit criticisms contained in the more systematic publications which came out in this same period, to wit, the articles "On Evasion" (1935–36), "Reality and Its Shadow" (1948) and "The Transcendence of Words" (1947), the first book on his own philosophy, *From Existence to Existents* (1947), and the transcript of lessons given in 1946–47, "Time and the Other." The last two works are best seen as preparations for *Totality and the Infinite*, which, in 1961, concludes the maturation of Levinas's systematic thought.[4] Whereas the period of his apprenticeship, critical distanciation, and emerging independence stretches from 1927, when Levinas was twenty-two, until 1950, when he was forty-five, his own philosophy took until 1961 to fully ripen. Obviously a complete study of the relation between Husserl, Heidegger, and Levinas would also include a careful analysis of other periods of his career and of other works, insofar as they criticize, transform, or integrate, implicitly or explicitly, various elements of Husserl's and Heidegger's philosophy. In particular it would include a series of essays on Husserl written after 1959, in which Levinas reevaluates some of Husserl's discoveries and suggestions. The sharpening of his polemics against Heidegger after 1950 also needs an explanation. Some elements of it will be given in chapters 5, 8, and 14.

Husserl

The Theory of Intuition in Husserl's Phenomenology (1930)

Since Levinas's first publication, his review of Husserl's *Ideen* (1929), is a faithful exposition of Husserl's thought without any criticism, a survey of his own evolution with regard to Husserl can start from Levinas's dissertation.[5] When Levinas prepared his manuscript during the years 1927–30, the only books published by Husserl were *Philosophie der Arithmetik*

(1891), *Logische Untersuchungen* in its first and second editions (1900–1 and 1913–21), *Ideen* (1913), *Vorlesungen zur Phänomenologie des innern Zeitbewußtseins* (1928), and *Formale und transzendentale Logik* (1929). The last book was published too late to be used by Levinas (TIH, 10); the *Philosophy of Arithmetic* did not seem, at that time, to be of any importance for the explanation of Husserl's phenomenology; of the articles published by Husserl, only *Philosophie als strenge Wissenschaft* (1910) was used by Levinas, and the courses on the inner consciousness of time played a rather modest role in his dissertation. Notwithstanding this rather sparse documentation, twenty-four-year-old Levinas succeeded in drawing a picture of Husserlian phenomenology that is still considered to be a very good introduction, and one he did not need to reject in later articles on Husserl.

Levinas wrote his book during the year he spent in Freiburg (1928–29). At that time Husserl had already resigned as professor, but was still giving a seminar; Heidegger, however, was at the peak of his career, and had become famous as the man who was accomplishing a far more radical revolution in philosophy than that of Husserl. In this context it is understandable that Levinas stressed those points in his interpretation of Husserl which were profoundly developed and radicalized by Heidegger, although Husserl did not follow the latter on his new path. Levinas is very conscious of the Heideggerian perspective he adopts in his dissertation, and devotes several pages of his book to justifying his approach. The essence of this justification consists in the following argumentation: If intentionality is the key concept that makes the relationships between consciousness and reality understandable, then a theory of conscious acts and consciousness is at the same time a theory of the meaning of their objects. From the very beginning, therefore, Levinas treats the constitutional problems of Husserlian phenomenology as ontological problems, stating that the *Logical Investigations* have founded "a new ontology of consciousness" (TIH, 11–19, 21–22, 33, 216–18).

Due to Husserl's new conception of reality in its relation to consciousness (or of consciousness as "intending" reality), Being is "defined" as meaning (*Sinn*) in its givenness to consciousness. Being is neither an appearance behind which some thing or some structure is ruling or happening, nor anything behind the appearances, but that which is meaningfully present to consciousness. The two fundamental modes of being are the being of the objects of external perception and the being of consciousness. The objects are related by a perception which is always and essentially inadequate; however, consciousness and its "lived experience" (its *Erlebnisse*) are always adequately given by immanent reflection. But the two modes of being converge insofar as they can be "defined" as the *presence* of the object itself to consciousness or as the *presence* of consciousness to its objects. The essence of intentionality is "to have the object before oneself" (TIH, 127).

The main model for every kind of intentionality is the perception, or even the vision, of an object which is there, facing consciousness as a *Gegenstand* (TIH, 135). The structure of the reflection through which consciousness knows itself is conceived of in analogy with the perception of external objects. In transcendental phenomenology, consciousness is studied as a sort of *Gegenstand*, while reflection, to which consciousness is given, is a sort of looking at something before it, a sort of *Vorstellung* (TIH, 184–85). The "objective" (*gegenständliche*) mode of being is central for Husserl's phenomenology, and knowledge is understood on the basis of objectification; it is primarily *Vorstellung* or *representation*. In this sense Levinas characterizes Husserl's philosophy, in a Heideggerian vein, as a *vorstellende*, "*objectifying*" or "*representationist*" mode of thought, a characterization maintained in later articles on Husserl, although Levinas insists there on the seeds of a postrepresentationist way of philosophizing in Husserl's work.

Levinas's dissertation skillfully develops the thesis summarized above. The central thought that self-givenness is the main form of being and that ideal knowledge is *adequacy* (i.e., the exact "fitting" of the world into consciousness) is expressed in Husserl's theory of truth as the "realization" or the fulfillment (*Erfüllung*) through intuition of the "signifying" act which otherwise would remain empty, but also in the fundamental role of evidence for all knowledge and in Husserl's theory of judgment as the direct intuition of a more complex object.

Perception, judgment, and naming are the privileged forms of intentionality in Husserl's thought, but *perception* is the principal model. The object of a judgment, the *Sachverhalt*, is understood by Husserl as a composite object, which differs from a perceived object not qualitatively, but only through its matter. Judging, too, reveals a mode of being which must be characterized as *Vorgestelltes* or *Gegenständlichkeit*. Levinas characterizes Husserl's preference for one *particular* mode of intentionality and being as a *primacy of theory* (TIH, 93ff., 107ff.), and this summarizes his criticism of Husserl as expressed in 1930.

Before we concentrate on this criticism, let us focus our attention on the hermeneutical method practiced here. Levinas understands Husserl's philosophy as a theory of consciousness which at the same time is a general ontology. This general theory claims to identify universal, often purely formal, elements and structures which determine the life of all human consciousness and of being "in general and as such." Levinas shows, however, that those elements are not really free from particular preferences or distortions; they testify to a specific theory of relating, thinking, intending, existing, and being. Husserl's preference for objectivity (*Gegenständlichkeit*), representation (*Vorstellung*), perception, evidence, adequacy, and theory expresses a specific orientation and a certain way of being, which presupposes a specific history. The Heideggerian inspiration of Levinas's hermeneutic is obvious. A question which he does not solve in his dissertation is whether the project of a universal and pure theory without any admixture of particularity can be realized. Are we able to pronounce truly universal statements not limited to a particular context? Is it possible to write a metahistorical ontology? Or is *it our* destiny to be, to speak, and to write in a necessarily particularized, nonuniversal way?

As far as Levinas's criticism of Husserl is concerned, some specialists may think it much too severe. In later studies on Husserl's work, Levinas makes more distinctions and stresses its positive and promising sides. He does not, however, change his central criticism. In his dissertation Levinas dedicates a long passage to the question of whether or not Husserl considers representation (*Vorstellung*) to be the basic form of intentionality (TIH, 97ff.). In the fifth of the *Logical Investigations* Husserl had stated firmly that not only objectifying acts but *all* noetic acts are equally intentional and constitute noemata of their own, but Levinas argues that nonobjectifying acts according to Husserl do not really contribute to the constitution of the *matter* of the intended noema. The specific character of a value or of utensils, for instance, does not enter into the constitution of the *existence* of objects, but is "grafted" upon the being of the noema which is posited by the objectifying act of representation (TIH, 142, 184). The fundamental structure of the world remains that of "objectivity" (*Gegenständlichkeit*).

Although in his *Ideen* Husserl stated even more clearly that the central place in knowledge is taken not by objectification and representation, but by "lived experience" (*Erlebnis*), Levinas holds that Husserl continued to consider the objectifying acts to be fundamental.[6] The doxic thesis is always included as the basic intention positing the existence of the meant object. Later on, however, Levinas puts the accent on Husserl's radical distinction between *meaning* (*Sinn, Seinsinn*) and *object*, a distinction effectively exploited by Heidegger, who thereby freed phenomenology from its representationist remnants.

Another of Husserl's radical thoughts, which came to be of the greatest importance to Levinas's own philosophy, is hardly at all expressed in the dissertation. As Levinas formulated it in 1963, it is the insight that the implicit *horizons* that transcendentally condition every noema form "scaffoldings" which "never become useless" and can never be dissolved into adequate representations. Through this insight, Levinas says in "Signature," "Husserl has contested that the place of truth is in representation," notwithstanding his intellectualism, which cannot be reconciled with that discovery.[7]

The primacy of theory which, according to Levinas, is the secret of Husserl's attitude towards Being, goes together with an *ahistorical* conception of Being. Empirical consciousness and history are looked at from a transcendental standpoint, the attainment of which is made possible by the phenomenological reduction. Through the description of the acts whereby the transcendental consciousness constitutes the empirical *cogito* and its time, the subject comes to coincide with itself. Human subjects are, as it were, present at their own genesis through their theoretical identification with the transcendental *cogito*: the subject of consciousness is its own father and son.

This interpretation ties the primacy of theory to a project of freedom and *autonomy*, which Levinas only touches upon at the end of his dissertation (TIH, 220–22); however, it is the central theme of the article on Husserl's oeuvre which he wrote in 1940, "L'oeuvre d'Edmond Husserl." According to this article the inner secret of Husserl's preference for the theoretical attitude is a desire for sovereignty. Transcendental phenomenology, as the inner consequence of Husserl's approach, makes it possible for the philosopher to coincide with the original consciousness and thus to master the true source of all Being (TIH, 203–14). Husserl does not explain, however, why it is necessary and how it is possible for a human subject to neutralize its immersion in the concrete world of lived experience and of history (TIH, 219), and how we are able to ascend to the heights of a detached observer. How can we *become aware* of the naiveté of our natural, dogmatically lived life, and how can we *detach* ourselves from it in order to overcome it by transcendental theory? Husserl neither answers nor asks this question, as Levinas remarks on the last page of his dissertation, when he states that "Husserl posits the freedom of theory just as he posits theory."[8]

Every criticism of a fundamental attitude or orientation presupposes as a minimum that the critic suspects the possibility of an orientation or attitude different from the one he criticizes. From what perspective, background, or inspiration do Levinas's critical remarks come? They suggest that, even for a philosopher, the theoretical ideal and the realm of representation are not the most radical and not a universal perspective. Later on, for instance in "Signature,"[9] Levinas identifies the theoretical ideal with the spirit of Western culture; but what other light or space enables him to attain the distance needed for a "neutralization" of Husserl's absolutization of theory?

If we set aside the religious tradition to which Levinas belongs—as do his own first works—the answer is clearly to be found in the thought of Martin Heidegger. Not only the hermeneutic method which Levinas used, based on the supposition that philosophy is a specific practice and mode of being rooted in concrete existence, but also the formulation of his criticism is inspired by Heidegger (and perhaps, to some very small extent, by Scheler). This is seen most clearly in his dissertation, where Levinas opposes Husserl's "intellectualism" by asking the rhetorical question: "Is our main attitude toward reality that of theoretical contemplation? Is the world not presented in its very being as a center of action, as a field of activity or of *care*—to speak the language of Martin Heidegger?"[10]

Even in "L'oeuvre d'Edmond Husserl," written in 1940, Levinas's critique of Husserl is wholly Heideggerian,[11] although he had, in the meantime, published some anti-Heideggerian studies. In his articles on Heidegger, beginning with "Martin Heidegger et l'ontologie" (1932), he also claims that Husserl's objectifying philosophy is not radical enough because it does not pay enough attention to its being preceded and inspired by the way of being typical of philosophical existence.

"The Work of Edmund Husserl" (1940)

Ten years after his dissertation, shortly after Husserl's death, Levinas wrote a long article on the whole of Husserl's philosophy for the *Revue Philosophique*.[12] In it Levinas also considers Husserl's *Formale und transzendentale Logik* (1929) and the works published after 1930, the *Nachwort zu meinen Ideen zu einer reinen Phänomenologie* of 1930, the *Cartesianische Meditationen* (1931), and the *Krisis* (1936), in addition to the works mentioned above. The topics on which Levinas concentrates in order to grasp the overall inspiration of Husserl's philosophy are (1) intentionality and evidence; (2) time; (3) the phenomenological reduction; (4) the crisis of European culture; and (5) Husserl's solipsism. Levinas develops and deepens the interpretation of his dissertation, but on the whole maintains what he said there. The main difference concerns his critical diagnosis of Husserl's work, as we will see in a moment.

As I have already pointed out, the importance of Husserl's distinction between *meaning* and *object* is now drawn more clearly than in the dissertation. In fact, this distinction destroys the privilege of the objectifying and representationist model of thought (EDHH, 21–24, 51–52). The nonobjectifiable horizons form a nonrecuperable precedence (*un avant non récupérable*) which invites a radical revolution in phenomenology. However, Levinas maintains his charge that Husserl continues to think from an objectivistic perspective. To show this he dwells on the essential connection of the identifying act, which is presupposed in every evidence, and the objectifying act, which functions in the doxic thesis.[13]

The new perspective of "L'oeuvre d'Edmond Husserl" is provided by the idea of freedom in the typically Western sense of *autonomy*, which Levinas traces out in Husserl's treatment of all the topics listed above. After extensive analyses his conclusion is that Husserl's thought is "a philosophy of freedom which realizes itself" as consciousness and defines itself through consciousness (EDHH, 49). I will summarize only a few fragments of his argumentation here.

In Husserl's view every being has a meaning for human consciousness; the latter is as all-encompassing as the universe; it fits Being perfectly and cannot be shocked by anything alien to its own being. Being is being constituted for and by consciousness. Consciousness is first, because all modes of being presuppose it in order to emerge, while consciousness itself possesses itself in adequate self-evidence. This conception entitles Levinas to call Husserl's philosophy a form of idealism.

According to Husserl the self is a total and universal openness, but as adequate self-possession it cannot go out of itself. Because it is coextensive with Being, consciousness cannot meet with meaningless or irrational beings. Its contact with reality is never a shock; it cannot be ashamed or overcome by horror or malaise. Being is being on the way to becoming evident for the mind, i.e., being able to be seized and integrated by a free subject. "The evidence of a given world . . . is the positive realization of freedom" (EDHH, 24). The light of evidence, in which every being is given bodily, enables us to behave as origins of Being. Intellection is the realization of sovereignty.[14]

On the other hand, the subject of consciousness is always able to take a distance from that which presents itself (EDHH, 50). One can withdraw from all engagements and choose to enclose oneself within the openness of a monadic universe (EDHH, 46–48). Intersubjectivity, social relations, the empirical ego, and history are constituted before a free transcendental ego can escape from the facticity of its birth, life, and death, liberating itself through evidence. The phenomenological reduction is a special mode of existence, motivated by a desire to be contemporaneous with and present at the origins of oneself and the world. In reflection upon the empirical consciousness the secret origin of the world reveals itself; the discovery of its constitution by a (transcendental but particular) subject establishes a total coincidence of the subject with itself and acquires, thus, the highest autonomy. Husserl's phenomenology tries to realize liberty rather than to question it.

In *The Crisis of the European Sciences*, Husserl himself clearly expresses his inspiration when he situates the origin of the sciences in the human desire to freely constitute our own existence.[15] Knowledge is a way of overcoming all strangeness; it is an instrument of liberation. Insofar as philosophy is humankind's struggle to understand itself through theory, it desires the power of giving a rational meaning to all beings and to Being itself. Philosophy liberates and is itself a way of being free. The crisis of our sciences can be solved if phenomenology helps us discover the original meanings that present themselves in evidence. Human self-knowledge is the only way to the restoration of an authentic spiritual life.

Besides his diagnosis of Husserl's oeuvre as a philosophy of autonomy, Levinas expresses hardly any criticism of it in this article. It ends with a short comparison of Husserl and Heidegger, in which it becomes clear on which side Levinas situates himself (EDHH, 51–52). To Husserl's celebration of the free subject which masters the passive synthesis of time and history, Levinas opposes Heidegger's view that consciousness and the clarity of evident meaning are always already preceded by the opaque drama of a concrete existence in a concrete history which cannot be mastered by theoretical evidence. Evidence is *not* the fundamental mode of understanding, and the clarity of objectification is not the authentic mode of spiritual life. Heidegger inherited from Husserl the method and means of uncovering the transcendental conditions of knowledge, but he practiced them in a more radical way. In comparison with Heidegger's ontology, Husserl's philosophy is still too naive and not transcendental enough.

Heidegger

In a very short passage of "Signature," Levinas formulates the essence of Heidegger's philosophy, reduced to its inner core, in these words:

> The phenomenological method was used by Heidegger to turn, beyond objectively known and technically approached entities, toward a situation which would condition all others: that of the apprehension of the being of these entities—that of ontology. The being of these entities is not another entity; it is neutral, but it illuminates, guides, and orders thought. It calls to man and nearly brings him forth.[16]

The brevity of this note contrasts with the importance of Heidegger's thought for the genesis of Levinas's own philosophy, the number of studies he wrote on Heidegger,[17] and the constancy of Heidegger's presence (as the former master and now the greatest of all adversaries) in Levinas's own philosophical work.[18]

In 1932, two years after his book on Husserl, Levinas published an article "Martin Heidegger and Ontology."[19] This publication contained "the first chapters of the first part" of a book which Levinas was preparing at that time.[20] After a French introduction to Husserl's phenomenology, he apparently wanted to write a book on the main lines of Heidegger's thought. The second part of this book was to have "identified Heidegger's place in the history of ideas and especially to have situated him within the phenomenological movement and in relation to Edmund Husserl, the philosopher to whom he owes so much."[21]

The article begins by praising Heidegger, but this praise was suppressed, when, after World War II, it was reprinted in *Discovering Existence with Husserl and Heidegger*.[22] Heidegger's philosophy is called "one of the apogees of the phenomenological movement" because of "the brilliant originality and power of his effort," and Levinas states that for once "fame has not been mistaken and did not come too late."

The essay approaches Heidegger from a question to which Husserl —as we have seen—did not give an answer: How does philosophy emerge from life? What and how are the relations between existence and philosophizing? Heidegger's answer shows that the philosophical way of understanding is rooted in human existence and is itself a special mode of being. The answer presupposes the ontological explanation and analysis of *Dasein* given in *Sein und Zeit*. Levinas explains the unbreakable connection between the question of Being and the hermeneutics of the special mode of being called *Dasein*. He explains how Heidegger's clarification of *Seinsverständnis* differs from the contemplative or theoretical knowledge that has dominated Western philosophy from Plato to Husserl. He opposes the objectivity of representationism and stresses the finite character of transcendence through an explanation of "thrownness" (*Geworfenheit*), "disposition" (*Befindlichkeit*), facticity (*Faktizität*), and "fallennness" (*Verfallenheit*). The fundamental and unifying role of anxiety (*Angst*) is emphasized and the radicality of Heidegger's analysis of *temporality* as coextensive with Being and as the essential structure of Being is brought to the fore.

The article does not contain any criticism of Heidegger, but expresses the same distance with regard to Husserl as was formulated in the dissertation.

In 1940 Levinas gave a lecture on Heidegger to the students of Jean Wahl, which was not published until 1949, when it appeared under the title "L'ontologie dans le temporel."[23] Since Levinas had already been looking for a way out of Heideggerian ontology since 1935, it is surprising that his lecture of 1940 dedicated only one page to a critique of Heidegger. Probably Levinas refrained from extended criticisms because the purpose of Jean Wahl's invitation was for him to focus on an explanation rather than a critical judgment.

His paper starts with the question of how we can understand (or comprehend)[24] reality. In order to understand beings we must not only understand their essential structures, but must first of all understand what and how Being in general and as such "is." The ultimate condition of all particular knowledge is thus the understanding of Being itself. This understanding, the *Seinsverständnis*, exists, is practiced and "lived" as the existence of *Dasein*. It is the implicit and fundamental understanding through which *Dasein* seizes its own possibilities. The most fundamental possibility of *Dasein* is not to be conceived of as an Aristotelian *dynamis* which can and should be realized by an act which is determined from the beginning by a final cause. This concept of possibility is valid for all sorts of secondary possibilities which belong to "fallenness" (*Verfallenheit*), but authentic existence recognizes and lives out its original possibility as a pure possibility, a "can-be" (*Seinkönnen*) that cannot be actualized in any way. Existing authentically means accepting this condition and submitting to this fate.

The structure of *Dasein* is care (*Sorge*), characterized through "thrownness" (*Geworfenheit*), "project" (*Entwurf*), and "fallennness" (*Verfallenheit*), and unified by "anxiety" (*Angst*). Anxiety is not directed toward any object or particular being; it understands that the end of human existence is neither a goal nor a possible reality which has to be actualized; it is *nothing*. This understanding reveals the nonimportance and nothingness of the world and of *Dasein* itself. At the same time, however, this nothingness is the condition of the possibility of the primary and authentic possibility which is the essence of *Dasein*. Only "running ahead of oneself into death" (*Vorauslaufen in den Tod*), only "being-toward-death" (*zum-Tode-sein*), enables *Dasein* to project itself toward its own possibilities by living them as possibilities. Only the *finiteness* of a being which can and must die enables it to have a *future*. A possibility that would be dominated by a final cause, i.e., by a (possible) actuality that determines it from the beginning, does not have a real future, because its predestination prevents all newness. Its future is already contained in the essence of its past. The present is, then, as Plato said—an image or shadow of an immobile eternity in which there are no differences between *possibilia* and *realia*, since everything is fixed in an eternal actuality. The *finitude* of mortality conditions human possibility and gives it a horizon within which it is able to have "projects" (*Entwürfe*). This finitude of time is thus a condition for the understanding of the essential structure of beings and of Being itself, on which Levinas concentrates his attention in the beginning of his article.

The article ends with a list of critical remarks, from which Levinas's later, more elaborate criticisms can be developed. He situates Heidegger in the great philosophical tradition of the West, which began with the question of Being in general and has always seen a connection between its ontological interest and its desire for freedom, mastership, and sovereignty. The Western attempt to master human destiny has always been connected with a movement of transcendence, but the traditional way consisted in the absolutization of one being, such as God, Substance, Idea, Spirit, or Eternity. Heidegger accomplished a revolution by arguing that the question of Being itself precedes the question of a highest being. He continued the Western tradition insofar as he subordinated all ontic truth to ontology, because in doing so he submitted all beings to the "reality" and the "truth" of one selfsame something, *to auto*, *le Même* (EDHH, 88–89), the identity of a self "which, by its existence, has a relation to being," and whose being is constituted by this relation.[25] This relation of existence to itself in the light of Being constitutes the closed circuit of an *interiority* that excludes any authentic otherness. Other beings cannot enter into the self-identity of a being in which the understanding of Being realizes itself without any appeal to otherness.

The closed character of Heidegger's *Dasein* follows also from his analysis of *death*. If nothingness is the secret of time and the authentic foundation of existence, the human person cannot rely on anything other than himself. The rejection of any reference to the Eternal and the insensitivity toward any otherness result in a tragic form of liberty. It belongs to our time, but "perhaps it will be possible to overcome it tomorrow" (EDHH, 89).

This last sentence of the 1940 lecture, pronounced in the first year of World War II, does not sound like the announcement of an imminent victory over Heidegger. During the war, however, Levinas began to develop a philosophy of his own, in which his debt to Heidegger does not prevent him from showing that we must leave Heidegger's thought behind. Fragments of this new philosophy were published in *De l'existence à l'existant* and *Le temps et l'autre*, both published in 1947. Their titles summarize an entire anti-Heideggerian program, but Levinas's criticism remains implicit for the most part. I will therefore pass on to an article of 1949, in which Levinas meditates on the phenomenological method as it was practiced, theorized, and transformed by Husserl and Heidegger: "*De la description à l'existence*" (EDHH, 91–107), but even here the explicit criticism is very brief.

Once again Levinas shows that Heidegger's philosophy is an ontology, after which he concentrates on its central thought, stating that the relationship between beings and Being, according to Heidegger, primarily consists in *understanding and comprehension*. Levinas's criticism is presented in the form of a few rather rhetorical questions. He suggests (1) that the relationship of comprehension is not the only and not the primary one between human existence and Being; and (2) that Heidegger's clarification of understanding is guided by the model of *domination*: the light of Being, within which we understand all beings, dominates us, but because existence is fundamentally comprehension, it too is a *pouvoir*, power and domination. Against a thought led by a certain affinity with power and slavery, Levinas looks for a way out, as he already did in his *De l'évasion* of 1935. Without much elaboration he points to two directions which are also suggested in other publications of the years 1940–50: createdness and sexuality.

The article that completes Levinas' first critical period is "*L'ontologie est-elle fondamentale?*"[26] From the very beginning it presents itself as a questioning and contesting of the primacy of ontology, but a short summary of Heidegger's central thesis precedes the attack.

Heidegger's merit has been to see that philosophy is not the same as a contemplative theory; it rather is the explication of the understanding of being, the understanding that constitutes human existence. Existence has taken over the *transitive* nature of thinking ("I exist the world," "I exist my future, my *Verfallenheit*"), but it cannot transform all the implicit horizons of its direct intentions into clear phenomena. Still, Heidegger maintains that existence is first of all *Seinverständnis*, comprehension, and that being is the light or the openness by which that comprehension is possible.

Levinas's main argument against this position radicalizes the objection he had made since 1930, with Heidegger, against Husserl's identification of philosophy as an objectifying theory. Heidegger opposes that contemplative ideal, but he himself remains subservient to the Western tradition by declaring that the fundamental *Existential* is a form of comprehension (*Verständnis*). Despite his transformation of Western ontology, the structure of *Seinsverständnis* remains that of an understanding which grasps a particular being against a background or horizon or context that has the character of generality and totality. The traditional explanation of knowledge as seizure, definition, or circumscription of a universal essence, concept, or form continues to dominate Heidegger's ontology.

So far, so good. But why should this schema be rejected? Why should a philosopher refuse to state the primacy of understanding and comprehension? For the first time in one of his articles on Heidegger,[27] Levinas answers this question with the clear statement that Heidegger's understanding of existence and of understanding does not permit another human being (*autrui*) to present him- or herself as he or she is. This thesis is the center and source of Levinas's development from the 1940s until the appearance of *Totality and the Infinite* in 1961. The article of 1950 is a first mature explanation and defense of it.

Autrui, the Other, does not affect us in the light of a broader concept or against the horizon of universal Being. To grasp the Other as a particular case of some universal reality is to destroy that which distinguishes another human from all other beings in the world. A Heideggerian defender of ontology will say that being-with-others (*Miteinandersein*) is an essential structure of *Dasein*'s being-in-the-world, and that an authentic relationship with others presupposes a "letting be" (*Seinlassen*) which permits the Other to present his or her proper (mode of) being. But it is not true that the Other appears as a being which we can understand in the light of Being. He/she is not something which has to be looked at on the basis of a preceding *Seinsverständnis*; the Other disappears when reduced to an object of thematic reality. *Autrui* is encountered in the vocative. Meeting with an Other cannot be separated from the invocation by which we address ourselves to him/her. Instead of appearing as a particular entity illuminated by the *Entwurf* of a preceding comprehension of the all-encompassing Being, the Other is an associate who invites me to greet him. *Language* in the sense of talking to (including also the possibility of refusing all communication) is an appropriate response to the self-presentation of another person. The Other's independence escapes every attempt to integrate her as a moment within a horizon. Although the word "totality" is not pronounced in this article, the idea is present, when Levinas writes that the relation to the others "joins, in human faces, the Infinite" (EN, 20). The Other is not the object of a vision— the later Levinas will even say that he is not a phenomenon at all. To look at another's face, the face-to-face of an encounter, has a different structure than that of vision or perception: it has the structure of speech and *language-as-discourse* (*discours*).

From the perspective of ontology one could ask whether the "understanding of Being" cannot be extended to the attitude which has just been described and whether "Being" could not be comprehended in such a way that it separates itself from the model of a horizon or a light within which beings present themselves. Levinas's answer is: not insofar as comprehension always includes a going beyond, a surpassing or a transcendence (*dépassement*) towards something else (EN, 19). As the projection of a horizon within which it captures beings, Heideggerian comprehension repeats the gesture of Western reason. "Letting be" (*Seinlassen*), the permission given to all beings to present themselves in the splendor of their being, has in fact been practiced as an exercise of power and domination. The reduction of particulars to universality is the first theoretical form of violence. The true "order of reason" is an order in which we talk to one another.

It is impossible to get hold of another without reducing her to what she is not, i.e., without killing her. The only way for another to come to the fore is to confront me with the nudity, i.e., the nonuniversality, of her face. The source of light, due to which we "know" another, is not to be found in Being, but in the face that looks at me. The Other's face breaks open the closed circuit of my finite, solipsistic interiority, and thus can be called a manifestation of Infinity. Levinas's long meditation on the meaning of phenomenology and the roots of philosophy has resulted in the following answer: the primary truth and source of all truth is found in the attitude that enables another human to present him/herself as he or she is, i.e., in *moral consciousness*. Conscience is the primary condition of all disclosure (*dévoilement*) and ontology (and not the other way around). If we want to stress the difference of this insight from Heideggerian ontology, we can use the catchword "metaphysics" and state that the post-Heideggerian *metaphysics* of Levinas has the character of a fundamental *ethics*.

From Intentionality to Responsibility: On Levinas's Philosophy of Language

Levinas presents his meditation on language as a central part of his persistent reflection on Edmund Husserl's principle of intentionality.[1] By systematizing somewhat the elements of a theory of language that can be found mainly in *Otherwise than Being or Beyond Essence* (AE, 39–76, 167–218; OB, 31–59, 131–71) and the essay "Language and Proximity" (EDHH, 218–36; CP, 109–26), I shall try to give a succinct picture of Levinas's critical retrieval of that principle and his passing beyond it toward a trans- or pre-intentional origin, which, in fact, is not an *arche* but an *an-archical* point of departure.

The Principle of Phenomenology

Let us follow the main line of Levinas's argument in "Language and Proximity" and start from intuition, "the principle of principles," as Husserl calls it in *Ideas* I, section 24:

> Every originarily given intuition is a source for the legitimation of knowledge; everything that presents itself originarily to us (so to say in bodily actuality), must be simply accepted as that as what it gives itself, but only within the limits within which it therein gives itself. . . . Every enunciation [*Aussage*] that does not do anything else than to give expression to such givens [*Gegebenheiten*] through mere explication and adequately corresponding significations, is therefore actually . . .

an absolute beginning [*Anfang*], that is, in a true sense, called to be a foundation [*Grundlegung*], *principium*.[2]

Many questions may arise from the reading of this text. An important one concerns the expressions "originarily present" and "given." If, for this moment, we grant Husserl that the search for an absolute foundation of knowledge does not rest on dogmatic or false assumptions, we might ask: Where do we find a given that has the character of an origin and can function as foundation? We know Husserl's answer: it is the intuition of some *x* that presents itself as though it were a living body there in front of our eyes. Intuition is claimed to assure a firm ground on which we can build other layers of a solid construction called "true and ascertained knowledge." This answer, however, provokes the following critical question: Does the metaphor of an eye seeing bodies render adequately a primordial evidence that is able to function as an origin?

Plato is the original authority for the seeing metaphor. In the *Republic* (507d–509c) he stated that a truthful contact between eye and phenomenon would not be possible without a specific mediation that accords light to both the phenomenon and the looking eye. His meditation on this necessary medium resulted in a metaphysics that proclaimed the source of light itself to be more eminent and more originary than either the world of phenomena or the seeing psyche recognizing them as phenomena.

There are other possibilities of making contact with reality. The mediation on which the hearing of a sound depends is less obvious, and the distance between the hearer and the heard is smaller than that of visual perceptions, but distance and mediation cannot be abolished altogether. Feeling, however, seems to be the most immediate way of being in touch with phenomena or their primordial constituents.

The most elementary sensation is the most immediate contact between a sensing and a sensed, so immediate that we may call it a fusion or confusion. If there is no experience of any distance at all, the feeling and the felt are not given as distinct elements. Can we, in this case, speak of anything given? To whom, to what, *as* what, then, would it be given? If this immediacy were the most radical and the all-encompassing dimension of human existence, the origin would be the unity of a pure confusion without contours or relations; a chaotic and "formless void" before the emergence of any profile (AE, 40–43; OB, 32–34).

In *Otherwise than Being* (AE, 41–43; OB 32–34), Levinas observes that when Husserl introduces the notion of an arch-impression (*Ur-impression*) as the absolute start of all experience—a sort of first creation—he hints at a sort of timeless presence "before" all possible modifications and before the scission that splits consciousness and Being. If consciousness and Being have not yet separated, the "presentation" or "giving" of something to, for, or by consciousness is impossible. And since consciousness is understood by Husserl as "having present before" or as "presenting or re-presenting something to itself," there is, at this level of first creation or *archi-presence*, neither consciousness nor givenness. Intentionality and phenomenality have not yet emerged.

In order to be presented or given, that is, in order to appear or become phenomenal, a being must deploy itself *in time*. A being becomes a phenomenon (or an element thereof), the hidden becomes perceptible, a timeless presence becomes a given presence, by unfolding itself within the openness of temporality. The exhibition of something before consciousness is conditioned by the temporal ekstases of its unrolling itself from a past to a future, while the ekstases through retention (memory) and protention (expectation) are gathered into the horizon of a concrete presentation or representation.[3] Intuition, the principle of principles, is conditioned by temporal modifications that do not alter the content of the given. Disclosedness implies, or rather *is*, the deployment of time. The phenomenality of all phenomena presupposes and essentially implies temporality. Time is the light without which perceptibility would be impossible (AE, 33–38; OB, 26–30).

For the experience and the concept of presence, this insight involves, as a consequence, that "the present" is *either* that which, as a moment of the primitive flow of time, is never present—one comes always too late to capture it—*or* something that comes "after" the originary gathering of temporal ekstases: something captured and arrested—for example, as a theme—by an identifying gesture. To become conscious of an *x* as "this-here-and-now," one must come back onto that which already has passed or is being passed. By a most elementary sort of *anamnesis* (recollection), one must remember what already has escaped. Without time, consciousness would not awaken from its immersion in the indistinct confusion (EDHH, 222–23; CP, 113–15). The "bodily presence" of a phenomenon is constituted by the gathering of its temporal ekstases; it presupposes a presentification, and this is, as we will see, possible only as an active identification.

Indeed, the presentification to which a phenomenon owes its possibility of appearing before consciousness demands more than temporality alone. To appear as a phenomenon, Being must also be identified *as this or that*. Through identification the confusion-before-creation receives its first possibility of showing shapes and figures. In the absence of any identification, there would be only the rustling of a totally anonymous and shapeless "there is" (*il y a*) in which everything gets confused with everything else.

The identification of a phenomenon as this or that is its *thematization*: "Being manifests itself by becoming a theme," that is, by being gathered, centered, and posited as . . . The identity of a phenomenon is *thetic* in virtue of its being "seen" or "thought of" *as* an issue taken and stated as this or that. To "see" or "conceive" of a given as this or that is not a form of pure receptivity, but a specific way of looking at or "taking" and positing as. Consciousness "takes" or "*means*" the given *as* . . . Identification is a *Meinen* and *Vermeinen*. The *as-structure* indicates the position achieved by consciousness in every possible intuition to lay hands on a phenomenon.[4] Intentionality implies the capturing of givens through the recollection of their sensible multiplicity by taking or positing them as thetic realities. There is a sort of sovereignty in this way of getting in touch with the given. Consciousness leads the game and determines the positions of the pawns (see EDHH, 218–19; CP, 110–11).

By taking a phenomenon as a theme, I perceive it in the light of a specific meaning expressed by the "as" of the as-structure. To use Husserlian terms: I impose an ideality on a given. Being cannot become phenomenal if it does not appear as having this or that meaning. This meaning, however, is not given immediately before any temporal synchronization and thematic recollection. The given must be meant in order to have a meaning. In a way, its meaning is not given, but rather imposed. To mean this *as* this, is a claim or allegiance (*prétention*) through which consciousness *intends*, or even—in a prebehavioral sense—"wills" the given as an appearance. To make this constitutive moment of phenomenality and perception understandable, Levinas uses the ambiguity of the German word *meinen*, which means "to have the impression, the belief, or the conviction that" as well as "to intend," "to aim," or "to have the purpose," and of the French *entendre*, which means "to understand" as well as "to want" or "to will."[5] The original understanding of a phenomenon is not a purely passive reception through which it would produce a corresponding "idea" in a perceiving consciousness, but an *intention* in the strong sense of an intending (*entendre*) that is a claim, a pretending (*prétendre*) or pretension (*prétention*), which may be justifiable or not. The difference between the immediately given and the meaning claimed or "pretended" by consciousness cannot be abolished by any evidence. This difference does not lie in the distance between the emptiness of a signitive act and the originary given of a bodily present phenomenon, a distance that could be bridged progressively, at least in part, by a series of new experiences; it is the difference of two different dimensions (EDHH, 218; CP, 110). The meaning is neither given nor not-given; it is meant, claimed, pretended. The fulfillment of the empty signitive act is therefore necessarily delayed. For the presence of a phenomenon it is essential that consciousness subsumes, gathers, and synchronizes the given multiplicity under a theme. The intending or meaning of a phenomenon as a present this or that achieves a *synopis*. Without such a synopsis, intuition would not be possible. The authority of Husserl's "principle of all principles," thus, rests upon the meaning or "intention" (including a "pretention") by which a synthetic and synchronic, thematizing and identifying consciousness presents and—as temporal consciousness—represents the given.

Meaning and Language

If the identification of a being presupposes its thematization in the light of an ideal meaning, the imposition of this ideality on the given—its being taken and claimed as . . . —presupposes its being illuminated and consecrated by a prelingual doxa: an "*Urdoxa*" or naming for which Levinas uses the expressions *epos* and *fable*.

From the outset a given is perceived, taken as . . . , thematized, and identified in light of and as an instance of something that goes beyond the given as simply received: a sort of "already said" (*déjà-dit*) that is not yet heard or spoken, but is already more than a perceptual grasping of the given (AE, 45–46; OB, 35–36). If Levinas uses the word "fable" to indicate this *verbum mentis* or fore-word,[6] he probably alludes to the character of an exemplary story that can be illustrated by many cases. The word "epos" (AE, 46, 48; OB, 34, 36) stresses the narrative context of our thematizing of phenomena, as well as the (pre-)linguistic aspect of our "meaning" them as meaningful. The "already said" of this doxa or epos precedes, however, all particular languages of history.[7]

In going beyond mere givenness, the ideal meaning is a universal, but its universality cannot be understood as that of a genus or species of which the phenomena of human experience would be the individual realizations. The identification of *this as this* does not proceed by individualization or exemplification of a universal idea that would be present as an a priori. Even the very first phenomenon that strikes us is necessarily seen as the appearance of a meaning that is not exhausted by this appearance. But neither is it a case of a general idea remaining equal to itself in all the instances concretizing it. Even a *singulare tantum* like Socrates is perceived as an instance of a certain way of being that could be called "Socratizing" (AE, 53; OB, 41).

Although the ontological status of the prelinguistic epos or fable is not easy to determine, there must be such a sort of fore-word preceding actual speech or writing, because the thematizing identification, by which a phenomenon is constituted as such, would not be possible, if it were not guided by an affirmation or affirmative gesture, which normally expresses itself in linguistic discourse. The affirmative character of identification is *kerygmatic*: to identify a being is to pronounce a kerygma or proclamation; consciousness proclaims this phenomenon to be this and such. The most explicit form of such a proclamation is a philosophical judgment, but the same structure can be found in any narration, myth, tale, or story. All of them gather things, events, and relations into the synchronic unity of a whole, in which the fluency of time is punctuated by the identification of knots and relations. Predication, as contained in a philosophical theory, is an explicit form of kerygmatic identification by which immediate experience is laid open as a world of phenomena. The overcoming of the prephenomenal chaos and the emergence of an order from the anonymous grumbling of Being before "creation" is conditioned by the logos of a saying or writing, which—in its turn—is conditioned by the emergence of givens from the persistent flow of time.

The appearance of a phenomenon implies, thus, the essential structure of *phenomenology*. Intentionality is a specific union of consciousness and Being, made possible by a thematic way of Saying (*Dire*). Every phenomenon is (a) Said (*Dit*). The exhibition of being, its disclosure or manifestation, the very idea of phenomenality presupposes *and* conditions a particular mode of language: the *apophantic* language of gathering identification and thematic presentification of a said; kerygmatic proclamation; phenomenology.

Language and Being

We remain within the dimension of the phenomenologically said when we reflect, with Levinas, upon the "amphibology of being." As with the French *être* the English word *being* can, indeed, be used to *name* a single being or the totality of all beings, but also used as a *verb*, to indicate the being process, which—as Heidegger showed—must be understood as the active and transitive essence, or *essance*, thanks to which beings are, in various ways, what they are. Without entering, at this moment, into a discussion of the ontological difference as understood by Heidegger and reinterpreted by Levinas, I would like to dwell a little while on the linguistic difference through which the ontological difference is said.[8]

If Levinas is right in pointing out that the identification of phenomenal being implies a kerygmatic proclamation, which is the core of apophantic language, then being and language are so intimately connected that an adequate distinction between them is impossible. Being is inseparable from its spoken meaning. Then, also, the ways in which beings appear or "are" can be heard in language.

The designation of a being by a *noun* identifies it as a characteristic unit emerging from the constant flow of time. It is fixed and, to a certain extent, immobilized. By denomination one takes a being from the anonymous "there is" (*il y a*) of confused and chaotic sensation. Designation by nouns presupposes a preceding epos or fable: the speaker must already have heard a fore-word; he obeys a pro-phetic doxa when he tries to name the being that happens to him. To capture a being by a noun is a sort of consecration, without which that being would not be what it is.

The Said is not exhausted by *nouns* alone, however; *verbs*, too, belong to its possibilities of proclamation. Verbs do not immobilize beings; thanks to them the fluency and the modifications of beings' Being as a process of temporalization becomes apparent and audible. In a verb we can hear the vibration of sensibility, the modes of essence, the adverbiality of beings, the ways in which things and events pass as modifications of the ongoing deployment of disclosure. A noun does not suffice to say what happens or what is the case. The Being of what there is—i.e., the temporal essence of things, relations, and events—needs apophantic predication to become perceptible. There is no essence or appearance behind the Said; the verbally Said *is* the ostension and disclosure of Being. In the predicative proposition the verb "exposes the silent resonance of the essence" (AE, 51; OB, 40). In a verb, Being is meant and heard as time. Temporality is the verbality of Being.

The power of verbality is best expressed in contemporary art. This is not only an example, but the very expression of the secret of the Said and its attractive realm. Instead of fixing figures and profiles, or telling tales about events, today's art celebrates the ways in which essence and temporality pass, appearing and resounding in their modifications. As mere ostension of modalities of Being, art is absolute exhibition without fixed quiddities. All representations of things are liquified in order to show colors, contrasts, timbres, rhythms, sounds, qualities. Everything must sing. The modalities of essence must beam and dance before eyes and ears. This demands a continuous renewal. Conformity to once-accepted standards and iconographic codes would result in the withdrawal of Being's modalities. In art the language of words, forms and sounds has become a "pure how" ("*un pur comment,*" AE, 52; OB, 40). Not only music and architecture but all sorts of art show the adverbiality of Being, which is forgotten if we concentrate on nouns and substantives.

It is, perhaps, not fortuitous that in philosophy, too, art has become more important than morality since Hegel dedicated much of his courses to aesthetics, whereas moral philosophy was made a subordinate part of his theory of law, economy, and the state. Heidegger too thought that he could delay indefinitely the questions of ethics, whereas poetics and visual arts were as important as philosophy itself for him. As we will see, for Levinas morality is as important and originary as the questions of metaphysics and more important than ontology and art. In order to understand why this does not represent a simple backsliding into the pre-Heideggerian tradition of philosophy, we must continue our analysis of language.

To conclude the first stage of this analysis, we may state that the amphibology of Being belongs to the dimension of the Said. The hesitation of language between nouns and verbs, its switching from beings to Being and the other way around, characterizes it as logos, *apophansis*, Said (*Le Dit*). Language is more than that which is or can be said, however; it is more than the resounding essence of beings and their essance, more than an epos, myth, or *Sage*, more than the disclosure of a difference that would be restricted to the realm of ontology.

Saying

Perception and language have been described so far as belonging to the realm of "the Said" (*le Dit*). By this expression Levinas does not want to suggest an opposition between spoken and written language—on the contrary, written texts are the clearest examples of the Said. As opposed to the Saying (*le Dire*), the Said encompasses all discourses or narratives in which beings are identified and essence verbalized. The opposition between Saying and Said is neither a difference of two species belonging to one genus nor a dialectical contradiction like that between Being and non-Being. It is simultaneously a separation and an intimate relation between two dimensions that cannot be synthesized or integrated into a totality. (See for this and the following explication AE, 55–61; OB, 43–48).

According to Levinas, the whole history of Western philosophy has been dominated by the idea that the philosophical problem of language can be identified as a problem of texts in which beings and Being show themselves by being worded in speech or writing. The whole of philosophy would coincide with *phenomenology*, and since the phenomena cannot show themselves as meaningful if they are not worded, philosophy would also necessarily be a *logology*.

Heidegger has awakened our consciousness to the ontological difference, but, in Levinas's interpretation, Heidegger's diagnosis of our civilization and his search for a more originary origin have remained captive to the phenomenological and logological intentions of Greek-Western philosophy. Without minimizing the importance of the ontological difference and its oblivion, Levinas indicates a more radical oblivion when he points at a very simple fact, which surprisingly never has been taken into serious account by philosophy: *the fact that a discourse or epos (or Sage) always is said by someone to one or more others (or to oneself as listener or reader)*.

The saying of a said is certainly one of the most ordinary and basic events of everybody's everyday life, as well as a root of the whole enterprise of civilization, unfolding itself in communication, social institutions, moral codes, skills, science, philosophy, religion, etc. Why, then, has the Saying as such never become a theme of philosophical reflection? Why has this always concentrated exclusively on the Said, without thematizing the Saying through and "in" which the Said exists?

The first answer is that Saying resists becoming a theme. As we have seen, the very structure of thematization makes every being into a said, i.e., into a being that is identified as a phenomenon within the context of a story or discourse. Saying a said is not an element of such a context; it signifies a text and a context, but stays out of them by preceding all saids.

If it is true that Saying cannot be treated as a special sort or case of Said, how then can we describe and analyze it? Descriptions, analyses, characterizations, theories, etc., are, indeed, ways of identification and thematization. If Saying is not a phenomenon—i.e., if it is neither a being nor Being as such—and if it is not a structure or form that can be identified as an element of Being, how can we, then, give it a place in philosophy?

Levinas uses the Husserlian word *reduction* to indicate a way of writing and speaking philosophically about Saying without simply reducing it to a variety of the Said. When we try to give a description and an analysis of Saying, the theme from which our reflection takes its departure is the Said. In a retrogressive and backward-thinking way we must, then, hint at the otherness by which the Saying, prior to all Saids, differs from any theme. The difficulties met here are analogous to those of Heidegger's attempt to name Being itself in its difference from the universe of beings and to those of neo-Platonic thought in trying to transcend the realm of noeta toward the One that cannot be treated as a subject of apophantic language. In a way somewhat similar to but also different from the pseudo-Dionysian negative theology, Levinas tries to solve the paradox of a discourse on that which precedes but cannot enter into any discourse, by defending the necessity of alternately saying (*dire* in the sense of stating) and unsaying (*dédire* in the sense of denying) all that ought to be said about Saying. But before we draw our attention to this apology for his texts about Saying, let us first concentrate on their content.

Language is not only and not primarily enunciation, apophansis or expression, but *communication*. In talking or writing I always address my words—and myself!—to someone: I speak to another person who I suppose hears me. Even if I speak or write to myself, I, the listener or reader of my words, differ from myself as writer or speaker. Speaking or writing, thus, includes necessarily a relation between someone and some Other. This relation is the fact or event forgotten by Western philosophy.

One way to obscure it or leave it unnoticed is by simply not talking about it, as if it were self-evident that and how we can communicate, whereas everybody's relationships to world, society, Being, and oneself are considered to be problematic and worthwhile to be reflected upon.

Another way of hiding the peculiarity of Saying is to distort it by treating it as a phenomenon comparable to other phenomena. To speak to someone is radically different from treating somebody as the noema of an intention of mine, however. The Other to whom I speak is not there before me as a phenomenon who I can observe, study, analyze, reflect upon, but as someone to whom I offer something that I have observed, felt, heard, studied, reflected upon, written, or said. Of course, I can take the measures of someone's body, look at the color of human eyes, appreciate the beauty of somebody's nose, but these intentions are separated by an unbridgeable abyss from the relation constituted by speaking to—or by facing—another. The phenomenon seen by looking at the color of someone's eyes or the peculiarities of a human individual's anatomy belong to the universe of beings that can and must be described by an overall phenomenology, but the other to whom I speak is not such a phenomenon, and my relation to him or her does not have the structure of intentionality. By treating or observing another in a way that would be appropriate to a phenomenon in the normal sense of the word, I prevent myself from having an encounter with this person. In facing a face that looks at me and in speaking to someone, I separate myself from the identifying and thematizing attitude that is characteristic of a theoretical, a technical, or an aesthetic approach. By seeing another as an interesting variety of phenomenal being I reduce the Other's otherness to an element of the thematic universe or context over which I preside by giving a place and function to all beings, relations, and events. By describing another as someone with green eyes, an elegant mouth, a sportive suit, a sweet voice, brilliant ideas, great erudition, and a pleasant character, I miss exactly the element that makes it possible that this person can face me and that I can speak to her or him. The one to whom I address myself in speaking or writing is not an element of any context; as long as we think in terms of phenomenal beings that have a place and function in texts and contexts, the Other is a hole or absence: in contrast to the phenomena that I can observe, the Other whom I meet as Other is *invisible.*

According to Levinas, to whom phenomenality, as we have seen, is equivalent with the possibility of being identified and thematized, the Other is not a phenomenon, but an enigma.

The Western fascination with theory and thematization has neglected or repressed the truth of the Other's emergence from the context of noematic beings. This is the second answer to the question why Saying and facing, and, in general, the relation between one human and the Other, have been hidden in our civilization. The theoretical intention is essentially inapt to take this most trivial experience of everyday life seriously; it cannot do justice to the fact that words are *addressed to someone.* The problem with philosophy is that, as soon as we want to concentrate on this experience, we make it into a theme and in so doing betray its truth: by becoming a theme, an address hides or loses the very moment of Saying and, therefore, that by which its "signification" is communicative or signifying. By reducing it to a theme we cut the Saying off from its orientation toward an actual or possible hearer and thus kill it as Saying. The "to" has changed into the "in front of" or "before" of a noema that is present before consciousness, or into the "*with*" of our similarity or equality as cohuman participants in a collective *we.*

A *third* way of forgetting or repressing the otherness of Saying is to identify the problem of communication from the outset as a question of participation. If communication can be understood as a way of sharing common views or arguments, the relation of speaker to listener can be reduced to the universality and fundamental sameness of all human beings who recognize one another as participants in a common culture or ethos. This is the way followed by Heidegger when he treats communication as a form of *Mitteilung* and analyzes it as a particular mode of the existential *Mitsein* (SZ, 214–21).

In *Sein und Zeit* (sec. 34), language is defined as the being-spoken-out of discourse (*Rede*), and discourse as the "signifying" articulation of the understandability of being-in-the-world. *Mitteilung,* sharing-with or the communicative aspect of language, comes to the fore if we notice that being-with (*Mitsein*) belongs as an existential constituent to being-in-the-world and that this always exists in a determinate mode of being-with-others (*Miteinandersein*). Among the constitutive moments of discourse (*Rede*), sharing-with (*Mitteilung*) must, therefore, be listed with the "what about" (das *Worüber*), the articulated (*das Geredete*), and the announcement (*die Bekundung*), (SZ, 216). In a strict parallelism with the relation between *Dasein* in general and its constituent *Mitsein*, which in sections 25–26 was introduced briefly as an introduction to and for the sake of the analysis of *das Man* in section 27, Heidegger treats *Mitteilung* in section 34 as a moment of language that comes after its primary essence, which is the articulation of *Dasein*'s understanding of its being-in-the-world. Apophantic communication is a special case of the fundamental communication that is contained in the existential being-with. On this fundamental level there is already a sharing of disposedness (*Befindlichkeit*) and understanding (*Verstehen*) of being-in-the-world and being-with-others. Before any linguistic communication these existential structures are already revealed to those who share those structures as well as their being revealed and understood. The newness of the *Mitteilung* lies *only* in the explicit sharing (*Teilung*) of the *with* (*Mit*) by which they are joined in *Dasein* (SZ, 215).

Hearing is analyzed by Heidegger in a similar way (SZ, 217–18). The most original *Hören* is the existential openness of *Dasein* to its own capability of being. It is a belonging (*Hörigkeit*), made possible by the understanding in which Dasein as being-in-the-world-with-others hears and listens (is *hörig* with regard) to itself and belongs (is *zugehörig*) to itself. Speaking and hearing are considered exclusively to uncover the structure of *Dasein*-with-others-near-innerworldly-beings. "With" (*mit*) and "near" (*bei*) specify the "*in*" of the "being-in." The relation to other humans is reduced to the "with" or the side-by-side of common participation, and this is subordinated to the overall relation of *Dasein* and *world*. No attention at all is given to the confrontation of two persons who speak to one another or to the encounter of two facing faces. The exchange of words, the alternation of addressing and responding essential to *all* speech—even if an answer is not given actually, but only expected—is not even mentioned, except, perhaps, in one place, where its importance is denied rather bluntly: "A denial as answer, too, results at first directly from the understanding of the 'shared' what-about (*Worüber*) of speech."[9]

Our conclusion must be that Heidegger was not interested in that aspect of communication which is *not* reducible to a preceding and already present understanding common to people who meet and speak. For Heidegger there is nothing radically new in a speech I listen to or in the face that looks at me; communication is primarily, even exclusively, sharing and explicitation.

In *The Origin of the Work of Art,* Heidegger is still more explicit when he states that—notwithstanding the current opinion, according to which the essence of language is a sort of communication (*Mitteilung*)— "language is not only and not primarily an expression by sounds or writing of that which ought to be communicated." Its primary essence is its "bringing all beings as beings into the open" (*die Sprache bringt das Seiende als ein Seiendes allererst ins Offene*). In the absence of language there is no openness of Being. In naming beings, language—by proclamation— "brings them from their being to their being" (GA, 5, 61). Here, all Heidegger's attention is directed toward the triangle Language-*Dasein*-Being, as in *Sein und Zeit* it was concentrated on *Dasein-Rede-*World. The possibility of transcending myself and the world by addressing them to another who is not contained in them, is hidden by the caricature of "a transport of experiences, e.g., opinions and desires, from the interiority of one subject into the interiority of another subject" (SZ, 215). According to Levinas, the alternative presented before the reader—either to vote for this caricature or to accept a description that reduces all intersubjectivity to shared participation in an anonymous instance fully present in *Dasein* as such—distorts the actuality of speaking and the human face-to-face. Although our speaking depends to a very large extent on the sagas and myths, the literary traditions and current sayings of the contexts in which we have become what we are, it is *not* true that language, understood as an anonymous power, speaks. The sentence telling us that language speaks[10] may be a rhetorically justified provocation meant to awaken our thought to a forgotten truth, but exaggerations like "the death of the subject," "the repression of all individuality," and "the indefinite delay of ethics" are refuted by the simple fact that all saids and texts are addressed by someone to some Other. There is always a vocative in our language; the irreducible relation to the addressee is clearly expressed not only in greetings that do not contain any message ("Hello!" or "Hi!"), but also in very informative sentences, since they are always spoken *to* or written *for* someone, who thereby is provoked to an answer. The fact that both the provocation and the answer, as to their content and form, can be understood as variations on the traditional patterns of a shared culture and ethos, does not abolish their being uttered and addressed by a saying that does not enter, as a contextual or intertextual element, into any said.

Whereas Heidegger's search is dominated by the quest of Being itself, Levinas points to another beyond: the Other who faces me, awakens me to a "dimension" beyond the universe of beings and their Being. In speaking to somebody I transcend the realm of Being by accepting my being meant to be there for the Other.

Responsibility

In saying something to you, I not only present a text, but I expose, discover, present, and offer myself to you, who happen to hear me. You surprise me by coming to me. Even if I invited you, your coming disturbs my world. Indeed, your entering into my dwelling place interrupts the coherence of my economy; you disarrange my order in which all things familiar to me have their proper place, function, and time. Your emergence makes holes in the walls of my house. If I could see and treat you as a being amidst other beings, like a knot in the all-encompassing time flow, or as an element of a universe unfolding its riches before my mental eye, you would have been bereft of everything that justifies my calling you by the pronoun "you." You would be a peculiar part of my realm.

To speak is not a special sort of intention that would be comparable to other noetico-noematic correlations; it is *transcendence*—the happening of a relation that "precedes" and conditions all sorts of intentions by offering the *whole* of my identifying and verbalizing acts, that is, the whole of my world, to someone who is not a part or moment or event within that whole. You and I are not to be found "*in*" the world, because you come from afar and, in speaking to you, I do not coincide with my being-in-the-world. The relation by which you and I are connected and separated, is not a constituent of our being-in-the-world; you cannot be seen as a worldly being, whereas my subjectivity, as response to your facing me, precedes any nestling in the domain of phenomenal beings. Your being you is your invisibility; my being me is the origin of all responsibility: responsibility for you, for others, for all the others, and also for me.[11]

If we understand "*Mitsein*" as an expression of our coparticipation in a common culture, it is an existential constituent of our being-in-the-world, but neither "mineness" nor "yourness" can enter into this concept, except, perhaps, to indicate the characteristic style of your and my works and words. If, however, we take "*Mitsein*" to mean the originary—or, as Levinas calls it, the pre-original—relation from which all intersubjective and social contacts between humans spring, we must say that it does not belong, as a constitutive element, to the world and our being-in-it. The totality of our being-in-the-world (its *Ganzheit*, as Heidegger persistently calls it in *Sein und Zeit* and in the courses of the late 1920s)[12] either forbids the entrance of another or is broken by it. The Other who looks at me is not a phenomenon; a face is invisible, because it cannot be identified as a theme; it is not the noema of an intention in the sense that was described before. The "epiphany" of a visage cannot become familiar as a piece of my surroundings or a part of my social context; the Other pierces the skin of my world when she visits me as an absolute stranger coming from beyond.[13]

My speech, too, comes from a "beyond," insofar as it precedes everything which is or can be said thematically. Saying is and remains exterior to the totality of texts that can be presented by it. The exteriority, which, according to its subtitle *"Essai sur l'extériorité,"* is the subject of *Totality and the Infinite,* is an otherwise than the being of phenomena, and, if phenomenality is synonymous with Being, it "is" an *otherwise than* or a "beyond" of *Being.*

Even if my saying is a thematizing one, it cannot enter, as an element, into the discourse offered by it. It cannot be interpreted or appropriated because it precedes all contents and forms or structures. In its contentless and nondiscursive repetition it is always new, it has always already passed when its message is heard. It comes from a past that never can become a present. Its originality consists in the fact that it cannot be treated as a cause or ground, an *archē* or origin within the horizons of phenomenology and ontology. This is the reason why Levinas does not call Saying an origin of the Said, but rather calls it the pre-original past from which the Said comes—a past that never can become a graspable or identifiable present.

The subject of my speaking to another is the I who is responding to the stranger who visits me. Finding myself facing another awakens me to *responsibility*: an infinite responsibility for the Other, who is in need of everything that is necessary for a human life. By addressing myself to another I practice this responsibility, be it reluctantly or not. A total refusal of it would express itself through murder. Total acceptance would coincide with perfect love.

Speaking can never become a theme or noema because its structure is radically different: it establishes a *contact* and a *proximity* which are neither forms of knowledge nor possible themes of a theory. The relation between speaker and listener is not a theoretical or thetic intention; it precedes the scission of theory and practice but includes an ethical moment. The pretheoretical responsibility practiced in proximity is analyzed by Levinas as *substitution, obsession, accusation, election,* and *persecution.* The existential structure of "the one-for-the-other" marks every human life as a "me" in the accusative (the accusative of my responding to an appeal by the words *"me voici"*—"See me, here and now"). The subjectivity of this "me" is being the one—the unique one—who is responsible for any Other who arises in front of me. Affected by the defenseless nudity of another's face, I am exposed and inescapably delivered to an orientation that does not rest upon a choice of mine. The human subject is not dead, but it is not absolute autonomy either. Against the dogma of an original and originary liberty, and against its total abolition by some writers of today, Levinas shows that the obligations of my responsibility do not stem from any decision or contact or convention originating in my or our will. Before I even could think or choose or freely accept, I have become responsible. My responsibility for the Others has begun before I became aware of my own being. Before my capacity to will, there is a more profound *passivity* in me. Human subjectivity has been determined by a past that never was and never will be a present. An immemorial and irretrievable past has made me this individual here and now, who came from nowhere, to be responsible for these Others.

Responsibility can be described as a prephenomenal and pre-ontological inspiration, but this should not lead us to the idea of an ethereal something, a soul or ghost that hides behind the skin of a human body. Against all forms of anthropological dualism, Levinas's analyses show that human subjectivity exists as a sensible, affective, working, speaking, and suffering body, whose skin is the possibility of contact, proximity, and vulnerability and whose respiration is the dynamism of a moral inspiration and the expiration of someone who lives for Others who may continue to live after one's death.

The human body with its sensibility is not an exclusively altruistic possibility, however. As directed toward Others it also enjoys earthly satisfactions and pleasures. The appeal to responsibility is heard by someone who already has been immersed in an ocean of lust and pains. Even after the discovery of Other-directed responsibility, enjoyment still remains a necessity. Indeed, what could I offer the Others, if it were not in any respect pleasant? Or what could I give, if I did not know by experience how good it feels to receive these gifts?

Signification

If speaking and writing are, first of all, responding to another's entrance into the world of the speaker or writer, the basic structure of language is the contact between one singularity indicating itself as "I" and another singularity called "you" by "me." The anonymous language of grammar and semantic theory comes after that. Language does not speak: it is the realm of all that has been or can be said; human subjects, however, speak, for example, when they greet each other without saying anything that has the character of a thesis or information. The realm of the Said is the realm of Western ontology. In it the truth of body, language, perception, culture, and subjectivity is confined to meanings that are perceptible from a phenomenological perspective. The individuality of speakers and listeners and the peculiarity of their relationships disappear behind the universality of the noematic correlates of the theoretical approach. This can be illustrated by an analysis of human *signature*.

If, in our reading of a text, we concentrate on that which therein is said, it will be difficult not to agree with those who state that every text is an exponent of a common heritage made up of ongoing myths and discursive practices that do not belong to anybody. In this context a signature does not indicate more than an act of appropriation, which may still be justified to a certain extent, insofar as the author of some new text has marked the anonymous heritage by a more or less original style. From the perspective of the Said a signature is the name of a work or style that differs from other works or styles in the history of a culture. The individuals behind the work are not interesting except insofar as the peculiarities of their texts and their affiliations can be understood better through information about their life.

If language primarily is not an anonymous condition or source of Saying, but Saying itself, a signature is a gesture by which writers signal their responsibility for possible readers. By a sort of greeting they expose themselves as subjects who do not want to escape from their obligation to approach possible readers in a responsible way. Without having the pretension that we can originate or possess the content and the presuppositions of our texts, we still agree to our responsibility for them. Being the guardians of the language, the ethos, and the culture that have become ours through education and practice, we are "condemned" to give apologies for particular traditions. Nobody has invented the sources of our being human, but no individual, not even the most empty or stupid one, can be reduced to his work as if he were an event of language. For everybody's speaking or writing comes from a pre-original or anachronic past before culture and transcends the boundaries of any phenomenology.

Saying and Denying

The difference between the Saying and the Said cannot be the last word of a philosophy, because the relations by which they are connected demand reflection. However, such a reflection necessarily thematizes those relations and the two terms they relate, just as the foregoing and all possible reflection on transcendence betrays it in the very act of distinguishing it from intentionality. What is Levinas's answer to this paradox?

The program that must be executed in order to solve this paradox embraces three main questions: *First,* one must justify the enterprise of philosophically talking about a reality—transcendence, Saying, substitution, subjectivity, etc.—that does not permit us to treat it as a phenomenon, a noema, or a theme, and to which Levinas even denies the name of Being. Once a philosophical discourse about a "beyond of Being" has been justified, one ought, *secondly,* to show how the two incomparable dimensions of the Said and the Saying can be brought together in a philosophy of their difference and connectedness, that is, how phenomenology (or ontology) within one text can go together with nonphenomenological transcendence. *Thirdly,* a metatheoretical reflection is needed in order to determine the mode of thought by which this philosophy of both essence *and* transcendence can save itself from absurdity. Since it is impossible to treat here these questions in a satisfactory way, I will conclude by giving only a very succinct summary of Levinas' answer to the first question: How is it possible to approach philosophically the pre-original or *an-archical* beyond that cannot be captured by the normal, reflective, and thematizing methods of our philosophical tradition?

Levinas agrees that his whole discourse on the Other, Saying, subjectivity, transcendance, etc., betrays these nonobjects by thematizing them. Although they are neither themes nor parts of the Said, within philosophy they are necessarily treated as if they were. Still, Levinas could say that his work shows that one can thematize and (re)present these "nonphenomena" in a way that makes their radical difference from phenomenal beings understandable. Thematizing language apparently has two possibilities: besides the normal one, it is capable of pointing at, and of somehow determining, the borderlines of the thematizable as well as that which "is" beyond. Because such a determination necessarily involves a negation with regard to the essence of phenomenal, identifiable, and thematizable being, it involves a denial of whatever has been and must be said in a thematizing way. This denial cannot constitute a dialectical negation, which would lead to a synthetic concept. For if this were the appropriate method, transcendence, Saying, and otherness would reveal themselves to be moments of a thought that has all the features of a present panorama identified by a solitary eye. The thetic treatment of transcendence and its subsequent denial, thus, create a tension that cannot be overcome by a straightforward discourse. A reconciliation within philosophy is not possible, if the concept of reconciliation implies a synthetic and synchronic view in which the two dimensions are understood as parts of one whole. Stating and denying, saying (*dire*) and unsaying (*dédire*),[14] evoking and revoking are both necessary to bring our thought into a good relation with the transcendent. But since they cannot be thought simultaneously, their mode is alternation. Instead of the synchronic time of traditional philosophy, the *diachrony* of successive affirmations and denials is the only possibility of being true to "what there is and happens" and the conditions thereof. According to Levinas, all discourses must result in the undoing of the tissue they wove. Is Penelope, more than Parmenides, the patron of philosophy?

A repetitious and never-ending succession of saying and unsaying of the thematically Said does not constitute a satisfactory theory. It seems to indicate a dead end, an "end" or frontier of philosophy itself. Levinas goes one step further when he states that the destination of apophantic language (the Said) is in its "ancillary or angelic" function (AE, 7; OB, 6). The subordination of all said to saying contains the seed of a metatheory of philosophy, in which there is, perhaps, more than the repetition of affirmations and negations without end. When Levinas, at the end of *Otherwise than Being*, explains the word "philosophy" as meaning an understanding on the basis of and from the perspective of love (*sophia tes philias*, "*une sagesse de l'amour*," AE, 207; OB, 162), he points to a source beyond philosophy that might be approached more closely by a devoted life than by the profound reflections of ontology.

Through Being to the Anarchy of Transcendence: A Commentary on the First Chapter of *Otherwise than Being*

I t is very difficult, if not impossible, to understand *Otherwise than Being or Beyond Essence* (1974), which Levinas himself finds more adequate to his purpose, without having studied *Totality and the Infinite* (1961), the relation between the two being somewhat comparable to the relation between Heidegger's *Sein und Zeit* and his later work. Having already offered a commentary on *Totalité et Infini*,[1] I will concentrate in this chapter on *Autrement qu'être ou au-delà de l'essence*. Instead of following all the chapters of that book, however, I will explain its main problematic and structure by giving a running commentary on its first chapter, which Levinas himself presents as a résumé (ix/xli).[2] This approach will occasion a few repetitions of material already presented, but these can hardly be avoided if the purpose of a more or less complete explanation of chapter 1 should be maintained.

Title and Dedication

At least some knowledge of Heidegger's use of "*Wesen*" (*essence* or *essance*) and "*Sein*" (*être*, Being) is necessary to understand the title *Otherwise than Being or Beyond Essence* as a double translation of Plato's way of characterizing the Good (*to agathon*). As *epekeina tes ousias*, "beyond Being" (or Beingness, or Being as Being, or Being in the transitive sense which indicates its "active" "giving") the Good is one of the names (a provisional name or a pseudonym) for that which is neither Being nor non-Being, and which transcends the distinction and the solidarity between Being and non-Being.

The expression "beyond Being" suggests that we must *start* from a consideration of Being, i.e., from ontology, after which we can go beyond Being in order to discover something else. As Levinas himself remarks: "[Goes beyond]—that is already to make a concession to ontological and theoretical language, as though the *beyond* were still a term, an entity, a mode of being, or the negative counterpart of all that" (123/97). However, we are not looking for a hidden superentity or a no-thing which could be intuited or conceived if our understanding were perfect or infinite. "God," whose name in philosophy is "Being's Beyond" (199/156), cannot be represented as something or some no-thing; "he" or "she" or "it" neither is, nor was, nor will be ever present as the correlate of any logos or intuition. But then a theology seems not to be possible at all, and any attempt to write a theory of the Good betrays what it wants to show. This is the reason why philosophy cannot approach the beyond of being without using ethical language, as Levinas has argued and practiced in *Totality and the Infinite*. The ethical language should not then be understood as a normative dimension that is built on a primary level, which would be purely theoretical, but rather as the primary answer to the awkward question: what "is" the Good? The ethical interrupts and bends the language of logos (logic, phenomenology, ontology, etc.) into an attempt to formulate that which precedes the split between theory and practice, apophantic discourse and imperatives:

> Ethical language, which phenomenology resorts to in order to mark its own interruption, does not come from an ethical intervention laid out over descriptions. It is the very meaning of the approach which contrasts with knowing. . . . A description that at the beginning knows only *being* and *beyond being* turns into ethical language." (120/193, n.35)

As we will see, the connection with Western ontology, expressed in Levinas's borrowings from Plato and Heidegger, is maintained throughout the whole book, even though it is inspired by a breath from outside— or rather, from before—the Greek and Germanic traditions of European philosophy. This breath and the rhythm of its respiration is thematized in the last two chapters of the book (179–94 and 228–33/140–52 and 181–85), while it is announced in the two dedications and in the five epigraphs that precede the table of contents. The Hebrew dedication, written in the form of an epitaph, devotes the book "to the memory of the spirit of" Levinas's father, mother, brothers, and parents-in-law, and adds the liturgical prayer "that their souls may be kept in the bundle of life." The French dedication extends beyond the memory of "those beings who were closest among the six million assassinated by the National Socialists," to "the millions upon millions of all denominations and all nations, victims of the same hatred by the other human, the same anti-Semitism." The equivalence expressed here between antisemitism and antihumanism lends the reader a key to the interpretation of the book. The persecution of the Jews is understood as the realization of a hatred which is not limited to a particular nation, race, ideology, practice, or faith; it is hatred of the human, of humanity as such; this hatred is *the* root of any form of antihumanism. The victims of this hatred, be they Jews, gypsies, blacks, or Vietnamese, symbolize humanity as such: they are hostages, subjected to suffering and persecution, humiliation and death. If "hatred of the other human" is indeed the root of evil as expressed in anti-Semitism, then the understanding of the Holocaust coincides with the most important question of all time: a question which a responsible philosopher cannot ignore or suppress. We *must* ask *and answer* the question of how and why gratuitous persecution and antihumanism emerge and develop, how we can fight it, which radical turn or reversal can free us from it, and so on. Levinas's answer, which he seeks to justify in *Otherwise than Being*, states that anti-Semitism and antihumanism have their roots in a specific way of relating to the world, others, society, history, oneself, and Being as such; a way of relating expressed in Western civilization, especially in its philosophy.

Preliminary Note

In the last paragraph of the "Preliminary Note" (ix–x/xli–xlii) to *Otherwise than Being*, the author summarizes the topic of his book in the word "*subjectivity*." It is neither the Other, nor the world, nor God, nor Being as such, which forms the center and focus: it is rather the subjectivity of "me," of "*le moi*" or "*le soi*," "the me" or "the self." The focus is on the "me-ity," if one could venture this expression, or on the subject's selfhood in its contacts with the world, Being, the Other, history, etc. Selfhood or subjectivity is presented here as an exception, an *Ausnahme*.

In hearing the word "exception" as an allusion to Kant and Kierkegaard, we are warned that the subject for whom Levinas's book seems to be an apology, is utterly different from all those subjects which can be discussed within the context of laws and universality. Although Levinas claims later in the book that subjectivity is the source of all morality, he does not simply return to the transcendentality of an ego along the lines of the modern tradition. Against Kant's condemnation of all exceptions as immoral attempts to escape moral universality, Levinas holds that reason and universality cannot be the source because they ignore, neglect, or even deny the unicity of the Other (you) as well as the subject (me). Subjectivity does not fit into the dimension in which philosophy has made itself at home. It distorts and deregulates this home, although—as we will see—it incessantly relates to it in an ex-ceptional way.

The dimension of modern philosophy (or—as Levinas claims—of Western philosophy in its totality) is evoked here in Heideggerian terms as "the conjunction of essence, beings and 'difference,' " and a little further on—in less Heideggerian terms—as "the praxis and the knowledge inherent to the world" (*la praxis et le savoir intérieurs au monde*). The word "difference" in this context primarily evokes the ontological difference between "Being itself" (here presented as "essence" in the transitive sense of Heidegger's *Wesen*) and the ensemble of all beings. The quotation marks surrounding *"différence"* suggest, however, that Levinas also hints at the general trend of French philosophers to use *"différence"* as a keyword for post-Nietzschean and post-Heideggerian thought. The practical and theoretical mode of existence of "the world" and the conjunction of Being and beings in their ontological difference is portrayed in certain sections of the first three chapters, where Levinas retrieves the basic insights of phenomenology and ontology in his own way. It is important to read these sections as an attempt to rewrite and to reposition ontology, and not as mere refutation. Levinas objects to any thought that maintains the question of Being and the ontological difference as the ultimate or the most radical, but he does not reject the necessity of a phenomenology of Being that stays within the limits of its own dimension. In this sense he does not reject but confirms and retrieves the tradition of ontology. However, the exception of "subjectivity" enigmatically and efficaciously disturbs and refutes the supremacy of essence and difference.

The continuity between *Otherwise than Being* and *Totality and the Infinite* is obvious if, in "the conjunction of Being, beings and difference," we recognize a new, more adequate name for the Hegelian expression "totality"; and if in "subjectivity" we hear an emphasis on one side of the relationship between the Other and "me," which in *Totality and the Infinite* was called the metaphysical relationship. Whereas that book concentrated on the epiphany of the Other's face and speaking, *Otherwise than Being* stresses the selfhood of the subject as always already subjected to responsibility for the Other. The relation between the Other and me is a transformation of Husserl's intentionality[3] and, although it has a different structure than the adequate correlation of a noema and a noesis, neither the Other nor I can be isolated. The "separation" which characterizes the "metaphysical relation" is an unbreakable tie, a bond and an alliance determining the Other's core as well as mine.

By way of anticipation, the "Preliminary Note" summarizes a host of (quasi- or trans-)intentional analyses in characterizing the subject as a unique "substance" whose "incomplete identity"[4] with itself lies in its being a hostage to the Other. The incompleteness of this identity, its deficiency or gap, is not a negation, either straightforward, or dialectical or "differential"; it is rather an "abnegation" in the sense of tolerance, suffering, and mortification: the subject loses its own life by being for the Other. All these expressions must, however, be heard in a nonvoluntaristic, nonmoralizing and pre-ethical way. No choice is involved, not even an attitude or a weak kind of willingness, as for example in a half-forced, half-voluntary consent. "Before" any possibility of willing or resisting, "always already," the subject transcends the order of Being and essence toward the Other, in the impossibility of circling back upon itself for a complete identification with itself. The subject, born into transcendence, is turned toward the Other, without having a choice. "Passivity" could be a name for it if our understanding of the passive would not immediately place it, together with activity as its opposite, within the horizon of a world of praxis and poiesis, initiative and neglect, moralism and antimoralistic violence or indifference. Levinas's task consists in distinguishing the *pre*voluntary, *pre*virtuous, *pre*conscious and *pre*moral "passivity" from the constellation of free will, choice, consent, or denial, and, in *this* sense, of autonomy and heteronomy. In going back to Kant's sharp opposition between (universal) reason and (subjective) *Willkür* (as the faculty of choice), we might discover a certain kinship between Levinas's concept of "passivity" and Kant's analysis of "moral feelings," by which Kant shows that conscience, as a matter of fact (a "fact of reason") is a humiliated consciousness.

As subjection to the Other, transcendence has always already declined the subject's desire for self-identification. It has exposed and wounded the subject before it discovers and finds itself as consciousness and will. When Levinas calls this nonvoluntary "susceptibility" "nonassumable" (*inassumable*), he cannot mean that it is impossible to consent or agree with it; rather, he stresses the fact that my being for-the-other, my being responsible, a hostage and a substitute, does not wait for my consent to make me fulfill this responsibility. I am not capable of preventing this transcendence; if I tried, I would at the same time be involved in destroying my being what I always already am.

"Am"? "My being"? Can this "subjectivity," "this being (a substitute) for the Other" be called a kind of beingness or essence, a prevoluntary and preconscious mode of *Being*, a "nature" or "*physis*" which characterizes humans as such? Don't these words "*physis*," "Being," "essence" carry with them a particular point of view? Don't they imply an ontological denial of transcendence, and thus of "passivity" and "subjectivity"?

In his descriptions of the "conjunction of essence, beings and 'difference,'" Levinas tries to show that "essence" and "Being" are necessarily such that they absorb, level or assimilate transcendence and infinity, hence denying the susceptible, pre-autonomous, vulnerable "passivity" of subjectivity. To "save" the subject, i.e., to do justice to subjectivity, we must transcend the essentially finite order of Being, but not without passing through it. To think susceptibility is to think beyond the dimension in which the categories of activity and passivity, finitude and infinitude, etc., have received their traditional meaning. It is to think new, "transcendent" meanings of the words that are at our disposal, to think beyond the world of theoria, poiesis, and praxis; to think passion as "un-worldly" and the metaphysical as the "invisible" ex-ception of speech and face. Such thinking goes beyond the essence of Being, *epekeina tes ousias*. This explains the title of the book, in which Plato's characterization of the Good is translated twice: "beyond the essence" is neither a mode of being different from other modes of being, nor is it Being at all.

After this firm denial of Being's all-encompassing universality, one might be surprised to read that "the notion" of "beyond Being" lays no claim to originality. In mentioning its antiquity and the "ascension" of a "steep slope" (*son antique escarpement*) Levinas seems to allude to Plato's allegory of the cave; but very probably he simultaneously hints at another, non-Greek tradition: a prophetic tradition which has always challenged the achievements of logos in its Greek and European forms. That tradition can be heard in Levinas's identification of the beyond with the idea of the Infinite: one should try "to hear a God non-contaminated by Being." The coincidence of this attempt with the investigation of "subjectivity"—i.e., the meaning of Levinas's overcoming of the double death of God and man—lies in his plea for transcendence as the secret of human existence. Perhaps Levinas's remark about the "nonoriginality" of "beyond the essence" also alludes ironically to the fact that his book does not claim to be "original" in the sense of a sensational and trend-setting discovery of new insights or a brilliant retrieval of the entire Western heritage. Although, like most post-Hegelians, he speaks of Western philosophy as if it were a whole, Levinas does not repeat the Hegelian attempt to present his own thought as the necessary end-product of that heritage. His thought does not move within the dimension of history in its world political, cultural, or monumental sense. It rather attempts to uncover the most common and elementary facts and events of everybody's everyday life, such as eating and drinking, having a body and enjoying it, being born and suffering, speaking, listening, learning, and laboring, having a conscience and being confronted with injustice.

The unspectacular everydayness of the investigated phenomena might partially explain why our epoch does not display a strong tendency toward creating a Levinasian fashion comparable to the Heideggerian or the Derridian fashions. Is it still to come? Does the absence of epigonism prove the failure of Levinas's theory? The "ordinary" character of Levinas's subject matter does not imply that it is easy to write about it or to understand what he wrote. The difficulties that hinder access to the simple but fundamental and most common realities express themselves in a language that seems to be out of breath. The exhaustion (*essoufflement*) which a radical thought inevitably runs into, this radical handicap and source of numerous misunderstandings, testifies however to a breath (*un souffle*) which is not completely within the power or the choice of the writing or reading subject. As Levinas shows in chapter 5 of this book, the respiration by which all language lives precedes the origination of thoughts and deeds in the author's consciousness. The breath of authentic thought is an ex-ceptional alternation of inspiration and expiration: not the magical enthusiasm of mythical gods, but the emergence of a prophetic witness.

The last sentence of the "Preliminary Note" warns the reader that the author does not aim to replace philosophy with prophetism; he attempts rather to translate some insights of a prophetic tradition, whose traces are *also* found in Greek and European thought, into the language of logos. Is it simply a sign of modesty that Levinas juxtaposes, on the one hand, "to hear a God non-contaminated by Being" as "a human possibility no less important and no less precarious" and, on the other, Heidegger's attempt "to bring Being out of the oblivion in which it is said to have fallen in metaphysics and onto-theo-logy"? Levinas denies that "the conjunction of *essence, beings* and '*difference*' can be the ultimate horizon, or, if it is not a horizon, that it can be the 'first' and 'ultimate.' " By identifying that conjunction with physis, as analyzed by Heidegger in his commentary on Aristotle's concept of physis,[5] *Totality and the Infinite* proclaimed the necessity of thinking beyond the physis of ontology in a *meta-physics* of the beyond. In *Otherwise than Being* the word "metaphysics" rarely appears,[6] but the same claim is repeated: one should neither ignore nor neglect the dimension of Being (although we might criticize the ontologies factually unfolded within that dimension), but any and all ontologies must be developed in the awareness that the essence is relativized from the outset by a beyond to which it owes its most radical significance. Levinas even uses the word "to desire" in formulating the relation between the "world" of ontology and the non-worldly, nonhorizontal, and nonessential beyond: one of the proposals of *Otherwise than Being* is "to derive the *praxis* and knowledge that belong to the world from [*à partir de*] the inassumable susceptibility" of the pre- and meta-ontological, pre-original and an-archic passivity (x/xlii). Not against, but through (an amended) phenomenology and ontology, Levinas works toward a thinking of transcendence as relation, movement, and difference between the exception of subjectivity and a beyond which is neither Being nor non-Being.

Structure of the Book

A program for the investigation can be developed out of the formulation of the question. In the "Preliminary Note," Levinas states that the book was "built" (*bâti*) around chapter 4 (ix/xli). What sort of building or construction does he mean? In *Otherwise than Being* we find at least three ways of proceeding. The first chapter, which in Levinas's own words, "sets out the argument of this book" (ix/xli) by way of an introduction (23/19), offers one possibility of structuring its content. Chapters 2–4 follow other lines of exploration, and the concluding chapter 6 illuminates the argument in yet another way (*l'éclaire autrement*, 23/19).

I will comment briefly on the outline of the argument as described on pages ix–x/xli–xlii and 23–24/19, and then turn to the commentary on the first pages of chapter 1.

Since subjectivity is the central topic, it is not surprising that the book is centered around a chapter on *substitution* (chapter 4), where subjectivity is shown to be a primordial and unchosen form of subjection to and responsibility for others. As will become clear from a careful reading of chapter 1, the subject's exceptional substitution cannot be discovered philosophically unless one starts from the dimension of ontology. Ontology will then be shown in its own grandeur, but also in its incapacity to do justice to certain basic "phenomena" like desire, transcendence, conscience, passivity, etc. The distance between ontology and the heterology of *substitution* must be measured by a phenomenological analysis of constellations in the dimension of beingness and beings. This will lead to a threshold or limit, where an exodus from ontology becomes inevitable. The perspective of *Otherwise than Being* is determined by the question of how subjectivity relates to the realm of Being. The turn or jump which is necessary in order to radically undermine the all-embracing absoluteness of the essence is the proper "topic" or "theme" of this book.

Chapter 2, which is the real beginning after the introduction (or the résumé) of chapter 1, starts with a rewriting of ontology, by considering— in an amended phenomenology—various modes of being, the "essence" of truth, Being as such, presence and time. Without denying the correctness of the phenomenology thus sketched, the author then points out that it ignores and is blind to a "phenomenon" or an event which is experienced by everybody although it cannot be presented or represented, or even thought of *as* an object, a phenomenon, or a theme. This is the Saying (*le Dire*) upon which all that can be said or written depends. The order of Being, truth, simultaneity, and presence is the order of *the Said* (*le Dit*): the order of texts, cultures, worlds, world history, economics, politics, etc. As belonging to a world, a heritage, the museum of civilizations, or the history of humankind, each and every phenomenon is caught in a web of "inter-essing," inter-esting, and interested beings, held together by the *Wesen and Walten* of Being's essence. It can be said, and as a said, it can be thematized. Saying, however, evaporates or changes into a Said as soon as it is made into a theme or topic. Following the indication contained in its title, chapter 2 can be summarized as a conquest of the most originary, the "pre-originary," dimension via a critique of Husserl and Heidegger: "From [consciousness as] intentionality to [subjectivity as] sensibility."

Chapter 3 is an attempt to show that Saying is given in human *sensibility* before any utterance. All the words used for the quasiphenomenology of the beyond or before as revealed in Saying, the Face, the Trace, should here be put between quotation marks, since descriptions and analyses are only fit for thematizable phenomena. However, it is impossible to determine the conditions of world, Being, society, and history, without being a part of the conditioned. Under the title "Sensibility and Proximity" Levinas presents a phenomenology of the inspired body; its sensibility *is* proximity.

Sensibility is being affected, in touch, in contact with the Other; it is vulnerability, an affective proximity which, without ever having been chosen, has always already confined me in my body *and* brought me in touch with the otherness of others. The analysis of proximity reveals it to be a never-begun responsibility: since time immemorial, and in spite of myself, I am the Other's hostage, her/his substitute. This is brought out in chapter 4: I (or rather the "passive," "susceptible" *me* expressed in "*me voici*") am the achievement of the "otherwise" than the essence of Being. *Me voici* breaks with and jumps out of ontology. "Substitution" is the name for the ultimate signification of subjectivity.

Chapter 5 ("Subjectivity and the Infinite") shows that transcendence, as the structure of subjectivity, is double: the one-for-the-other is both moral and religious; "the Other" is *autrui*, as well as the *Most-High*, as Levinas wrote in the beginning of *Totality and the Infinite* (TeI, 4; TaI, 34), although he did not in that book explain the coincidence of these two heights. In *Otherwise than Being*, the metaphor of height and ascension in trans*ascence* is infrequent. In accordance with the accent being displaced from the Other's (your) illuminated face to the humble passivity of my never-chosen obedience in spite of myself, the *au-delà* of the essence is revealed now in the *en deçà* of an underlying, "subjected" before. My pre-original passivity is shown to be the passing of the Infinite: a passage and a passion through which the Infinite occurs (*se passe*).

After analyzing the difference between the order of Being and the disturbing enigma of the "before" and "beyond" of transcendence and subjectivity, Levinas dedicates a part of chapter 5 to the question of the justification and the meaning of "the Said." This expression is another name for the ontological economy of reason, universal laws, theory, and politics. Toward the end of chapter 1 Levinas, in the following words, sketches how it would be possible to complete his task: "Starting from [*à partir de*] the Saying, as real in substitution, we must justify the order of the Said, [i.e.] of thought, justice and Being, and understand the conditions under which philosophers, in their Said—in ontology—can signify truth" (24/19).

Despite its brevity, this passage and section 3 of chapter 5 act as important antidotes against a possible reading of Levinas as anti-ontological. Ontology is not the ultimate or the absolute, but it is needed as the penultimate condition for the unconditionality of subjectivity and transcendence. We must return to this question of the sense of the *epekeina*, the character of the difference between ontology and the thinking of transcendence, and the necessary bridge between both constellations.

Chapter 1: The Argument—Essence and Dis-inter-essence

The main structure of the ten sections which make up chapter 1 is quite clear. If it is true—a truth which still has to be proved—that subjectivity, as an exception, is other than Being, the difference between Being, or essence, and otherness must be shown and analyzed. Levinas prefers transcendence to "difference," but as I have already stated, the dimension of height should not be stressed;[7] the below and the inferior is as good a metaphor for the beyond as is the sublime and the heavenly.

Otherness and transcendence are the "themes" of section 1, but since they cannot be conceived without reference to beings, it is necessary first to characterize the essence of Being (section 2). Looking for a phenomenon or quasiphenomenon that shows that Being is not the ultimate or absolute, Levinas no longer gives a description of the other human's face or speech, as he did in *Totality and the Infinite*; he rather focuses on the fact that language does not coincide with what people say. Besides and "before" the Said, speaking, or writing there is a *Saying*. This is the exposition of a subject who offers words, and thereby exposes her/himself to another. The Saying somehow "precedes" the Said, and this "precedence" is an "*en deça* that "shows" the exceptional character of human subjects (section 3). The fourth section briefly anticipates the analysis of subjectivity as an extraordinary kind of reflexivity, and the fifth section reveals the transcendence in the subject's responsibility for the Other. Responsibility testifies to the passage of the Good as having no place in the order of essence. Section 6 then, concentrates on the significance which the subject owes to its finding itself in the trace of the Good, in contrast to the meanings it can find within the horizon of the essence. Section 7 shows that the ethical connotations of responsibility do not point toward some idealistic or spiritualistic conception of human nature. Arguing against all forms of anthropological dualism, Levinas holds that the transcendence of subjectivity is found in the very structure of *sensibility*. In section 8, the unbreakable ties between transcendence, on the one hand, and Being, on the other, are reaffirmed. It is impossible, and it would be unjust and disastrous, to dismiss ontology or to prevent its unfolding in philosophy. A new ontology must be developed from the "perspective" of (*à partir de*) transcendence, as discovered in subjectivity: "Being must be understood starting from [*à partir de*] Being's other" (20/16). The difference between Being and the beyond, despite their interrelation, is again developed in section 9 under the title, "Subjectivity is not a Modality of Essence." Section 10 concludes the chapter with some remarks on method and an outline of chapters 2–6.

It is clear from this overview that Levinas concentrates on otherness, transcendence, subjectivity, etc., without neglecting their connections with the dimension of ontology, even though they have no place in that dimension. The Saying and the Said are not homogeneous: yet there must be a way in which their difference holds them together. Similarly, in *Totality and the Infinite*, the Other and the Same are related, despite their separation.

In the following commentary on the first chapter of *Otherwise than Being*, I will pay special attention to the function and the character of ontology. My study takes place, of course, within the framework of Levinas's book, whose very title announces an overcoming of ontology. The questions involved here are important if we wish to gain clear insight into the relation between Levinas's own attempt to conquer the nihilism of Western civilization, and his assertion that ontology as such cannot overcome nihilism. The question of whether he is right in seeing Hegel and Heidegger as the greatest representatives of the spirit that led to nihilism is an important one, not only for the reconstruction of modern and contemporary history, but also for the diagnosis of our own philosophical situation. However, if Levinas is more than just a commentator, then a more important and more urgent question is this: Does his retrieval of ontology present us with a possibility of thought and practice which is, on the one hand, inevitable, and in that sense true, while, on the other hand, it cannot be the ultimate truth since this would destroy some more originary or "pre-originary" signification? And, as part of the same question: Does Levinas's "otherwise," his way of pointing to the exceptional subjectivity revealed in the face, present us with a turn that can save our thought and practice from nihilism by showing the possibility of a non- or meta-ontological, "an-archic" signification?

In my commentary I will argue for the following answer to these questions. As a brilliant phenomenologist, Levinas offers us an origi- nal rewriting of Heidegger's ontology, on the basis of which he shows that some simple but extraordinary "experiences" or "facts" of everyday existence cannot be "placed" or understood within the horizons of any ontology. Thus, he sets up a nonontological, non-"comprehensive," non– properly-phenomenological, "transphenomenological" and "transonto- logical" view of an enigmatic beyond, which is more radical, "more" originary or "pre-original" than the categories, principles, or *archai* of the ontological constellation. Such a beyond cannot, however, be evoked *philosophically*, except by discovering it to be the constellation of another dimension, which is easily masked. This latter dimension appears neither as essence, nor as a superworldly or supernatural above or behind of the world of ontology. A sort of transcendental illusion constantly threat- ens the "otherwise than Being" by trying to conceive of it as a "being otherwise."

Levinas himself is very much aware of this danger; one of his main concerns in *Otherwise than Being* is to prevent the Good as *epekeina* from turning into the supreme being of a *Hinterwelt*. He knows and thematizes the fact that any thematization or problematization of the "beyond" and the "otherwise" inevitably turns into ontological discourse. He concedes that, *within philosophy*, a language "uncontaminated by Being" (x/xl) is hardly possible, and that the expressions used to evoke transcendence have an ontological ring about them. The self-critical judgment already quoted ("goes beyond—that is already to make a concession to ontolog- ical and theoretical language, as though the *beyond* were still a term,

a being or a mode of being or the negative counterpart of all that"
[123/97]), can also be applied to the word "otherwise," since the different way or "-wise" it points to cannot be heard otherwise than as a mode
of *being*. The distinction between "otherwise than Being" and "being
otherwise" (than Being) is therefore very difficult—perhaps impossible—
to maintain, at least within philosophy.

In *Totality and the Infinite* Levinas insisted, much more than in
his later work, on the necessity of using an ethical rather than an ontological language to express that which is more originary (or rather
"pre-originary") than the split between the theoretical and the practical. Within the philosophical discourse, however, all ethics turns into
thematizing, and inevitably uses phrases like "being obliged" or "being
for-the-other," leaving no possibility of avoiding the copula in most of its
discourse. The language of philosophy seems to be ontological through
and through. In order to escape ontology, one can only stop doing
philosophy, or leave it behind.

Intermezzo

I personally believe that Levinas's critique of what he calls "ontology"
can be expressed in another, somewhat less aporetic way. The philosophical theories criticized in his work, especially Hegel's systematics and
Heidegger's thought, do not exhaust the possibilities of ontology. It is
perhaps true that the Western—or the modern—tradition of thought
has neglected, forgotten, or suppressed the otherness of *autrui* and the
infinite (though I will not consider this question here): this neglect or
oblivion or hatred indicates a restriction and limitation, a narrowing
down of its understanding of Being. Western ontology would then have
been a partial view of the universe of beings and their modes of being.
The ways of appearing, being, coming to the fore, and existing of you
as you and me as me; the ways of otherness, transcendence, difference,
infinitude, and subjectivity, have then been ignored or distorted due to
a certain fascination: other modes of being and appearance, like *Vorhan-
denheit, Zuhandenheit*, universality, ideality, objectivity, etc., have captured
our thought, so that we have become blind to the "transcendent" ones. It
is not necessary, however, to continue the identification of the essence of
Being with the giving and gathering that are characteristic of those Greek
and Western perspectives on being. Being as such does not abandon itself
to any of its modes, nor to any particular ontology, which, as a kind of
second-order mode, inevitably privileges certain perspectives and modes,
tonalities, rhythms, melodies. If the face, otherness, "you-ness," "me-ness,"
singularity, Saying, addressing, greeting have not been respected by the

thinkers and traditions of ontology, this does not necessarily mean that ontology is exhausted or is essentially incapable of taking the neglected phenomena into consideration. It rather means that *ontology has not yet properly begun.* Levinas's oeuvre itself is the illustration of an expanded phenomenology and ontology. He must continue to use the copula in most of his sentences, and he recognizes that the language of theory is necessarily and unavoidably ontological. Both the essence of "the Same" *and* the constellation of transcendence, infinity, otherness, and subjectivity *are* in their own ways. The paradoxes that emerge from their relations belong to beingness itself, but Levinas's perhaps too polemical writings have sharpened our senses for the detection of various ways in which the meaning and scope of Being is particularized and wrongly identified with certain figures or masks of Being. Neither Hegel's conceptual symphony, nor Heidegger's "phainaisthetic" celebration of the cosmic fourfold, nor, perhaps, Levinas's ethical severity simply *coincide* with the essence of Being as such. Insofar as all of these have at least some authenticity, however, they are discourses or logoi of Being in its enigmatic diversity and unity.

There are many parallels between the paradoxes on which Levinas concentrates and the paradoxes that puzzled the classical metaphysicians. There are also profound differences, such as the difference between a more onto-theological approach and the concentration on intersubjective phenomena and moral consciousness. Although Levinas denies any similarity between his own procedure and that of negative theology, certain convergences invite a thorough comparison. Plotinus and pseudo-Dionysius call the One or God *hyperousios* and state forcefully that to call that "reality" a being would betray the exceptional character of some-no-thing before all thought and beingness. But, in so doing, they state that "it" or "he" (or "she") *is* such, while in the same breath they fiercely deny that this "is" expresses any coincidence with a past or present being or essence. Levinas chose to avoid the terminology of ontology: But is it possible to do so?

It is obvious that this reading of Levinas's work makes it look more traditional than it is meant to be. In *Totality and the Infinite* there is evidence to support such a reading, however, as I have argued elsewhere.[8] It is also true that Levinas himself finds the language of *Totality and the Infinite* too ontological and tries in *Otherwise than Being* to speak another, less "Greek" language. Although I do not believe that a nonontological language is possible within philosophy, this impossibility need not destroy—it may even reinforce—Levinas's criticism of a certain type of ontology: a type which has prevailed in modern and contemporary philosophy, perhaps also in the Greek classics, and maybe even in the great European metaphysicians from Plotinus to Cusanus, notwithstanding their fascination with originary and infinite donation, word, love, and creation. In countering the prevailing caricatures of "metaphysics" and "onto-theology" Levinas has not only resuscitated the basic questions of desire, subjectivity, ethics and the Infinite; he has also shown, as none other has done, that the most radical, (pre-)originary question goes through a confrontation with facing, speaking, responsibility, and giving.

1. Being's "Other" (l'"autre" de l'être)

The title "Essence and Dis-inter-essence" (*Essence et dés-interessement*) (3/3) spans the horizon of the argument by pointing to the two economies between which human existence is lived: on the one hand, the essence, as the beingness (*Seiendheit, essance*) of beings-as-a-whole (*das Seiende im Ganzen*) and, on the other, the possibility of evading that essence, disengaging from our existing amidst beings and our connection to them through mutual interests which Being (*esse*) weaves between (*inter*) us: a "*dés-inter-esse-ment*" or "dis-inter-essence." As Levinas's sometime italicizing of the suffix -*ment* suggests, the word "*dés-intéressement*," like "*essence*" or "*essance*" (ix/xli), must be heard in a dynamic, "active" and "transitive" sense: over against the *Wesen* and *Walten* of Being, which weaves all beings together in an economy of mutual interests, transcendence and subjectivity are ruled by a disengaging movement, a breath or inspiration which makes the subject pass over to " 'the other of Being' " (3/3). The conjunction "and" between "essence" and "disinteressence" hides a transition from Being (or "essence") to the Other (or "disinteressence") beyond the opposition of Being (*on, Sein*) and non-Being (*me on, Nichtsein*, or *Nichts*), beyond their contradictory or contrary, dialectical or differential opposition. As the book shows, passing from Being to the Other accomplishes itself in a profound "passivity," older than any ontic or ontological passivity: a nonchosen, pre-autonomous, and in that sense pre- or an-archic patience or passion, the patience of a passion preceding and therefore questioning all attempts or thoughts of autonomy and autarchy; passivity as a dynamic fact that uses, empties, wears out, disactivates, and undoes or "de-fects" (*dé-fait*) its own facticity. The ambiguity of this *fact* and the impossibility of wording it without suggesting that it is a mixture of Being and non-Being summarizes the main difficulty of Levinas's enterprise: How is it possible not only to put into words (for example, in greeting or praying) but to thematize the "Other(wise) than Being" without changing it into a "being otherwise," that is, into a mode of being?

An escape or "evasion" from Being seems impossible, since all attempts to negate it are immediately neutralized by its all-encompassing invasion. Neither Hegel's "nothing," nor Heidegger's *Nichts* can abolish or overcome the essence. In taking away all determinations of Being, the most radical of all phenomenologies is still confronted with the irresistible universality of Being. Stripped of its qualifications, it still "is"; not in the rich and generous way suggested by the "giving" of the German "*es gibt*," but rather in the poorest and yet most basic poverty of all poverties: the indeterminate rumbling and mumbling murmur of the French *il y a*, in which the "there" in the "*y*" still suggests too much. If the essence of Being is the ultimate horizon, it excludes the possibility of exceptions; and if the existence of human life (and thus, of human death) is understood or lived as a mere moment, an incident or accident of Being's ruling, then the monopoly of ontology would take away any exceptional significance. Life and death insofar as they are yours or mine would be without meaning. In Hegelian terminology, life and death would be no more than a moment whose meaning is exhausted by the meaning of the totality: absolute Spirit's history. Being's "undethronable royalty" would submit humans and gods to its repetitious murmur. Transcendence is then possible only as the discovery or conquest of other beings, for example of some highest entity in a world behind the world of visible phenomena. This would justify the caricature according to which "Western metaphysics" is said to have treated God and humans as entities, without first considering, in awe and wonder, the enigmatic mystery of Being's essence.

At the end of the first section (4/4) Levinas rejects—perhaps too quickly—the possibility of asking and answering his questions within the framework of an ontology which, from the outset, would allow for all the differences in the modes of being. Even an analogical unity would gather worlds and subjects, beingness and transcendence into one realm whose ruling and structure would not permit living, speaking, caring, and dying to be what they are. But *aren't* there exceptions? Or does the use of the verb "be," imposed on us by our languages, signify no more than the inevitability of a transcendental illusion?

2. Being and Interessence

There is an abrupt transition from *il y a* at the end of section 1, to the *essence*, as described in the second section (4–6/4–5). Both are names for Being, but whereas the *il y a* names it in its nakedness stripped of all determination—a sort of chaos before all creation—"essence" translates Heidegger's "*Wahrheit des Wesens*," interpreted by Levinas as the transitive beingness through which all beings are given in their coming to be, in their shining forth, and in the persistence of their being. In section 2

Levinas gives his description of essence as the beingness to which all beings owe their being-there. Like Parmenides's Being, it is well-rounded and completely full, without any holes, filling in all the gaps between entities, gathering and relating them in one cosmos. Being(ness) is being interrelated, being as a moment, an incident or accident of an ongoing unfolding. The truth of essence lies in its refutation of all non-beingness, an *Aufhebung* of nothingness by which becoming is no longer different from Being.

Essence is also the fundamental urge of all beings to be, to maintain their being, and to persist in being there. Using an anthropomorphic metaphor, we could say that all beings are egoistic and self-interested. This would involve their being "allergic" to one another. This allergy, together with the interrelatedness of their gathering, necessarily results in a state of war. As already stated in the preface of *Totality and the Infinite*, *polemos* is the dramatization of (the Truth of) Being as essence.[9] The simultaneity of the interest and urge of all beings, the synchrony of their *conatus essendi*, the overwhelming power of a universal self-affirmation and perseverance in being, excludes patience and passivity. On the basis of Being (I would rather say: on the basis of such a *way of* being) one can neither wait, nor suffer; victory, satisfaction, and autarchy must be immediate: the will to be cannot be postponed. The way of being thus identified as the essence of Being is recognized here to be the root of all violence and evil. If this were the whole truth, if Being and ontology were indeed the first and ultimate, there would be no place for goodness in the form of patience or dedication. The fourth epigraph of the book we are reading resumes the adventure ("*la geste ou le drame*") of Being in a quote from Pascal: " 'This is my place in the sun,'—that is the beginning and the usurpation of the entire world" (5/4).[10]

For the correct interpretation of Levinas's (re)description of Being, as well as for his reading of Heidegger's *Sein*, we must understand that *Sein* (*einai, ousia,* Being) or *Wesen* (essence) cannot, in his opinion, be separated from the beingness of existing beings, and we must understand why this is so. *Sein* cannot be conceived of as a hypostasis or as equivalent to the universe of all beings. Although it gathers and binds *ta panta* together in the totality of *to pan*, it is neither a highest being, nor the universe as such. If there is some *x* to which all beings in their beingness owe what they are, this *x* cannot "be" of the order of Being, beingness, or essence. It should "be" "not contaminated by being" (x/xlii), but how can such a non-thing neither be, nor "be" nothing at all? Or, in other words, how is it possible to prove that "the subordination of all thought to the comprehension of Being" is a "myth" that has to be destroyed? (8 n. 4/187 n. 5).

If Being is essentially at war, how would peace ever be possible? What are the conditions of peace? Over against the dramatization of the essence in *polemos*, peace would be the dramatization of a "beyond" or an "otherwise than Being." This would demand patience, the ability and the disposition which permit rupture with the striving for self-unfolding in the simultaneity of a universal *conatus*. Where and how can such an arrest or delay, such a "hole in Being," be found?

Can *reason* deliver us from generalized violence? Levinas briefly evokes the tradition of social philosophy from Hobbes to Hegel, remembering perhaps also Eric Weil's renewal of this question in the 1950s and 1960s.[11] According to them, reason is the means to rule, transform, and sublimate violence such that its energy becomes useful and good, or beautiful, rational, and reasonable and a necessary moment of a concrete humanism. However—and this is Levinas's critique—the source and basis of this rationalism lies in the essence whose unavoidable polemic is manifested in Levinas's phenomenology of Being. The patience and the postponement of a peace that is founded on reason, emerge from interests and calculations in line with the fundamental interestedness described above. All kinds of abnegation demanded by diplomatic concessions to save the peace are motivated by the computation of future compensation. The question of peace is then a purely technical one. Utilitarianism is the preferred kind of ethics for the world of exchange and commerce realized by the *Mitsein* of its citizens.

One might, in Levinas's critique of the calculative character proper to the rational interpretation of violence, hear an echo of Heidegger's diagnosis of the essence of technology. When—rarely—Levinas writes explicitly about the merits and dangers of technology, however, his tone sounds very different from that of Heidegger. As we will see, technology, calculation, legal, political, and economical generalizations, and the repression of violence by a just and calculated second violence, in the style of social philosophy from Hobbes to Eric Weil, are necessary for the realization of justice. The philosopher's task includes the derivation of these from the Good, which does not itself belong to their dimension, although they could not exist without its having gone before.

The time upon which reason must work is the present of a representation in which the adventures of the past and the expectations of the future are gathered by memory, history, and calculation. By integrating the original violence of interested entities, reason builds an impartial and balanced economy of rights, power, and consumption, ruled by the standards of equality, reciprocity, and lawful universality. This kind of pacification depends upon the possibility of bringing the past and the future into the synchrony of an overview. The time for reason is the simultaneity of the present: a present which remains unstable, threatened as it is by the "swarming" (*grouillement*) of the essence and the conflicting interests of all beings that go with it.

In the preface to *Totality and the Infinite* Levinas "defined" politics as "the art of foreseeing and winning the war by any means" (TeI, ix/TaI, 21). If politics is warring under the cover and behind the appearance of peace, a radical rupture with war, which is not just a pause or a means for the essential polemos of opposed interests, presupposes some kind of gratuity, an exception to the realm of the essence, a disengagement with regard to Being, a more originary disinterestedness. This thought is "dramatized" in the second quote from Pascal, the fifth and last epigraph with which *Otherwise than Being* opens: "They have used concupiscence as best as they could for the general good; but it is nothing but a pretense and a false image of charity; for at bottom it is simply a form of hatred."[12]

Reason is autonomous and self-sufficient; the evasion from the essence, transcendence, is impossible. The death of "God" necessarily follows from the endeavor to close the horizon through rationality, and atheism is the normal, only reasonable way of thinking. The word "good" should be read as "useful" or "interesting" or "fitting" for the order of beingness. Obviously, any attempt to reopen the question of God in philosophy will find itself out of breath (*essoufflé*), or at least without the breath which dominates and inspires modern thought (or, as Levinas claims, all Western thought). Speaking of a transcendence beyond the essence is the losing of your own breath, a sort of expiration, or, at least, a respiration that is not owned but received and in which a wholly different spirit than that of ontology can—enigmatically—be heard. Is it still possible to search for a different meaning of "spirit," "transcendence," "inspiration," and "expiration" from the meanings which have been tried and worn in our tradition? Can Plato's pointing to "the Good beyond the essence" encourage us? Can the unphilosophical prophets of Israel, either by a breathless ah, or by a courageous but helpless "Here I am" (*me voici*) inspire us? Perhaps the spirit speaks through the silence of those who hold their breath, while suffering its most extreme possibilities.

In *Totality and the Infinite*, Levinas concentrated on the Other's face and speech in order to awaken the reader's philosophical mind for the "epiphany" of such an extreme possibility. When he used the word "language" (*langage* or *parole*), he most often meant the Other's speaking to me. In *Otherwise than Being*, language is thematized primarily as "my" or the subject's speaking or writing to one or more others. As "Saying" (*Dire*), it is distinguished from the message or the text through which it is delivered and addressed: "the Said" (*le Dit*). In neither of these books is the answer to the question of signification and transcendence sought in any other mode of essence or in any other essence of language, such as an aesthetic, "poietic," evocative, or mythical *Sprache* or *Sage*. All kinds of message, epos, fable, poem, oracle, or kerygma, belong to the order of the Said, the textuality of literature, the works of civilization, the monuments of history, the world of politics, the economies of life and societies. The essence of art realizes the structure and the movement of Being in wonder, beauty, and monstrosity, but its seductions do not permit transcendence. On the contrary, they easily imprison the elementary realm of the gods within the limits of physis or nature.

3. Saying and Said

It seems that any attempt to name the beyond inevitably falls back into the language of ontology, where only beingness can be said. Does the fate of philosophy lie in this incessant metamorphosis of transcendence into a theme, a topic, a thesis, an argument, or—to gather all of them—into "the Said" of a thematizing text? The very logos of philosophy would then imprison all beings in a circle without issue and thus guarantee the absence of the transcendent, the Other, the One, or the Infinite. As thematization of the divine, theology would be an excellent way of killing God. Theology and atheism are then very close.

Within the ontological framework there is no other space for transcendence than that of a "being otherwise": another figure of beingness that can be treated as a superphenomenon or superworld, a backstage or *Hinterwelt* whose mysterious events manifest themselves in the thaumaturgic gods of the earth. Their supernaturality belongs to the economy of interessence, an economy of conflicting egoisms—and thus of war. Without the breath of true transcendence the closure of this economy is without "spirit"; its obsessional perseverance in being is governed by the death of uninspired matter. The inescapable destiny of ontological theology is materialism and war.

Is this fate inherent to thought as such, or is it typical of the Greek and Western logos, the logos of ontology? Within its horizon all events and exchanges are governed by mutual interest; even death does not stop this game if it is interpreted as a transition to the compensating happiness of eternal life. Since interestedness does not generate responsibility, the play of Being is hardly serious. The extreme gravity of responsibility—one cannot laugh in the midst of a holocaust—goes together with an imperative disruptive of that frivolity, an imperative without compensation, not even in an "afterlife," but which demands disinterestedness, or even suffering and sacrifice, as the necessary passage from the essence to the Infinite. Such a gratuitous but serious imperative cannot be heard in the oracular or kerygmatic text of objectifying discourse. It is enacted however in the Saying itself through which a human subject addresses him- or herself to another. No "said" goes without "saying"; and without at least some sort of expressed or "said" content no saying is possible. Philosophy has not sufficiently thematized the unthematizable "moment" of human discourse: that is, its being spoken by a subject who thereby approaches another. A single "Hello" or "Hi" signifies not through its message, but through its accomplishing my proximity to you, and thus expressing a difference which is neither interested nor indifferent, a "non-in-difference," as Levinas writes later on. Although Saying is inseparable from its Said, it is not a component of the delivered message. The latter can be treated ontologically, while forgetting its being addressed to someone else. To formulate the difference, Levinas states that the Saying "*precedes*" the Said. It is a fore-word (*avant-propos*) to any word, a silence ahead of all words. Saying is the very signifyingness of all signification: the making of a sign thanks to which signs are more than a text in reaching the Other. We might be tempted to call the Saying original or originary, but like "principle," "*arche*," or "cause," "origin" belongs to the language of ontology and is thus inapplicable to the "beyond" or "before" of beingness. To underline the exceptionality of this "precedence," Levinas uses the expressions "pre-original" or "an-archical."

Ontological descriptions and analyses of a proposition, a discourse, or a text are not sufficient to bring out what happens in their being spoken or written. As belonging to a world, a literary heritage, a linguistic economy or a mail system, utterances can be studied according to their semantic, syntactic, aesthetic, ideological, "metaphysical," and ontological features. As soon as we discover that "before" and independent of their "content," they already signify, we must ask the question of what sort of sense this "before" reveals? What are the implications of the ordinary yet exceptional fact of a human subject's addressing herself to others in speech or by other means? Levinas wrote a phenomenology (or "transphenomenology") of that which cannot be "seen" by those phenomenologists who are completely taken up with the worldly, cultural, historical, and ontological aspects of language. Within the horizons of a language that speaks of its own accord (*die Sprache spricht*), Saying is too insignificant to be noticed, but its humility could well contain the secret of a passage from Being to transcendence.

The quintessence of Levinas's thought lies in his pointing out that Saying implies the disclosure that a subject is close to another through a proximity which has "*always already*" made the subject responsible for the Other. Without having had a chance to say yes or no, I am— always already—supporting the child or man or woman who happens to be nearest. I have been taken hostage before I know it. That is my condition, a condition which can neither be refused nor changed: it is the unconditionality of the absolute lack of a good and happy condition.

Immediately after the introduction of his distinction between the Saying and the Said, Levinas shows how difficult it is to maintain that distinction in writing or speaking about it. Indeed, as soon as we speak about the Saying, it turns into a theme, a said. It shows itself in the words through which we try to formulate its difference from a text, thus converting itself into a text. Although the Saying precedes all essence and interessence, by being thematized it becomes part of an ontological economy and a linguistic system; it is conquered by Being and language. By saying the Saying, we transform it into a Said, simultaneously revealing its exceptionality *and* treating it as an essence. To word it is to betray it (*traduire* is *trahir*).

The ontologization of the nonontological is what happens "in this very moment," in which Levinas is concentrating on the difference between "being otherwise" and "otherwise than Being." The ambiguity is inevitable, at least if we stick to a reflective language. It reveals that the language in which the Saying shows *and* denies its exceptional transcendence, cannot be transcendence or pre-original precedence itself.

As a way of revealing the transcendence of Saying, while at the same time inevitably masking and distorting it, language shows its own relativity. Alluding to the medieval idea that philosophy is a maid (*ancilla*) of the highest wisdom (*ancilla theologiae*), Levinas characterizes the reflective language as ancillary. It is neither the ultimate horizon, nor anything absolute. Like a messenger who speaks about the sender without being able to speak the sender's own language, a phenomenology of the Saying is *angelic*, but not divine. Here the biblical allusions are obvious: God himself never appeared. When He visited human beings, it was through his angels or his words as spoken by prophets. The unsayable needs the Said, but at the same time holds it at a distance.

Levinas seems to implicitly agree here that the order of the Said—ontology—can be redeemed from its atheistic and "theological" denial of transcendence. If we understand the relativity of ontology, i.e., if we can circumscribe its dimension (with its own ontological difference and amphibology) and indicate how this dimension is subordinate to the absoluteness of transcendence as revealed in the Saying, then a certain peace between Being and its beyond (or Other) seems possible. The "if" does not forbid a certain veneration for words, although it definitely condemns any idolatry of language. To the oracles of Greek *theologia* Levinas here opposes the saying of prophetic demands. The mediation of the latter is a special one; as neither dialectical, nor hermeneutical but angelic, prophetic words testify to the impossibility of capturing in a said the Saying which precedes all true sentences of a monstrative, or—as Heidegger and Aristotle call it—"apophantic" text.

Phenomenology, monstration, and apophansis are not the only possibilities of Saying, however. Neither are they the primary possibilities. They presuppose the language of responsibility. Before it can show, represent, investigate, or problematize, Saying is a response that cannot be avoided. The entire book revolves around this "thesis": as the pre-original "form" of language, Saying (or "being-for-the-Other") is a nonchosen, inevitable responsibility. All language games presuppose and emerge from a supremely serious fact: everyone is infinitely responsible for the Other.

The seriousness of responsibility is contrasted with the play of essence, which shows itself to be comparatively superficial. Responsibility does not play an important role in the order of Being, yet far from being a diminished sort of essence or a mixture of Being and non-Being, responsibility (or Saying) is that which ultimately counts. Its necessity reveals itself in the impossibility of refusing responsibility, an impossibility which becomes phenomenal in the remorse that follows attempted refusals and in the scrupulousness of consent and obedience.

Levinas's reproach that ontology is not serious enough might surprise us, especially when we think of Heidegger and the Heideggerians whose texts are hardly more playful than the treatises of classical metaphysics. Their attempts at monstration or justification by appealing to the originary do not lack depth or weight, but all the seriousness of their thought can be interpreted as a shield against the stakes of responsibility. Responsibility forbids us to see the play of Being and language as the ultimate from which all call and donation arise. Responsibility interrupts their play with its unconditional demands. Its structure differs radically from that of ontological thought. It is not one kind of a general attitude which lets all things come and be as they are; it does not fall under the conditions of Being or phenomenality in general. Things, language, space and time, the fourfold, logos, destiny, etc., belong together in the tragicomedy of a *condition*; but to be responsible for another is not a condition, it is the noncondition (*l'incondition*) of unconditionality.

Since responsibility and essence belong to different dimensions, they do not exclude but need one another, yet without forming a dialectical whole. The central problem which follows from their differential connection concerns the structure of this connection: How are transcendence and essence related and interwoven? How does responsibility belong to world history? How do Saying and the Said form one discourse?

In this section Levinas stresses only the relationships between the pre-original "an-archy" of Saying and the "archic" or "archeo-logical" and, in general, ontological structure of the Said. More specifically, he formulates the methodological problem of whether and how it is possible to save that which cannot be a part of the Said (e.g., the Saying itself) from its becoming a said as soon as one focuses on it. If focusing on everything, or a certain "indiscretion," is essential for philosophy, it seems that philosophy is incapable of not betraying Saying and responsibility. Propositions, doxic theses, the language of Being and beings can serve as an ancillary and angelic mediation on the condition that they are accompanied by a critique, a denial and an "unsaying" (*dédire*) of their betrayal. Still, every denial will be a new betrayal, insofar as its negation once again transforms the formerly expressed transcendence into a new said. The play of yes and no will never escape the realm of the ontologically said. The succession of Saying and unsaying suggests another dimension, but are we capable of getting beyond the ancillary language described above in order to expose the transcendence of Saying and responsibility in themselves and as such? The question itself is an ontological one. It demands that Saying and unsaying be gathered in the simultaneity of a concept or intuition of which they are two moments, thus constituting one (super)entity. Over against the simultaneous presence of contrary or contradictory moments in one essence, the endless succession of Saying and unsaying generated by transcendence seems to be the only possibility to converse *philosophically* with the pre-originality that supports all forms of apophansis and reflection. The way transcendence speaks in philosophy is successive, nonsimultaneous, diachronic. Presence and synthesis, including dialectics and all other systems and networks of oppositions, rule in ontology; the beyond of Being demands and reveals itself in a nonsynchronizable time. Such a time is needed for authentic surprises, adventures, and history, but it resists the supremacy of a gathering philosophy.

The structure of the "ancillary" and "angelic" language demanded and held off by transcendence has now been briefly described. Further analyses are necessary, but at the end of section 3, Levinas already anticipates a startling development which will be given later in the text (213–18/167–71). Here and there he compares and contrasts the diachrony of the angelic language with the language of skepticism, which he calls "a legitimate child of philosophy" (9/7; 231/183). From its beginning, skepticism has accompanied philosophy; after every refutation it comes back, unimpressed by the logically irrefutable remark that it professes the impossibility of truth proclaimed by it. What could explain this audacity?

Without defending skepticism as a doctrine (since it is a negative thought of the nonontological) we might perhaps say that Levinas wants to argue for a skeptical element in the thought of transcendence. Indeed, it cannot be silenced by the classical refutation which seems logically correct. For although it is true that it denies *in actu exercito* the impossibility of truth as stated in the Said of its Saying, the logical refutation of skepticism demands that, *after* having heard the content of the Said ("truth is impossible"), we make explicit what is implicit in the very positing of this thesis ("this statement is true") in order to compare these two statements and establish their incompatibility. According to Levinas we need time to realize, *first*, what the skeptical thesis states, *second*, that the stating of the thesis entails another thesis, *third*, that the two theses are incompatible and cannot be maintained at the same time. The possibility of skepticism and the feeling of being cheated by its purely logical refutation are thus explained by the successive or *diachronic* structure which is hidden and masked in the skeptical position. Logic would triumph if all the elements of the skeptical thesis were contemporaneous, i.e., if we were entitled to gather all propositions in one present. This right is precisely the presumed right of ontology as a philosophy of synthesis and presence. If "the truth" reveals itself as diachronically dispersed, i.e., in events, surprises, adventures, and (hi)stories rather than in systems or overviews, then logic, in solidarity with ontology, has lost its *absolute* validity.[13]

4. Subjectivity

Being or essence is the realm of a destiny which gathers all beings and all modes of being as moments of one order with an economy of its own. Even death does not break with this economy: corpses themselves contribute to its perpetual regeneration, as, for example Plato's palingenesis shows.

Modernity was the attempt to escape from destiny through the redemption of human freedom. The deterministic mechanics of matter can and should be conquered by the autonomy of choice and self-projection; the conflicts which follow the confrontation of individual and collective liberties with the order of essence should and can be overcome by emancipation and democracy. However, modern freedom is not capable of breaking with that order. On the contrary, it is its cornerstone. As philosophy from Descartes and Spinoza via Kant, Hegel, Marx, and Sartre has shown, freedom has revealed itself to be an event and a function within history; notwithstanding—or rather due to—its opposition to destiny and determinism, freedom belongs, with its opposites, to the temporal order of the essence.

"Freedom" or liberty (*liberté*) here is the name for that which has been thematized in the "epic" of modernity.[14] Its main characteristics are selfhood, choice, and rational self-regulation. Levinas does not want to repress or belittle the admirable emancipation of humanity from social and cultural slavery. Responsibility would be an empty word without adult selfhood. He contends that freedom by itself cannot be the origin of meaning, however; it needs a direction which cannot be chosen but only obeyed. Responsibility precedes all choices or projects; it constitutes, or even precedes, the self of subjectivity.

The escape from ontology does not abolish or diminish freedom, but reaches back to something more "original" than being, freedom, history, epics, literature, and destiny. Is it possible to conceive of such a "pre-original" or "an-archic" "reality"? Where could we go in order to escape the all-invading essence?

Levinas seems to allude to Heidegger's use of the verb *er-örtern* (to clarify by situating) and the substantive *Ort* (place, site), when he says that transcendence does *not* deliver us from Being to bring us to a specific site or situation, condition, country or home; it frees us from all places. The unconditional is not a place. It does not "take place." The French word "*non-lieu*" is a legal expression; it indicates a judge's decision not to pursue a case. This meaning does not seem to fit here. However, *non-lieu* also refers to the verbal expression *avoir lieu*, which means "to happen" or "to take place." The word can thus be read as a polemical neologism for the exceptional out-of-placeness or "nonplace" which contradicts Heidegger's insistence on the links between understanding and being placed or situated, being at home, being rooted in a soil, conditioned by a landscape, etc. The question of "where" transcendence will bring us is then answered by the remark that it cannot be dated or located in time either (*n'a pas lieu*); it does not belong as an event in history. Not only is responsibility free from attachment to any particular soil, country, space, or race: it also eludes subjection to the temporality of history. Transcendence does not belong to a specific language, culture, or period, because it is foreign to any homeland and marginal to history.

All the traditional oppositions of being—like Plato's non-Being (*me on*), Hegel's negativity, Heidegger's *Nichten* and Sartre's nihilation—are too much attached to their opposite to initiate the authentic difference of an exception. This difference is, however, found in the human subject as marginal, anarchical, prehistorical and pre-ontological self, simultaneously unique and incomparably different from itself. Selfhood is here not the triumphant and self-certain unfolding through which a person realizes original possibilities in final perfection. The self does not, by becoming actual, coincide with its own promising essence; it is rather the inescapable restlessness by which a unique subject finds *itself driven* out of itself to the Other, beyond the circle of possibilities that can be realized. The subject's self is not the dialectal difference between the ego as subject and object of its own consciousness or life. Oneself, me, myself, yourself, herself, or himself precede any possibility of a total reflection which would enable a subject to reach the actualization of its potentiality. If such a reflection were possible, I would be able to be the end as well as the origin of my life. The impossibility of a coincidence between the subject's possibility and its realization indicates that the subject can neither recuperate the origin of its task, nor identify itself as a reality in which this task is fulfilled. The reflexive pronoun "oneself" (*me, moi, te, toi, se, soi*) does not indicate any mirroring of an original or transcendental ego in the reality of some accomplished personality. Such a correspondence could be proclaimed the *entelecheia* of which the human essence is the *dynamis.*

Just as in section 3 where Levinas focused his analysis on the Latin word "oracle," so here he uses a Greek word, *kerygma,* to sketch the difference between the presuppositions of the way in which the philosophical tradition defined essence, subjectivity, reflexity, etc., and the exceptional nonidentity of the nonessential or pre-ontological subject. Its nonidentity differs radically from all other differences, insofar as it is a doubly negative but nondialectical difference: a non-indifference. Indeed, indifference with regard to the Other's interests constitutes the identification through which an egoistic self returns to itself; the impossibility of coinciding with oneself, however, is the split which makes a subject interested in the Other and unconquerably different from itself.

Levinas finishes section 4 with references to some historical prefigurations of his own descriptions of subjectivity. As in *Totality and the Infinite,* where Plato's "idea of the Good" and Descartes's "idea of the infinite" are quoted as extraordinary gestures toward a beyond of ontology, so now he points at Plato, Husserl, and Nietzsche as flashes of exceptional anarchy. I will not dwell on this passage because the allusions are all too summary. The passage suggests ideas for a revision of the standard history of philosophy, but in no way claims to encapsulate a reinterpretation of Plato, Husserl, and Nietzsche.

With regard to the much debated question of the subject, I would like to note that Levinas does not take sides in the battle between those who maintain the ideals of the Enlightenment and those who abundantly argue for "the death of the subject." His response to the solidarity of modern and antimodern reactions to the ideal of an autonomous subject consists in a redefinition of subjectivity. It is other than and prior to freedom as it is classically understood in opposition to determinism and oppression. This enables him to avoid the sensational trivialities of the positions that are stuck in the worn-out patterns of modernity. Levinas's "pre-originality" might become the origin of something refreshingly new.

5. Responsibility for the Other

Section 5 approaches transcendence from the perspective of time, and only focuses on responsibility toward the end. Levinas starts by asking: How "is" the time of the beyond? Again, as always, the approach is conditioned by a reflection about the time of ontology.

Levinas begins by excluding a classical answer. He refers to Kant's treatment of the fourth antinomy of reason, where a refutation of that answer is apparent: the beyond of Being is not the timeless dimension of eternity. If it were, the question of how something eternal could command temporality would arise. However, Kant proved that we cannot know anything about a non- or supratemporal reality.

The refutation of eternity given here does not seem sufficient. Perhaps Levinas also implicitly appeals to an opinion widespread in the twentieth century. In any case, as we will see, the thought of an eternal *presence* (for example, in the form of a *nunc stans*) belongs to the tradition of ontology; it cannot characterize the Other of Being. If eternity is not the dimension of transcendence, it seems to fall under the temporality of Being. Or is a different temporality possible?

We have already seen that transcendence does not take (a) place, but is its rupture with the essence not an event in time? If Being and time belong together, how then can transcendence, or responsibility, happen and continue? Haven't we said that responsibility is always already there, before freedom, and that it can never come to an end? If transcendence has a time of its own, this must differ from the temporality which governs Being and non-Being, phenomenality, monstration, causality, and so on.

The time of the essence is presence. Within ontology, the past and the future, and all temporal transitions, are variations of the present, as St. Augustine proved in the eleventh book of the *Confessions*. All beings and times are presented or represented as configurations of some present constellation or movement. The temporality of Being is synchrony, made possible by the gathering force of the human mind. Past events are retrieved by memory, the future is anticipated by planning and expectation. Husserl's analyses showed how retention and pretention stretch the present and reduce all past and future to the gathering here and now of the instant that can be said and inscribed.

If transcendence, too, is temporal, its time cannot coincide with such a presence. According to Levinas it cannot coincide with presence at all because presence, synchrony, and essence belong together. If another temporality is impossible, transcendence is an illusion.

To escape from the essence, we need a time which resists all attempts to reduce it to presence, a time that can neither be present, nor re-presented by memory or anticipated by imagination, a time of absolute surprise, in which new things can happen and old events can pass without being kept as an integral piece of our memory or as a function of synchronic history. Levinas looks for such a temporality mainly in the dimension of the past. Although *Totality and the Infinite* dedicates a chapter to the eschatological questions which also guide his commentaries on certain messianic texts in *Difficult Liberty* (DL, 83–129/59–96), in *Otherwise than Being* and most texts after *Totality and the Infinite* he stresses the past that cannot become a present, i.e., a past that cannot be remembered, recollected, brought to mind, an "immmemorable" past, "more" past than any memorable or recuperable past. Only such a past leads out of the circle and the repetitions of the encompassing presence in which the three tenses are fused. Only the difference between ontological temporality—in which presence swallows the past and the future—and the nonpresentable, irrepresentable, nonhistorical, and "pre-prehistorical" past, can provide transcendence and responsibility with a temporal lapse, and thereby give them the means to detach themselves from Being's history. Such a lapse is diachronical, and no longer the synchrony of the memorable past on which science and philosophy of history are based.

Synchrony and diachrony, Ulysses and Abraham, ontology and transcendence, the Same and the Other owe their difference to *different temporalities*. This clarifies Levinas's use of the term "pre-original." Since "origin," like "*arche*," "cause," "principle," etc., belong to the realm of the essence, the "past" of transcendence cannot be an origin because it cannot be thought of as a beginning, which then, "at the beginning," would necessarily be a presence. A past that cannot be recalled or represented, is a past that never was (a) present. It "precedes" all possible presents, including all beginnings. It is therefore not at all similar to what we commonly think of when we hear the word "past." Also, the "pre" of "pre-original" and the precedence constitutive of transcendent diachrony are differently "before" than the "before" with which we are familiar through the ontological understanding of time characteristic of our culture. In some sense, which it remains difficult to make more precise, all the expressions here become metaphorical, and as soon as we try to clarify them, we transform them into elements of a said, which, as said, obeys the temporal commands of ontology. However, we can understand that the gap between diachrony and synchrony exempts transcendence from the persuasive interestedness of Being, in which nothing should be lost and everything is retained, collected, and connected. In contrast with the "interesting" synchronization of ontology, the time of responsibility cannot be possessive; it does not master the time in which it is practiced.

"Time" thus hides two radically different temporalities: the time of essence, and the time of responsibility. The latter happens in Saying, not in the *epos*—the "word" or the "epic" of the Said—of thematic and historical syntheses. Saying signifies otherwise than the Said, for example in greeting, but it inevitably turns into a said whenever someone thinks about its signification. Saying is therefore equivocal; it wavers between two times, connecting and disconnecting them. The secret of its enigma is its difference from Being, insofar as this difference is expressed *in time*. The task of a quasiphenomenological characterization of Saying envelopes the detection of temporal adventures that cannot be understood as a past or future present. Stretching our memory (or, for that matter, our expectation or hope) does not lead to such quasi-events. Levinas nonetheless gives examples of a temporality in which a present action presupposes a past that never was (a) present: a person can be grateful for being (*already*) grateful, without being able to remember when this preceding gratitude began—it never did begin, but always already preceded every possible being grateful for it.

The last part of section 5 finally mentions the responsibility for the Other announced in the title. The diachronic structure of transcendent time, which has, in abstract form, been the topic up to this point, is made concrete, not by an example, but by the basic constitution of human existence: responsibility for the Other, i.e., being (not guilty but) responsible for the Other's faults and misfortunes. In responsibility we are related to a past which cannot be remembered because it was never present. Responsibility did not start at any particular moment; it was certainly not the result of a choice or a contract. It precedes not only my own freedom but also that of the Other for whom I am responsible, although the Other's will and mine have always been separate. Neither can responsibility be explained on the basis of human fraternity if this is conceived in a synchronic concept of which I am the master. Responsibility precedes all possible remembrance and surpasses all future achievements (because its demands can never be satisfied by any final accomplishment). It has its own nonspatial and nonsynchronical quasi- or pre-originality.

6. Essence and Signification

In section 5 "responsibility" appeared only at the end, although it was announced in the title. Likewise, the opposition announced in the title of section 6 is not thematized until its last page. First, the structure of responsibility is analyzed further and its implications for temporality are brought to the fore. The issue which receives the most attention, however, is "the Good," a pseudonym for the One whose name should not be pronounced frivolously.

The reference to the Good is set up by the question of the relation that ties a responsible person to that which has made her responsible. Is responsibility a conclusion or an application of some insight, a piece of wisdom to be conquered? Can philosophy lead to responsible behavior? Do we need philosophy for it? The answer is "no," because the an-archic "origin" or "pre-origin" from which responsibility comes does not let itself be caught by any insight or concept or thought; its impact, stronger than any other, cannot be thematized as a topic, a being, or a phenomenon. This is clarified from different perspectives. Without pronouncing the word "God"—but without lacking the courage to do so, as the essay "God and Philosophy" clearly shows[15]—Levinas at this point presents a summary of an entirely new version of philosophical theology. In fact, this version is neither theological nor ontological, for it contests the capacity of logos to speak about "God."

Levinas begins analyzing the diachronic structure of responsibility in contrast to the synchronical time of ontology. Over against all attempts to (re)collect beings and events into one overview—the synchronic totality of an imaginative or thoughtful simultaneity or "presence"—responsibility demands another kind of response. It reminds us of something that "happened" to us before we even had a chance to accept or refuse it, in an immemorable past at which we were never present, a "past that was never was a presence." The diachronic relation to such a past resists all seizure; the memory it involves is that of neither a historical reconstruction, nor of a kind of *anamnesis* through which one could re-present a forgotten truth.

To respond to responsibility means that we enact a relation to that which cannot be contained in any presence, given that it is unseizable, incomprehensible, and immense or im-measurable for any consciousness. It surpasses by escaping from any perception, thought, or image, and especially from that of a supreme being. The "superlative" (which is the Latin equivalent to the German *Aufhebung*) of its infinity is thus hardly perceptible; it impresses and obsesses by the "nonpresence" of humility. As the (pre)-origin of responsibility it is the Good itself.[16]

Since the Good cannot be seen, felt, imagined, conceived, or represented, it is separate from the universe of beings, different from Being itself, holy (*saint*). This has consequences for the relation of the Good to human freedom.

To be free means to do and to be what I choose or agree to do or be. This presupposes that I can dispose of the elements which play a role in my situation and actions, or at least that I can accept them voluntarily as they are. Freedom therefore presupposes that the elements which determine my being are present for my choice or consent. The presence of perception or representation, and thus remembrance, history, and synchronization, are essential moments of human liberty. If the Good does not let itself be presented or represented in such a presence, it cannot be chosen; it does not leave us free to enter into a relation with it, but has "chosen" us before we could even have an idea of it. Since the Good was never present to us, there was never a time in which we were able to choose it. In this sense, "subjectivity has no time," and never had, "to choose the Good" and nobody's goodness depends on his will ("no one is good voluntarily"). However, everybody is good to the extent that the Good has always already penetrated him or her with its diffusive goodness[17] before any awakening of consciousness or will to the presence of beings.

Freedom is *not* the basis and origin of humanity, as some existentialists wanted to believe. It is preceded by the pre-originary exception of a nonfree obsession. Since ontology does not permit this exception, it must interpret nonfreedom as the opposite of freedom, i.e., as slavery. Within an ontological framework, Levinas's work would present a pre-Nietzschean, pre-Feuerbachian, and, in general, premodern, or even pre-European defense of moralistic slavery, instead of a philosophy of human autonomy. His criticism of absolute freedom would then push him into the camp of those who proclaim determinism and the death of the subject to be more truthful, thus remaining within the oppositions of ontology. Levinas's rehabilitation of morality does not defend any slavery, however; responsibility presupposes free initiatives, choices, autonomous agreements, and so on, but these presuppose a direction which is neither chosen nor lived as a condemnation or repression. The Good is not able to enslave or repress—because it is good. Like love, it cannot be chosen but only welcomed: "it loves me before I [can] love it." Its influence is compared to the investiture of a knight or to the appointment of a substitute: "the Good invests freedom" with powers: the powers of being good. Nothing escapes the reach of the Good.

Instead of enslaving me, the anarchy of the Good makes me a hostage to the Other. Its command "ordains" me by making me close to the Other in a relation of being responsible for the Other's freedom. The service[18] that follows from it contains a form of negativity: responsibility involves sacrifice. This is why Levinas very often qualifies the "being-for-the-Other" by the clause "*malgré moi*" ("despite me") or "*contre mon gré*" ("against my will"). Slavery is not constituted by pain or by the sacrifice of certain enjoyments but by the loss of selfhood. This is not found in the ethics of "*me voici*" (here I am), however: the self in the accusative (*se, soi-même*) is the core of human significance. Employing an expression from the Gospels, Levinas reminds the reader that "losing" oneself in responsibility for the Other coincides with finding the true signification of oneself.[19]

At this point we may begin to understand how "the Good" differs from "the God of the philosophers, from Aristotle to Leibniz *via* the God of the scholastics." Such a God is crammed into the frame of a philosophy of immanence and autonomy; as fitting the dimensions of reason, it is a God that can be understood, and which therefore does not trouble the autonomy of consciousness. Consciousness is self-consciousness. Like Ulysses, it returns to itself in the end, having assimilated all surprises and adventures as enrichment of its wealth. Such a consciousness finds peace and enjoyment in itself and is thus atheistic. The unrest of Abraham, however, is the consequence of an orientation that does not permit establishment within the walls of such a home (cf. EDHH, 188).

Levinas's insistence on the exceptional "nonpresent," "nonorigi-nal," "nonperceptible," "nonphenomenological" character of the Good could give us the impression that he tries to renew the neo-Platonic and pseudo-Dionysian tradition of "negative theology," in which God, as "non-Being" and *hyper-ousia*, is thematized or evoked through a constellation of negative categories. He denies this both here and elsewhere because he wants to stress the positivity—an exceptional, nonontological positivity—of God's "nonpresent" impact as testified to by the ethical fact of responsibility. The positive category through which he describes that impact is the category of the trace, which he introduced in his essay "The Trace of the Other" in 1963.[20] Referring there to the fifth chapter of the fifth Ennead in which Plotinus speaks about the nature of the Good, Levinas quotes the following lines:

> With regard to the principle which precedes all beings, [namely] the One, this remains in itself, but although it remains, it is not different from that which produces the beings in agreement with itself. The One is sufficient to generate them. . . . The trace of the One gives birth to Being, and Being is no more than the trace of the One."[21]

Levinas's explanation of the trace can be read as a discussion with Plotinus but also as a translation of biblical wisdom into philosophical language. At the end of his essay Levinas refers to Exodus 33, where we read:

> And the Lord said: "Behold, there is a place by me where you shall stand upon the rock; and while my glory passes by I will put you in a cleft of the

rock, and I will cover you with my hand until I have passed by; then I will take away my hand, and you shall see my back; but my face shall not be seen."[22]

Levinas comments: "The revealed God of our Judeo-Christian spirituality maintains all the infinity of his absenc. . . . He shows himself only by his trace" (EDHH, 202; TrO, 359).

Levinas's justification of this reference is not by way of appeal to the authority of faith or theology, but rather through the suggestion that both the Greek and Hebrew tradition contain hints that point in the same direction as a twentieth-century phenomenology of transcendence. Before continuing my commentary on *Otherwise than Being*, I will summarize sections 5 and 6 of "The Trace of the Other" (EDHH, 197–202; HAH, 57–63; CP, 102–7) because the book seems to presuppose what the essay said about the trace.

The analysis of the nonphenomenological character of the face (EDHH, 187–97) leads to the question of what kind of signification we may ascribe to it. Since that which visits and provokes me in the face of the Other (or, to use the terminology of *Otherwise than Being*, since that which ordains me into responsibility) is absolutely absent, as a past that was never a present, the face can neither be its mask, nor its symbol, nor in general a direct sign or indication of anything that can be presented or represented. It does not, like a symbol, hide the presence of an invisible Absolute which could be revealed by analysis or unveiling. The Absolute is "ab-solute" because it has absolved itself from all participation in the immanence of the present world. As absolute past it left traces, in the Other's surprising me, or looking at me and speaking to me; the Other refers me to a past that cannot be transmuted into a phenomenon or the object of a thought. What, then, signifies in the significance of the face and in the responsibility that responds to its provocation? It disrupts and deranges the order of the world, but it does not do so by miracles or shattering events, as if eternity suddenly disrupted the normal order of history. A thaumaturgic transcendence can hardly be affirmed without affirming at the same time another world behind or above this world; that would only displace the enigma of the ethical, however. Eternity must be akin to the absolute past which has a real impact although it remains hidden from the horizons of our vision.

The trace thus signifies without manifesting anything. Although we could not say anything philosophical if we did not start from phenomenology, an approach to the trace demands some move beyond. Let's see how far a phenomenology of traces brings us on the way to the absolute.

The trace can be seen as a special kind of sign, insofar as a detective, a hunter, or a historian examine it for clues to the reconstruction of the activities and the character of those who left it behind. They did not intend to leave traces; they even tried to wipe them out, but in effacing them, they left other traces. A trace signals a certain past but contains no presence: the past it indicates is absolutely gone. The possibility of the trace and its specific form of signaling is based on the fact that it functions in a "world," i.e., in an order of things where everything is related to everything else. One can leave traces intentionally, for example in a game or in writing a check, but "the authentic trace" (EDHH, 200; TrO, 357)—the exceptional trace farthest from all other signs—disrupts the normal order. It is an imprint on the world left by someone who did everything he could not to leave a trace, for instance a criminal. He did not want to signify anything by it, but without or even against his will, his trace testifies that the world has been disturbed in an irreparable way. To leave a trace is then the same as to have passed in a self-absolving or "absolute" way.

In this sense, the trace is a common phenomenon. All signs, all words or gestures, are also traces: they are delivered by someone who passed. The signification of a sign is passed on by someone to someone. The sign is left as the trace of those who communicated it; it traces the speaker's or writer's passing by.

Levinas's distinction between sign and trace runs parallel to his distinction between the Saying and the Said. The meaning of a sign, the style, the subconscious intentions symbolized in it can be studied, but such a study does not touch upon the bare fact that someone passed and has become an absolved, absolute, and irreversible past.

To what extent are the Other's face, and my own responsibility, traces? They have no beginning, but come from nowhere and from a past before all past presents. As points of contact with the ab-solute they point to that which left a trace without ever having been present: the one (*ille, il*) who is always already gone, leaving us with a nonchosen infinite responsibility. The Other signals the transcendence of an irreversible and immemorial past.

Most often Levinas says that the Other dwells "*in* the trace of God," seldom or never that the Other *is* his trace.[23] The visage and responsibility do not simply coincide with the trace of God, because their absoluteness and infinity is bestowed on them by his passage from out of a "time" before all times. *Ille* is not identical to anything in the time of the world. The condition of all transcendence frees the Other and me from the world, while referring me to the Other and the only world in which we meet. The enigma of the absent Infinite refuses to be treated as a phenomenon, a being, a topic, or a theme. The humility and silence of the ultimate can be ignored or denied although its trace suggests a recognition which has the structure of an *à-Dieu*.

The positivity of the trace left by illeity is an excess: the Infinite exceeds the essence by its exorbitant demand. It converts the subject to the Other by an a priori responsibility that includes obedience even before the awakening of any liberty (cf. 16/13).

The structure of that demand differs from the *Sollen* as thematized by Kant and Fichte, because responsibility grows when it is fulfilled, and thus becomes even more demanding and less satisfied, while *Sollen* orders the progressive approximation to an ideal which can, in principle, be realized. The tasks of proximity do not diminish, because the Good always demands more than what can be accomplished.

As responsibility, subjectivity is the point at which the Infinite's enigmatic transcendence exceeds and disrupts the ontologic order of worldly phenomena. In this point of rupture, which is also the point of connection, essence and the beyond touch one another and split or, as Levinas writes: "Subjectivity is the very knot and un-knotting—the knot and un-knotting of essence and essence's other."[24]

The ambiguity of the contact between transcendence and essence is the ambiguity of a trace. We would like to clarify the structure of that contact and develop a conceptual schema of the connection between essence and transcendence. This would mean, however, that we would bring transcendence and its excess back into the horizon of ontology. The trace cannot serve as a basis for a conceptual analysis or an onto-logical or phenomeno-logical argumentation. And yet we refuse to fall into the arbitrary assertions of irrationalism. The only possibility for a serious and methodically justified procedure is to start from the (quasi)phenomenal facts of face, Saying, subjectivity, and responsibility in order to discover the limits of (onto- and phenomeno-)logic.

Any attempt at prove God's existence would run counter to all that has been said up to now. We must understand that God is neither a phenomenon nor a being, and that neither God nor human subjectivity, freedom nor speaking can be understood as themes or topics of thematization. They precede any possible logic, as not only Levinas, but the entire tradition of Western onto-theo-logy knew (despite today's cheap condemnations of "metaphysics"). A God that could be proven would certainly not be Godly enough to be "*Il.*" He would fit our categories— and thus, perhaps, give us satisfaction—but this would disqualify him from being God.

Transcendence touches us by leaving traces which challenge and resist our comprehension. Their obscure and enigmatic character does not diminish the overwhelming certainty of their practical relevance, however: the Infinite "speaks" by creating subjects as already obedient delivered over to the infinite demands of responsibility. The theoretical difficulties and doubts caused by the ambiguity of the trace do not destroy the pretheoretical "traumatism" of the "conversion" which precedes the awakening of consciousness and autonomy.

The Infinite blurs and almost effaces its traces by turning our theoretical curiosity about its nature into responsibility for other humans. Before any possibility of asking theoretical questions, a human subject already practices the "for-the-Other" which constitutes subjectivity as substitution and being hostage. In awakening to self-consciousness, a human subject discovers itself to be not "*an* Ego" in the sense of modern philosophy, but the "me" of "*me voici*," i.e., the servant of the absent whose "glory" is displayed in the exorbitant and disproportionate demand of responsible humility.

To be in the trace by saying and obedience constitutes the signifying character of subjectivity. What makes me significant is my saying, greeting, being concerned, my signifying or "*signifiance*" to and for the Other. The problem of signification and the problem of subjectivity are the same. And "the problem of God and the problem of subjectivity . . . go together," as Levinas writes at the beginning of section 9, where he will continue his meditations on the connection between the Infinite and me.

7. Sensibility

In section 3, subjectivity was called an exception, because it cannot be understood as an element in a network composed of modulations of Being and non-Being. Human subjectivity does not have a place within the framework of ontology. Not even its dialectical versions can cope with this "excluded middle." The alternative of Being and non-Being—and thus the foundational claims of ontology—is refuted by the fact of subjectivity as responsibility, subjection, and substitution.

The structure of subjectivity is extensively analyzed in chapter 4. The central word there is "substitution," but a host of other expressions clarify, interpret, or deepen its meaning: to be human is to be "the-one-for-the-Other," a hostage, a mother, obsessed, persecuted, etc. The results of those analyses are not enumerated in the course of the first chapter, but are rather presupposed in its various sections, and especially in sections 6 and 7.

As infinitely responsible for the Other, I am (*me voici*) un-conditionally (without condition, place, or case of my own) "for-the-Other," the Other's substitute and hostage, not because of any choice or desire on my part, but by an election that preceded my birth. This, and not freedom or autarchy, gives humanity its ultimate meaning or "signification." By humanly existing, you greet the Other, you give signs, you willy-nilly signify that you are for him or her. This "significance" disrupts the web in which we are caught; it comes from outside of the world in which we form constellations, and it reaches further than any transformation of this world. To be a substitute is not to coincide with another ego, as if I could replace another as being-in-the-world; rather it is to carry the Other—as Other— in me, a kind of maternity as Levinas sometimes says (cf., e.g., 85–86, 89/67–68, 71). This strange relation of my nonidentity in the place of the Other, without destroying the Other's identity, proves that the Other and I do not fit into the world and cannot be understood within the limits of an ontology. The order of Being is broken by the signification of the *ethical* (see below). But where does the ethical come from? This question can be conceived neither as a question about ontological origins and ends, nor as a question about a context, world, or gathering mystery. The ethical does not belong to any world or universe. It does not have a beginning but comes from nowhere, from a nonspace and a (non-)time before time. It does not differ from human subjectivity but constitutes its core, though it does not constitute a quiet essence or the busy dynamism of a "nature." "The ethical" is another word for "animation" or "inspiration." A human body requires the psychism of a soul or "breath." Under the pulse of its breath, as animated body or incarnated soul (cf. 87–89/69–71), a subject is inspired without being able to inspire or inflate itself. Its inspiration has always already preceded the expiration of its greeting and its service, the Saying of its exposition to the Other.

An *epoche* with regard to the economy of essence and interessence is made possible by an inspiration that makes human life significant. The subject does not possess its own breathing, but is animated and obsessed by it. Through inspiration, subjectivity evades the dimension of economics, worlds, and contexts, but this evasion is not possible without unbreakable ties to concrete economics and situations.

The duality of an ethics that cannot be separated from ontology (and vice versa) is not the old duality of body and soul. "Inspiration" does not refer to a spirit that hovers over the corporeal dimensions of nature and animality. Rather it indicates the human mode of being corporeal: a body turned to and touched by other bodies in a world common to them and me.

This mode is neither corporeal nor spiritual; it is "psychism" or *sensibility*. This is shown in chapter 3, which the section I am clarifying here succinctly summarizes. Being touched by the Other is as corporeal and sensible as it is to enjoy the elements by respiration, bathing, or eating. The modes of sensibility here are radically different, however; indeed so different are they that it is difficult to speak of one generic form of sensibility. Yet, enjoyment (*jouissance*) and being touched or wounded by the Other (contact, vulnerability) or even suffering under the burden of responsibility (*souffrance*) belong together. For to give to another what he or she needs presupposes that I have experienced what needs and fulfillments are, and to suffer entails the experience of possible pleasures at least. Whereas enjoyment is lived in the mode of satisfaction and autarchy, being touched, carrying a burden, and suffering are forms of passivity (cf. 79–80, 91ff./63–64, 72ff.). A masochist can choose such passivity, but that would transform them into experiences and experiments of a perverse project of gathering satisfaction and self-realization. The passivity of being-touched-by-the-Other, however, cannot be chosen, because it precedes any possibility of choice. It is not even an experience, but that which, from before all memorable time, rules and purifies all experiences.

The way in which a human life is lived or "happens" (*se passe*) is a passage that cannot be planned; it happens to you, just as becoming older "happens." Subjectivity is subjection to an orientation of time that is out of reach of any activity the subject could deploy.

Chapters 3 and 4 develop this "pre-originary" passivity by showing its necessary expression in exposition, denudation, vulnerability, suffering, denucleation, persecution, and expiation. The signification of subjectivity as hostage is found in the "passion" of a passivity that is neither the contrary nor the dialectical counterpart of activity, but is rather the trace of a nonhuman passage: the passing of the Good.

The unavoidable exposition of the subject can also be shown through the analysis of the Saying, which was already thematized in former sections. By relating sensibility and Saying, Levinas clarifies the corporeal (and not spiritual or material) immediacy of the latter and the width of its signification. All human activities start from an anachronic innocence; at the back of our involvement in the imbroglio of half-truths, lies and violence, there is a pure, sincere turning and giving: a Saying inspired by the Good.

At the end of section 7 Levinas calls the alterity of the Good's passing a form of violence, but how can the Good be violent? Has Levinas, too, fallen victim to a certain fashion according to which every act or gesture or word is inevitably "violent"? No, on the contrary, he insists on the sincerity, frankness, innocence, and veracity of the Saying, and the fact that it involves its subject in suffering is no reason to confuse this suffering with an effect of violence. The "violence" that is inseparable from the Good's otherness is its unavoidable answer to all attempts to close the dimension of essence and interesse, as if the economy of Being could support itself. Since the closure of that dimension is the source of all violence (i.e., of all forms of contempt for the Infinite), the Good must reject it. However, its mode of acting is a most humble and tender—but not painless—refusal of participating in the game of those who "usurp the earth" by claiming, before others, their "place under the sun" (cf. the first quote from Pascal on vi/vii).

A Note on "Ethics"

Whereas "morality," "moral law," "moral duties," and "moral philosophy" have almost disappeared from contemporary philosophy, the word "ethics" is used with enthusiasm and in many senses. In Levinas's oeuvre, too, it has a certain equivocity, which might lead to misunderstanding. A systematic study of Levinas's ethical terminology would be helpful both for settling certain questions about the relevance of his thought for fundamental and casuistic considerations of moral problems, and for the relation between ontology ("is") and normative theory ("ought").[25] This study cannot be undertaken here, but I would like to insist on one point, which seems to me fundamental for any faithful interpretation of Levinas's work.

This point has been clearly formulated in the preface to *Totality and the Infinite*: "Already *of itself* ethics is an 'optics.' . . . The traditional opposition between theory and practice will disappear before the metaphysical transcendence. The apparent confusion is deliberate and constitutes one of the theses of this book" (TeI, xvii; TaI, 29). This declaration excludes not only the thesis of most modern philosophies, according to which ethics comes after epistemology and a non-normative ontology have established the foundations of all truth, but equally excludes the thesis that ethics (in the traditional sense of moral philosophy, including social, legal, and political philosophy) should be the foundation of epistemology and metaphysics or ontology. "Morality [which stands here for 'ethics'] is not a branch of philosophy, but first philosophy" (TeI, 281; TaI, 304). Thus "ethics as first philosophy" can become the title of an essay in which Levinas summarizes his thought.[26] I will not repeat what I wrote on this point in *To the Other* (123–24; see also, 63, 65, 223), but will only remark on the use of the word "*ethique*," which has its first appearance in *Otherwise than Being* at the beginning of section 7.

In the sentence "*la rupture de l'essence est éthique*," the last word is an adjective; it must be translated by the English "ethical," not by "ethics," which would translate the French "*est l'éthique*." As the preceding appositions prove, the rupture explained in this passage is the central topic of this chapter and, indeed, of the entire book: *transcendence*, which can be approached from a more theoretical side (as, e.g., in sections 1 and 3), a more practical side (as in chapter 4), or a more affective side (as in section 7 and chapter 3). The rupture with essence (as interessence and interest, as gathering and presentification) is accomplished by greeting, signification, respiration, as expiration of a pregiven inspiration, disinterestedness, gratuity as escape from the int. rested economy of merits and compensation, gratitude as thanking the Good for a nondeserved and unowned signification. The passage in which the predicate "ethical" occurs clearly shows that the importance of the rupture is simultaneously "theoretical" (transcendence of the Said by an exceptional *epoche*), "practical" (substitution), and "affective" (susceptibility, vulnerability, sensibility). *If* we must ask and answer the question of whether there is one side that is more important or (pre-)originary than any other, we will certainly not designate the theoretical, but rather the affective or "sensible" side. However, sensibility, affections, and emotions cannot be described unless the proximity by which they are constituted as af-fectedness is brought to the fore. The qualification of transcendence as "ethical" does not oppose any metaphysical interpretation; it does not privilege ethics over metaphysics, but it does insist on the simultaneity of metaphysics and ethics and their transcendence with regard to ontology and the privileging of any pre- or not-yet-ethical practice, feeling, or theory. "The ethical" belongs to transcendence; it is an unavoidable but partial name for it, just as the Good is not simply a name for the primacy of morality, but also the (pre-originary always already passed) first.

8. Being and beyond Being

Section 8 is very important, because it states clearly—and this does not happen often in Levinas's oeuvre—that ontology, the order of essence, is not at all bad, but necessary. Levinas does not want to eliminate ontology but sees it as a dimension which is subordinate to the *beyond* and the *otherwise*. He quickly sketches the main lines of both "dimensions" and he indicates how ontology is based on and can be "deduced" from the beyond.

The *otherwise* is presented here in its concrete form which is described in the first four chapters: "the proximity of the one for the other." That their relationship does not fit into ontological categories is shown in the slow and cautious analyses of those chapters, which are summarized here. It is contrasted with some other basic relationships, which *have* been caught in ontological categories. The ontological perspective is dominated by the unfolding of the essence as the interested adventure of self-accomplishment. In this light, the meaning of otherness is perceived and measured by the fact that it interests me. The Other then appears as a limit or as a complement; it functions as an obstacle or as a condition for my self-realization. It can, for example, resist my wishes or my desire to encompass or comprehend things; it might hinder my striving for perfection. In the form of another human subject it can also confirm my selfhood and condition the unfolding of my possibilities, for example through the recognition (*Anerkennung*) whose dialectical reciprocity is analyzed in Hegel's *Phenomenology of Spirit*. If the Other is my slave or servant, he respects me and works for me; as colleague, the Other reinforces and more than doubles my capabilities. If the Other is experienced as a God who can help and favor me, it is still the principle of self-maintenance and accomplishment which rules my relation to otherness. I am the center: a finite, threatened, and uncertain being who cares for itself and for the Other as elements of my own adventure.

Proximity, the relation of my being close to the Other through the exposition of my sensibility, is radically different; it cannot be thought in the categories of ontology. Saying and sensibility, exposition and vulnerability are nonontological categories which are clarified in the following chapters. They are the basic, or rather the "pre-original" names for that without which ontology and its categories would be impossible. *And here Levinas clearly states that ontology and proximity—or Being and otherwise than Being—are necessarily connected to one another.* Essence is not to be shunned. Ontology is not false, but it cannot claim to be the truth about the absolute. Being is not radical enough, but neither is the corruption or failure of a superior reality. Its ultimate meaning cannot be found in Being itself, but essence and ontology are necessary conditions for the absoluteness of the otherwise and of responsibility. In more concrete terms this can be said thus: in the ontological dimension, the human Other appears and is thematized as someone who shares essential desires and attributes with me. Classical social philosophies have thematized our being together in a network of interrelations which emerges from our common, yet individual nature, our essential inclinations and universal reason. Heidegger was more radical when he unveiled our being caught in the original structure of *Mitsein*, but the discovery of our being-with and its ontological, legal, social, and political ramifications, is not radical enough. Our being together emerges from and is rooted in the *pre*-existential and *pre*-original relationship of proximity.

The ultimate meaning of Being cannot be found in its own dimension; the interest that the essence holds for us owes its ultimate significance to the disinterested being-for-the-Other of responsibility, patience, and peace. On the other hand, responsibility for the Other demands the order of essence, *Mitsein*, equal rights, etc. In a very succinct way Levinas outlines the argumentation through which he will try to deduce the dimension of general justice and equality from proximity (cf. 198ff.;

155ff.). As a relationship between a unique *me* and a unique *autrui*, proximity includes a relation to *"the third"* who appears at the side of and associated with *autrui*. As I have tried to show elsewhere, the concept of the third is ambiguous.[27] *Either* the third is someone whom I do not encounter and whose face I do not see, or the third besides you is another you whose face I can see in the same way that I see your face now. In both cases, however, the multiplication of persons to whom I am close blurs their faces and makes them more or less anonymous. As instances of a sort of genus called "other persons," they urge me to perceive and treat them as equally entitled to my devotion. This way of coming to the fore identifies them as competing subjects of right and care. As such, they demand that justice be done to everyone. Their unicity is masked by the general qualities of human beings deserving and demanding respect. The ontological dimension of "being-with" and general justice is constituted thus; it is a dimension that can be characterized by the structures of administration, synopsis, comparison, synchrony, universal reason, etc. The classics of social philosophy have thematized this dimension and developed theories about the power of reason as the key to overcoming the violence that emerges from general competition.

Levinas neither criticizes nor retrieves these works, but he insists— and this is the main thrust of his own work—that the dimension of general justice cannot be liberated from violence, *unless it is inspired by the face-to-face relationship of proximity.* A radical overcoming of violence can emerge only from disinterested patience and anachronical passivity.

Thus we see that responsibility encompasses the domain of Being, conscience, thematization, etc. Levinas's insistence on the beyond is not an alternative to ontology, but a more radical inspiration. This is the thrust behind his assertion that "Starting from this *Saying* of substitution we must justify the order of the *Said*: of thought, justice and being; we must understand the conditions in which various philosophies in their Said—in ontology—can signify *truth*."[28] And: "The signification of the Saying goes beyond the Said: it is not ontology that raises up the speaking subject; on the contrary, it is the signifyingness of the Saying going beyond the essence, as gathered in the Said, which can justify the exposedness of being, ontology."[29]

We might wonder whether the "radicalization" of essence and justice—their being conditioned by and rooted in substitution—does not have consequences for their treatment in ontology and social philosophy. Since Levinas wrote neither an ethics nor a social philosophy, his answer is not given. In chapter 2 ("From Intentionality to Sensibility"), however, he presents us with fragments of a new ontology. In this chapter several Heideggerian motives and gestures can be recognized, as Levinas himself states in a note: "These lines, and those that follow, owe much to Heidegger. Deformed and ill-understood? Perhaps. At least this deformation will not have been a way to deny the debt" (49, n. 29/189, n. 28). It seems improbable that Levinas's transformation of phenomenology and his plea for the Good as beyond would not change the dimension of ontology.

If it is true that "the later birth" of essence, knowledge, justice, and the Said can be found *in* the signification of responsibility (199ff./156ff.), two conclusions seem to follow: (1) the Good cannot avoid concretizing itself in ethical and political discourses and practices; and (2) these discourses and practices must differ radically from those discourses and practices that start from ontological principles, such as all the moral and social philosophies and strategies of modernity. The difference must lie and reveal itself in the traces left by the Good (that is, by the obsession of absolute responsibility) *in* the texts and strategies of ethics, politics, and philosophy. Only then can we affirm that general "justice in no way is a degradation of obsession, a degeneration of the *for-the-other*, a diminution, a limitation of anarchic responsibility, a neutralization of the glory of the Infinite" (203/159). This is Levinas's version of the old question of the relationship between religion and ethics: moral responsibility and social justice are not sincere and not authentic, unless they "come from" the passage of the Good, which "made" human subjects or "elected" them as absolutely responsible for this and that and any unique Other. No other "rooting" or "foundation" than being in the trace of God can guarantee the signification of human thought and behavior.

It is not easy to clarify this relation between substitution and its ethico-political (as well as philosophical) concretization (or between the passage of God and human justice or between the Saying and ontology). Very often Levinas uses the expression "*à partir de*" in this context.[30] Obviously the relation between the dimension of Being, universality, justice etc., on the one hand, and responsibility (or the Good), on the other, cannot be formulated in ontological terms like "foundational" variations on the ideal of an origin or principle. The *metabasis* from beings to the Good and vice versa needs an expression other than the theoretical ones characteristic of all discourses *about* something, or practical projects in which something (for instance world peace) is planned. The metabasis cannot be performed by any element of the ontological economy; it can come only from the "height" of the Good, that is from the deepest humility of suffering subjects. Can this "from," the "*à partir de*" be made more precise? Levinas tries to do this by interpreting it as an exceptional "kind" of *before*: the before of a diachronic time whose "origin" is absolutely absent, the time of an irretrievable past, which never coincided with any present, the prehistorical past of a passage that preceded all kinds of human beginnings, the past of a creation that precedes any possibility of atheism.

9. Subjectivity Is Not a Modality of Essence

The first sentence of this second section on subjectivity connects subjectivity with God and outlines its coincidence with the central topic of the book: transcendence. One possible reading of Levinas's enterprise presents it as a new response to the question answered by Descartes's *ego cogitans*, Kant's transcendental apperception, Hegel's subjective spirit, and Heidegger's *Dasein*. As for Descartes and Hegel, so also for Levinas this question cannot be separated from God; like Kant, however, Levinas refuses to merge God, Being, and subjectivity into one whole. The unbreakable union between subjectivity and "the Good" is transcendence itself.

A rapid and extremely condensed reminder of Kant's, Hegel's, and Heidegger's views on subjectivity lays the ground for the summary of Levinas's analysis of subjectivity as transcendence. Kant is mentioned because he rejects the idea of the human subject as able to gather the dispersion of time in an encompassing concept of the universe from beginning to end by the conceptual work of his *Verstand*. Kant understood that the successivity of our experiences (i.e., the dispersed character of sensibility) cannot be overcome by a view from eternity or by any other kind of panoramic presence. The subject can neither conquer nor possess objective reality; all understanding is essentially incomplete and provisional. The idea of a totality in which all reality is present before the human mind is only an idea; the subject is delivered over to time.

Hegel and Heidegger, mentioned in one breath, tried to show the profound unity of the subject and Being. According to Levinas's interpretation, both of them conceive Being itself as temporal and deny that the subject is separated from it by an unbridgeable gap. With regard to Hegel, Levinas refers to the introduction of the *Phenomenology of Spirit* where Hegel, against Kant, argues that the opposition of subject and object has always already been overcome by the presence—or, as Heidegger's interpretation of that text says, by the *parousia*—of the absolute in the subject.[31] In the course of the *Phenomenology*, and in subsequent works, Hegel thematizes the unity of the human and the divine by showing how "subjective spirit" *is* the finite presence of "the Idea" or "the absolute spirit," which are his philosophical names for the God of religion. As a former student of Kojève, Levinas sees Hegel's thought as a philosophy of history, according to which "Being," i.e., the Idea or Spirit itself, is temporal. Levinas's point—the partial coincidence of human subjectivity with the absolute subjectivity of Being in its most authentic and full realization—can however also be defended through an interpretation of Hegel's absolute as primordially and ultimately eternal.

Whether Heidegger can be interpreted as the defender of a similar conception, according to which *Dasein* is a function of Being, is a question which must be left open in this context. Perhaps Levinas "Hegelianizes" Heidegger, but the later Heidegger does undeniably stress the initiatives of Being, language, and *das Ereignis*, while he sees the task of *Dasein* above all as obedience and listening to Being. Does this mean that *Dasein* is no more than "a modality of Being"? And should we understand this expression as a synonym for Spinoza's modes of substance, obsessed by their effort to maintain and expand their being?

In Levinas's view, Spinoza, Hegel, Heidegger, and their numerous followers, reduce the subject to the anonymous essence, of which they are only functions, instead of recognizing the subject as a "sub-stance" or *hypostasis* whose self cannot be lost in Being. The description of *hypostasis* was already a central topic in Levinas's first book, *From Existence to Existents*.[32] In later works, the expression does not frequently occur, but the separation between the subject—who is "me" as well as "ego"—and Being, remains a basic thesis. The difference between Saying and Said is a new way of stressing that separation: in Saying the subject expresses its nondialectical difference from Being, that is, from all that can be gathered in the Said.

Gathering presupposes light: at night an overview is impossible. Phenomena need a horizon for their shining forth; they belong to the dimension of the essence. The Good, however, rather than enlightening the subject, burns all interests other than those of living (and, thus, suffering) for Others.

The significance of the difference between the order of the essence and the subject's responsibility lies in the possibility or impossibility of the Good. To identify the absolute as Being or Idea (or as language, *il y a*, culture, etc.) is to nullify the Good, to destroy the possibility of goodness, donation, ethics. The choice between God and atheism is thus at stake; or rather, the choice between God and idolatry, perhaps. The proclamation that *the Sache* of thinking is Being does away with the Good, because the Good cannot stand subordinate to any other power. This explains its disinterest in economic calculations, and also its rejection of all cultures and theories in which it is not recognized as first. Over against the all-encompassing welcome extended to all kinds and manifestations of moral and religious cultures, which is typical to the relativistic museum of our time, the Good is too demanding to accept all cultures as equally valuable. Postmodern Western culture has a place for everything; it welcomes the indiscriminate manifold of existing opinions, symbols, ideas, practices, and experiences with a mixture of curiosity, aesthetic pleasure, and indifference. Altars, sacred places, and times, the entire geography and history of moral and religious codes, practices, and convictions are hailed as polymorphous revelations of Being or Spirit. The Good is not a monoculture, but it neither respects nor tolerates the erection of idols and human holocausts. Violence toward, or neglect of, individual humans, the denial of proximity, is evil. Against evil, against this denial which is the primary violence, the Good is not tender; even if evil is an expression of the essence, it is not admirable and it should not be preserved or enjoyed. This is the reason that the ethics of goodness (a redundant tautology) is not dialectical but destructive: "It destroys without leaving souvenirs, without transporting in museums the altars raised to the idols of the past for bloody sacrifices; it burns the sacred groves in which the echoes of the past reverberate" (22/18). Those who love the idols of all epochs will accuse the Good of being violent or antihumanist or even antihumane. They do not see that its "violence" is absolutely disinterested: it does not care for immoral beauty but is concerned about singular individuals, whom it does not permit to be sacrificed to cultural ideals or reasonable universality.

Classical ontology appealed to reason for the taming and universalizing of the violence of spontaneous inclinations and arbitrary decisions. The justification of cultural and educational constraints was sought in the demands of reason: ethics was the art of submitting the human animal to human reasonability. The violence of constraint was a reasonable reaction to a first, arbitrary, and not rationally justified violence. The Good, too, is nonviolent by itself, but evil necessitates destructive responses. Its "violence" in breaking certain altars and gas-chambers is the mask of pure devotion; it is an unavoidable side of its extreme humility. To be for the good is a farewell to undecidability. However, the ethics of proximity has a structure other than that of ontology, insofar as reason and universality belong to the economy of the essence. Even reasonability is still interested, because it does not reach the individual Other in its utterly destitute and culturally uninteresting poverty. The violence of reason does not stop the *polemos* of logos.

Goodness dedivinizes ontology, history, and reason; they are not absolutes. It refuses to serve any god or to venerate any of their sacred sites or times. Idols ("gods") create victims. The only responsible response to their arrogance is the burning of their groves and the deletion of their empire from the earth. The Good is better than reason, Being, light; it is the only right answer to all kinds of antihumanism. Its greatest danger is to be taken for a god or idol or sacred destiny, which would once again involve it in the wars and interests of the essence. And yet, isn't this almost or wholly inevitable as soon as we try to pronounce its exceptional goodness and transcendence? All discourses about the beyond betray its unsaid sanctity. As appearing in the text, it belongs to the ontology whose universality is judged by its diachronic proximity.

10. The Itinerary

The structure of the book, which is indicated in this section, has been exposed above. The succession of chapters and their division into sections suggests a linear unfolding, but in reading them one will be surprised by the entanglement of the various themes and concepts, similar to their intertwining in the nine sections of the first chapter, which comes to its close in section 10. The justification of this lies in the fact that transcendence does not let itself be said in a systematic text. The concepts through which it must be clarified do not present parts that can be delimited or de-fined and ranged besides one another within a whole. They overlap and partially or laterally include one another, but not in the way of dialectical moments. They "echo" one another and "project their shadows and reflections on one another." This fact does not facilitate a clear insight and it certainly prohibits a clear overview of the constellation at stake, but it respects the distortion which transcendence, Saying, substitution, and subjectivity undergo by being said. Levinas meets here with the old Platonic and Plotinian tradition of theology (and, we may add, with Heidegger's problem of a discourse about Being itself): that which precedes all thought and language cannot be caught in definitions, theses, theorems, or thematic philosophy.

Leaving aside the other methodological questions involved in Levinas's enterprise, the remainder of section 10 focuses mainly on the question of the "beginning," the source or "origin" or "foundation" from which thinking draws its possibilities. The central importance of "prephilosophical"—for instance, moral, religious, literary, historical, and autobiographical—experiences is affirmed, as well as the impossibility of separating these experiences from the philosophy to which they lead. Regarding the connections between Levinas's philosophy and his prephilosophical experiences, I will underline only one aspect here, namely that of the certainty which may be expected from relying on such a not-yet proven "beginning." It is not enough to appeal, with Plato, to the beauty of the risk[33] involved; at least it should be a risk imposed by the goodness of responsibility. As we know, this risk is the certainty of suffering for Others, but this does not seem to be accomplished in philosophy.

Hegel, Heidegger, and Husserl are called upon as thinkers who were extremely aware of the difficult question as to where philosophy should begin or even whether it has any beginning—that is, any safe and sure basis or origin—at all. Hegel answered by stating that a successful end confirms the correctness of the beginning. According to Heidegger the beginning is Being itself. Husserl, however, saw that we cannot do without some naivete: philosophy can neither wholly replace nor absorb philosophically uninsured "experiences," "intuitions," or "inspirations" which develop into the core of its explanations. Transcendence, responsibility, suffering are such "intuitions." They intervene and interrupt the play of philosophical textuality, but without them this play would be boring, uninspired, calculative, and insignificant.

The critique and the criteria necessary for checking the plausibility of the philosophical unfolding of prephilosophical "intuitions" cannot be exhausted by the skillful practice of the philosophical method alone. The author of a philosophy is steeped in her own experience which is partially unfolded in her theory. *Other* philosophers are needed to bring out the weak points of that theory. They have their own strong and weak points, but a dialogue is needed to give their points of departure a chance. If philosophy is not a science whose skills can be learned by any person who is intelligent enough, but rather an engagement in ontology and transcendence, the confrontation of those engaged is necessary for a nonegocentric critique of singular saids.

The end of chapter 1 is one of the very few places where Levinas defends a dialogical structure for philosophy. Most often he insists on the *asymmetric* relation between speaker and listener, which seems to exclude the reciprocity of a dialogue, but here, on the level of the philosophy he presents as his voice among other philosophical voices, he can only ask what Others think of his presentation. He does not forget to mention that the dialogue lasts as long as the history of philosophy, and that the classics never can be brought to silence. By stressing that the confrontation of engaged thinkers constitutes a drama, the drama of a nontotalizable history, Levinas distinguishes the structure of philosophical dialogue and the history of philosophy from the structure of scientific teamwork or of a Platonic dialogue, which can be told or written by one who composes different voices according to his theatrical imagination or memory.

Once again, time reaches further than the presence of a monologue; the temporality of Saying, Said, another Saying and Said, etc., distends the simultaneity of an oeuvre in the drama of the before-and-after of the-one-for-the-Others.

7

The Other, Society, People of God

The following reflections summarize, question, and expand upon some key points in the work of Emmanuel Levinas in a partially non-Levinasian language. They proceed in three stages, sketched here only briefly with a few quick strokes, but which refer to Levinas's descriptions and fine analyses, especially those found in *Totality and the Infinite* and *Otherwise than Being or Beyond Essence*. First, I will ask how three things come to be realized: the ipseity of the me, the alterity of the Other, and a certain form of society on the level of life which *Totality and the Infinite* calls *economy*. In a *second* step, I pose the same question on the level (if we can still speak here of a "level") at which the other person appears as really other and as human (that is, as a face which looks at me and speaks to me). What is the meaning of the I, the Other and of sociality, when we start with the irreducible alterity of one who is "higher" than a being similar to me? The *third* level where I, the Other, and society are concretized, is the world of administration and politics which opens up with the analysis of a "third": it is the order of general justice. Finally, I conclude with some suggestions about what could perhaps be called the "people of God," or the "communion of saints and sinners."[1]

Economy

A reflection on the meaning and structure of the relations separating and linking the Other and me must involve a provisional abstraction of these relations, focusing on an analysis of the relation which distinguishes and unites the I and its world. Although it is uncertain whether an adequate distinction between my world and the Other is possible, since my relation to the Other involves the relationships me-world and Other-world (and doubtless also a certain form of "us" in a common world), we can study these simplest relations only one after the other. In this sense,

121

the Husserlian reduction of transcendental consciousness to the sphere of ownness (*Eigenheitssphäre*)[2] excluding all other consciousness must be considered inevitable and provisionally sensible.

The ipseity of the I, which includes its free independence, is rooted in the earth, delighting in the elements that it needs to subsist and be free. It appropriates *all* other (including things and animals with or without spirit), and transforms the world in the name of the multiple needs which compose the *ego* as a natural or—in the Aristotelian sense of the word (cf. TeI, 81–149; TaI, 109–74)—"physical" being. Everything that exists appears as an element of the self-constitution of an ego dominating the world, in such a way that the Other can emerge only as a beautiful and intelligent animal, an animated tool, a slave or a cherished object.

I anticipate here in saying that the egoism of the economical I is not in contradiction with the exigency which comes to light in the ethical stage. Although this egoism must be subordinate to the imperative contained in the face which looks at me, and is thus limited in its ambition, it is also a necessary (although insufficient) condition of this imperative. Here we see a clear parallel with the ethics of Kant, for whom needs and natural desires and all egoism of happiness belong to the natural necessity (*Naturnotwendigkeit*) of being human, which—as such—has nothing to do with evil. The moral law or practical reason, however, is revealed as "the limiting condition" (*die einschränkende Bedingung*) that restricts the reach of the free play and satisfaction of this egoism. The hedonism and utilitarianism of the "economy" is not an evil, but rather the constitution of a provisional world which waits for and "desires" a more properly human meaning.

The relation between the hedonistic ipseity and all forms of alterity is, at this first level, a relation of utilitarian appropriation or of purely aesthetic contemplation. It is thus a relation of integration dominated by the freedom of a central subject. To describe the ipseity of this subject, it is necessary to appeal to a characteristic of its Other, because this Other has the function of a dialectical moment included in the essence of the central subject itself.

Hobbes and others showed that the utilitarianism of the hedonistic I presupposes, as context and indispensable condition, a social order formed of institutions guaranteeing the subsistence and self-development of those who maintain their egoism while restricting it through contractual limits. The reason that they consent to these limits is not ethically motivated, but lies in utilitarian prudence, or the conviction that infinite satisfaction is impossible. We could develop this thesis by showing that the world of utility is necessarily constituted as a society of needs, work, and technological sciences. Despite the much less violent character of a purely aesthetic or contemplative egocentrism, it still seems possible to discover in it structures analogous to those of masterful appropriation.[3]

Ipseity, alterity, and sociality therefore appeal to one another on the level of economic egoism. At the same time, the distinction between them is very relative: to think one of the terms, it is necessary to think not only the others, but also the specific way in which they (as constitutive elements or necessary conditions, as complements or dialectical opposites) include one another. We cannot help thinking the unity and the fundamental union of the three terms at play here. We should therefore attempt to interpret the constellation that they form as the unfolding of an ensemble which gathers the internal differences in the unity of one whole.

When we characterize this constellation as "economic," or as "the reign of the hedonistic ego," or as "the Same," we have already unified the trinity I-Other-society in reducing these moments to the identity of an *ego* which acts as their center and foundation.

Intersubjectivity

In proceeding to the "epiphany of the other" in another's face and speech, I will here not repeat the analyses of *the-one-for-the-Other* that Emmanuel Levinas has given us. I would, however, like to insist on the *dissymmetry* of this relation, which has given rise to many objections while being the key and the sine qua non of the work we are examining here.

The first truth that strikes me when I find myself before another human is that he reveals himself as an Other who is not identical, not similar, to me. What I see when I look at a face (that is, at an other who looks at me) is never presented and can never be presented to me as an appearance or phenomenon of myself. The phenomenon of another's anger—for example, his enraged eye or his raised fist—"tell" me immediately what I could never have observed in the same way in myself. As soon as I look at my own fist raised with a same fear, surprise, or indignation, I find myself ridiculous; my anger will immediately give way to another intention, which could be theoretical, humorous, or shameful. All the arguments that have been used to try to resolve the enigmas of intersubjectivity by relying on an analogy between my body as visible and the visible body of the Other sin against the first rule of phenomenology. However, it is clear that we have available knowledge of the similarity—or even the essential identity—of all human beings, and Levinas does not deny this evidence, since he uses it constantly: he associates, for example, the Other and "the third," and he notes that the "other person" (*l'autre homme*) is a *person* (*un homme*), though radically other and different from the person that I am. But although this identity is *contained* in the face of the Other, it does not abolish or reduce the radical alterity which transcends it. The experience that I have of the Other who looks at me or speaks to me is not a modification of the experience that I have of myself. I cannot look at my regard, not even at my eyes. I can observe a dead reflection of my face in the mirror or on a photo, but this image of my face is not the face to which another directs her gaze: it is precisely the moment of the "gaze" which is extinguished in the mirror, and which makes for the humanity of the human face. The fact of *addressing oneself to* me in looking at me characterizes the humanity of this being in front of me that I call "person." It is true that I feel within myself—"from inside," so to speak—that I too, *address myself to* something, to the world, or to someone, but the similarity between the two ways of addressing oneself can only come to light on the basis of a subsequent comparison. This presupposes a kind of knowledge that identifies an element of my visual experience of the Other (I see that the Other addresses herself to . . .) with an element of *kinesthetic* and *nonvisual* experience, through which I am conscious of my own active centrality. It presupposes, moreover, that my experience of myself in looking or speaking to someone else can be put on the same level (the level of the Same) as the experience[4] of the interpellation by which another interrupts the course of my auto-identification.

Yet, if we start from language, should we not say that the way in which I hear myself speak (as addressing myself to other humans through linguistic means) is not very different from the way in which I hear another speak to me or direct himself in words to other persons? The experience of communicative words shows clearly that visibility, with all of its particular possibilities, is not essential to determine the peculiarity and the structure of the intersubjective relation. Hearing seems to put my word and the word of the Other on a unique level, and to overcome our radical difference. However, this impression is also misleading, as we can see by the fact that many phrases (truths, exclamations, promises, etc.) not only have a different "tone," but also a different meaning, according to whether they are said by someone other or by me. The meaning of a "said" is not entirely separable from the "Saying" that proffers it. If an Other returns the confidence that I shared with him, it touches me in a different way than were I to repeat my own confidence to myself. This also perhaps explains that the words I say about myself affect me a lot more when I utter them in addressing myself to an interlocutor than when I say them to myself in the solitude of my own reflection. The saying by which someone addresses herself to me is animated by a force and an authority which, independent of all content, cannot leave me indifferent; they make an impression on me. My experience of another's saying (you speak to me) is different from that of my own saying.

To look at another who looks at me (and not observe the color of her eyes) or to listen to her saying (and not study the truth of the propositions which she holds), is to implicate myself and be constrained to take a stand in relation to the one who reveals herself in face and word. I can flee, or act as though I neither heard nor saw anything. I can also silence the voice that speaks to me and extinguish the look which is directed to me, for example, by adopting the look of an anatomist or the hearing of a specialist of linguistics or logic. In this case, I do not allow the Other to reveal herself such as she is, as Other. To the face, which is invitation, call, and interpellation, I oppose the brutality of an attitude that wants to hear and see only what fits into the solitary project of my egoism. The opening the Other needs to reveal what she is as Other is a reception which, by hearing and looking, welcomes her entry into the world occupied until then by my universal domination. From now on, this world is oriented differently: the admirable "high-ness" of the Other demands that I obey the authority of the exigency that speaks to me in her. If I neither kill her nor flee her, then I *respond* to her face, in correspondence to what she signifies to me as coming from elsewhere. The *correspondence* between my look and hers, between my hearing and her word, and also between my word and her hearing, is built from an *asymmetrical* relationship without which the authentic meaning of the Other's otherness and an ego's non-narcissistic orientation cannot be secured. By recognizing this situation, by obedience to the demands that the Other imposes on me, I am revealed to myself as *the-one-for-the-Other* responsible for what the Other suffers and does, and as a body in my own right, vulnerable and suffering for her.

It is clear that *ipseity* and *alterity* have a completely different significance in this new structure than they had in the framework of "economy." The question even arises whether the relation between the Other and me can still be thought through categories as general as those of the formal trinity ipse-Other-society. By submitting the Other's alterity and the separation between us involved in it to a categorical and universal logic, we exorcise and level the anarchy of the one-for-the-Other, and reduce its marginal existence to the law of order. On the other hand, we cannot deny that my said ("I am responsible for the Other") also holds, and in the same way, for the Other. The altruistic remark that the Other, not I, should be aware of the Other's responsibility for me cannot suffice *in philosophy*. For, the truth that the Other's responsibility for me "is his business" implies—and I cannot ignore it—that he also must know and practice it *for the same reason* as me.

As long as we remain involved in philosophical reflection—that is, as long as we do not stop the necessarily generalizing thought by an arbitrary decision or by the passage to a truer and closer dimension of the task of living humanly (a passage of which philosophy itself could perhaps demonstrate the necessity)—we cannot escape the *universalization of the asymmetrical relation* separating and inseparably tying together all me's and all Others. Thus *asymmetry* shows itself to be a universal relation and universally *reciprocal.* This reciprocity excludes neither alterity nor asymmetry; it does not necessarily make for a simple symmetry.

As Levinas showed in *Otherwise than Being,* it is inevitable that we think the anarchy of responsibility through the conceptuality of general structures (AE, 195–218; OB, 153–71). In trying to say the nonuniversal character of my unique responsibility, I fail because I change it necessarily into something universal. I then undo my said by denying its universality and try to say it again in another way, but again I fail because I miss the Saying itself. In engaging in the alternance of Saying, unsaying, and Saying again I become aware of the force of the universal logos that allows for no exceptions, without however being able to extinguish the desire to say and the necessity of saying the nondialectical and an-archic alterity and the unicity which are no instances of any genus. Must we get out of philosophy, or even out of all thought to affirm (but how?) this exceptional unicity and alterity? But can we ever stop thinking, once we have tasted the power of its lucidity? Even were we capable of doing so, would not *life and practice themselves* be confronted by a problem analogous to that of thought? In fact, life also must resolve the question of how such and such a person (me or another) can, in and by the unique time of her life, unite the responsibility for some unique *Others* and her responsibility for justice toward all humankind.

Before reflecting on this question, I will pose another question, which certain readers of Levinas have formulated by way of objection to a thought they judge too moralistic, and too little "ethical" in the Hegelian sense of this word. Is the relation between the Other and me not too immediate, too exceptional and too asymmetrical to allow development of this relation in society? Is the "society" between the Other and me not too exclusively personal to allow the apparition of collective and social structures in the sociological sense of the term? Certain expressions which often recur in Levinas's writings seem to suggest that immediate and exceptional relations between a small number of unique and chosen people form the supreme perspective that condemns all philosophy of society and history to lesser interest. Even if we agree with the thesis that the meaning of human life is ultimately decided in the "dimension" of the immediate responsibility of the "unique son," we cannot help thinking of the question of the *relation* between the unicity of exceptional responsibility, and the order of universal justice which cannot not be universal and political.

Sociality

The way in which Levinas moves from anarchical responsibility to the universal order of justice (with all its implications for general rights, sciences, administration, logical and dialectical thought) can be summarized in several ways. In all these ways, however, the key to this passage can be found in the apparition of a "third" who is neither the face of the Other as it was described above, nor directly an *alter ego*, but another Other who is *beside* or *behind* this one here and now. At least once Levinas wrote also that this third shines in the face of the Other.[5] The third is therefore as much hidden as presented by the one whose face concerns me directly and from the first. The multitude of others—including strangers and the wretched—is close to me in a second proximity.

The immediacy of the one-for-the-Other in the sense of a pure *amor benevolentiae* would turn bad were it to enclose me in the intimacy of those to whom I can and want to dedicate myself through direct contact: the members of my family, my friends and colleagues, some poor people whose names I know. Since *all* Others, independent of whether I have met them or not, have a face, *everyone looks at me and concerns me* for the same reason. *The unicity of the face is universal.* The third is one who, *with* and already *in* the primary Other, concerns me *like* the Other. The fact that I cannot get to know everyone and that most other people stay nameless for me cannot degrade them into a secondary species of human beings. "The third" seems therefore to be the name for the Other inasmuch as the Other is multiple and anonymous, but always having a face and speech. It represents the multitude of those who, *like this Other before me,* appeal to my devotion. All concern and obligate me, for exactly the same reasons as does this Other whose face and words reach me here and now.

Should we not then say that the third *is* the Other inasmuch as the multiplicity of its unicity imposes limits on my dedication to this Other here who obligates me now? Doesn't the order of justice, which begins with the *next to* and the *also,* oblige us to treat the Other as a *case* of the *universal unicity* which characterizes all other people? Should I not— even toward this Other here and now—combine my substitution of him as brother with an impartial and anonymous treatment under which he is only one of my fellow people with equal rights? Should we then put all people on the same level, share and compare, practice distributive justice and treat the members of the human community as statistical cases?

I am myself an Other for the Other: an Other whom both the Other and myself should look after. I therefore impose demands on myself which I can neither deny nor spurn, just as I do for the third and for all the Others. This consideration of myself, seeing myself as equal to all Others, presupposes a specific experience that differs profoundly from the egoistic experience belonging to the order of economy. I only know myself as subject of equal and universal rights if I have discovered my existence as a being-there which is *given to me to take care of.* "The care of my soul," as Plato would say, or the *work* of human being upon which Aristotle founded ethics, is perceived only if I distance myself from narcissistic self-realization. Then I am also *for me, but* in a radically *other* sense than that of economic delight. I must prepare myself for a *disinterested* love for myself. Despite all the hidden snares along this path, it is possible and necessary to love oneself as a being who needs justice and mercy.

The society that arises from the universality of the third is a community of rights and interests where the relations of love and intimacy are submitted to an impartial justice. This justice imposes limits on the demands and desires of those who would like to dedicate themselves unreservedly to a restricted number of others. The judge or the politician must abide by what the law prescribes, even in the case of his parents or children.[6]

The social world of right and interest is organized in different ways that we can symbolize by the word *state.* It is clear, however, that the national modern state, as a particular arrangement of the order demanded by justice, has still not resolved the problem of universality included in the commandment that all human faces proclaim. We do not yet know how a really universal justice could be concretized. Weak attempts to unify the social world, to practice a dialogue between nations, and to prepare a cultural ecumenism point to the messianic ideal of world peace, but the gap between the obligations of responsibility and the realizations of justice remains huge. Prophets and kings cannot yet come to agreement. Fundamental misunderstandings are inevitable, for example, when those who fight for the abolition of nuclear arms forget that the specialists of anonymous justice cannot leave their people without protection unless they at the same time abdicate their role as politicians. Universal justice, inaugurated by the apparition of the third, condemns the particularism of states. In the name of "substitution," universal justice demands the preparation of a unique fraternal world. On the basis of such a fraternity, it would be possible to dedicate oneself to any Other who presents herself here and now. But if we have to wait for the realization of a brotherly and sisterly world to practice the responsibility included in the "one-for-the-Other," the latter is an empty slogan. Responsibility tolerates no delays, and it is responsibility which provides the perspective to institute a more just world, as a condition of it being taken seriously. However, a complete responsibility will be impossible as long as the reigning injustice still corrupts and destroys our efforts to respond to the demands of the stranger who comes to our door and along our roads. The other person, as Other and as third, accuses me, because I do not know how to respond to her entirely as I should.

People of God

Can we say that where true acts of substitution happen we see membership in what has been named "people of God"? The effective realization of prophetic demands would constitute the communion of saints who accept living and dying for the other's salvation. If we follow this path, we will come to see God and his people only where the epiphany of the Other gives rise to adequate responses provided by those who incarnate the Messiah himself. In the face of the messianic and eschatological world of the prophets, politics trying to concretize justice without aiming at personal substitution would represent a Greek or pagan world deprived of true proximity; it would be obsessed by the demand for universality, but blind with respect to the unicity of the Other.

The obstacle that we encounter in following this route is that in philosophy we cannot help thinking the union of the two layers, levels, or sides that our analysis has just distinguished. We cannot avoid thinking the unity of the Other and the third, of proximity and justice, of prophetic anarchy and the orders of the king. And not only in philosophy! In trying to confine all dialectic and all synthesis to the field of thematizing reflection, while pointing to praxis for the execution of the demands of substitution, we notice that in practice too a union—or an attempt at union—proves inevitable. The unicity of life, which is my task and my destiny, constrains me and obliges me to unite in myself—in the acts and desires of my responsibility of the *one*-for-the-Other—what belongs to the anarchy of prophetic substitution with everything that characterizes me as a member of the social and political world in search for as universal a justice as possible.

Inasmuch as the "people of God" can be called a "church," it would seem that this "church" could only be the attempted union of two dimensions. In gathering a people under the two symbols of King and Prophet it interprets human history as the enterprise—always attempted, always failing and always begun again—of realizing a genuine unity of universal justice and immediate proximity. An authentic church embraces and tries to reconcile the political history of the world and the unapparent events of charity. Systematic religion (with its laws and orders, its dogmatic declarations and hierarchical institutions) must always let itself be put into question by the eruption of prophetic charismata. The history of the people of God is the history of the tension between love and justice.

8

Technology and Nature

> It is said that we must defend humankind against the technology of our century since man has lost his identity through technology by becoming a small cog in an immense machinery of turning things and beings. From now on, to exist is equivalent to the exploitation of nature; but in the turmoil of this enterprise which devours itself, no fixed point can be maintained. The solitary walker strolling through the fields, certain of his autarchy, is in fact an ignorant client of the calculations, statistics and planning of a tourist housing industry.

These are the opening lines of a sharp attack on Heidegger's thought under the title "Heidegger, Gagarin and Us" written by Emmanuel Levinas and published in his book *Difficult Freedom* (DL, 299–303). Although Levinas does not claim that these lines exactly match Heidegger's interpretation of modern technology (in fact, they summarize a widespread opinion for which no deep thought is needed), the remainder of his article concentrates on Heidegger as the main representative of the antitechnological tendency in philosophy. Before hearing Levinas's own view on technology, then, it might be helpful to remind ourselves of Heidegger's analysis, as presented in the essay "The Question Concerning Technology."[1]

Heidegger on Technology

Starting from the generally accepted view that technique and technology are forms of instrumentality, Heidegger shows, first, how "the Greeks" practiced and interpreted what they called *poiesis*. In order to guard against the widespread misinterpretation of this word within the framework of the "doctrine of the four causes," he shows how *hyle* (material), *eidos* (aspect or figure), and *telos* (the binding completion) are gathered either by "nature" (*physis*) itself, or by a skilled person, in order to bring forth a *poiema* or "pro-duct" into the presence of its appearance. Gathered by the "producer," material, form, and telos share the responsibility for the presencing of a marvel that shines forth. Poiesis is being responsible for a certain mode of coming to the fore, coming to presence and manifestation. In it, nature and humans allow a being to display the splendor of its possibilities. In an epoch in which skillful production had not yet separated itself from art, human production was still akin to the *phainesthai* (the shining forth) of natural phenomena. To be a good "technician" was still to be capable of letting beings unfold their own completion.

Through this interpretation of poiesis as a premodern mode of production, Heidegger has shown that *techne* and production cannot be confined to a handling of means for the realization of ends. Poiesis is a way of bringing to light what was hidden, of unconcealing or unhiding what was concealed, of being responsible for the presencing of a present, of *aletheuein* in the sense of letting or having a phenomenon emerge and reveal itself from out of the secrecy of concealment.

Modern technology can certainly be studied as a complex system of means and ends in which the experimentation of modern science plays a crucial role, but its *essence* is nothing technical or instrumental; again, it is a specific way of unconcealment or disclosure, bringing to presence from out of the dark of hiddenness. The mode of modern production is, however, different from Greek poiesis: it challenges nature to supply energy, which then is stockpiled and used for a great variety of chosen purposes. Nature is treated as a reserve supply of energies to be exploited according to human needs. The earth becomes a collection of mines and fields for mechanized food and energy industries; the rivers are reduced to sources of electrical energy. By treating nature as a stock of materials and energies that can be extracted, stored, rearranged, distributed, and purchased, modern technology reveals its essence as a mode of presencing which is very different from the "phainaesthetic"[2] production of the Greeks. Technological unconcealment must be characterized as a *Herausforderung* (a commanding exploitation) and a *Stellen* (a way of disposing and settling on the basis of choice and command). In the word "*Gestell*" Heidegger tries to gather the whole constellation of this mode of bringing forth through demand, exploitation, and stockpiling with a view to energy supply. It is a mode of unconcealing which cannot be abolished by human intentions or measures. Nor has it been caused by human action alone. On the contrary, we are caught and captured in this mode of presencing. The *essence* of technology, that which generates and rules the technological constellation and our activities in it, is nothing technological; it holds sway over us and over the entire technological enterprise in which we function as ordered, demanded, posited, and stockpiled parts. It is the dispensation of destiny that we are settled in this mode of existence, by which nature and world have been changed into a supply of deliverable energies. The emergence of modern science was ordained by this dispensation two centuries before the inventions of modern technology. Both science and technology are ruled by the same essence. Humanity and the world are dominated and motivated by the settling of the *Gestell.*

The greatest danger of the technological mode of production lies in the fact that it distorts or utterly obscures our relationship to that which hides and governs *within* that mode: the nontechnological "essence" of technology. However, since this essence itself, although hidden, is present in it, the greatest danger is, at the same time, the possibility of overcoming it. The possibility of a total tyranny of positing demand and exploitation cannot entirely be disregarded: it is possible that most or all human individuals and societies will be reduced to functional elements in a worldwide setting of technology, and that nature will lose all possibility of showing its splendor. Whatever the case, if we are to be saved from our captivity to technology, such a liberation cannot be the work of human will and courage. It, too, must be given to us by destiny.

Salvation would involve finding a free distance from the technological setting, but this distance can only be found in the free space which the essencing of truth may grant us. It may give us such a space if *we* experience the danger as danger and the truth of the essence in its distorted presencing. If we are open to its dispensation, and think the constellation of technology as an (albeit twisted and obscured) unconcealment of the secret of Being (*das Geheimnis*), we can experience coming to presence and monstration (*aletheuein* or presencing) as the essence that makes us free.

Levinas on Technology

After reading Heidegger's profound analysis of the danger with which technology threatens us, it is somewhat sobering to read Levinas's response to the charges brought against technology as summarized at the outset of his essay "Heidegger, Gagarin and Us" and quoted at the beginning of this paper: "There is some truth in this declamation. Technique is dangerous. Not only does it threaten the identity of persons: it may lead to the explosion of the planet." The surprising brevity of this seeming concurrence with Heidegger might be explained by the polemical character of the essay from which it is taken, but it also shows that Levinas does not consider technology the most urgent issue for humanity today. As far as I know, none of his numerous texts contain an elaborated analysis of technology and its dangers. The statement quoted above can be read as a succinct résumé of his views on the matter, however, as the following passage from his article "Secularization and Hunger" indicate:

> Nobody is so foolish as to deny the contradictions and miscalculations of technology, its murderous dangers, the new enslavements and mythologies with which it threatens us, and the pollution that follows from it, which poisons—in the proper sense of the term—even the air we breathe.
> (SF, 106)

The dangers enumerated in this passage are the following: (1) contradictions and miscalculations; (2) a new form of slavery that could result from the technological industry; (3) the murderous character of modern technology; (4) its creation of new myths; and (5) pollution and poisoning. Although Levinas has given neither a full analysis of these dangers nor a complete evaluation of their gravity, and though he has not listed all the advantageous aspects of technology, his comments point clearly in the direction of a rather positive appreciation. Let us look at the five arguments summarized in these comments.

From the quoted text it is not clear (1) whether Levinas thinks the contradictions introduced by modern techniques are only provisional, that is, symptoms of a still experimental stage, or rather indications of a dead-end which cannot be overcome by more science and further technological developments. Nobody can answer this question with certainty. If there are other compelling reasons for continuing the technological adventure (see below), we should perhaps set ourselves on a path that eliminates the negative features as much as possible.

Although Levinas does not explicitly answer the various objections which could be made on the basis of (2) the enslavements and (3) the deaths caused by the technological industry, we may assume that he counts them among the factual contradictions of an enterprise that was meant to liberate people from an all-too-needy, enslaved, vulnerable, and risky existence. In the same vein, (5) pollution could be seen as a negative effect of an intermediary stage of development. The heroes of modern technology are sometimes portrayed as half-gods of (4) a new mythology, but the character of twentieth-century myths seems hardly comparable to that of the ancient ones. Who, today, can really believe in the supernatural and superhuman powers of idols such as these?

> The moon is no more than a rock and no longer can be the object of a
> cult. But the astronaut is a half-god. This may be true, but then at least fifty
> percent has been secularized! And it is still to be seen whether the other
> half of that false divinity is sacred in the same sense as the idols of the age
> before technological development, and whether those who applaud the
> astronaut's courage are still lucid (SF, 107 n. 4).

On the other hand, mythologizing, even in our secularized epoch, does
remain a possible temptation, but this temptation is not specific to technique or technology. On the contrary, as we will see, this danger is much
greater within the context of an antitechnological return to nature for
which nature has become an object of awe and veneration.

Against all-too-massive attacks on technology Levinas stresses the
following points:

1. We lack a standard by which we can establish a balance of its positive
   and its negative aspects.
2. The condemnation of technology has become comfortable rhetoric
   which uses all the inventions and refinements of communication
   technology; without this parasitism such a rhetoric would certainly
   be less comfortable.

Whereas the first point postpones a final evaluation, the second—if taken
in isolation—could be heard as an *ad hominem* argument, and therefore as
rather rhetorical. We could answer it, for instance, by stating that indeed
we are not capable of escaping from the realm and essence of technology,
although we are very much aware of its unnatural and inhuman character
and suffer greatly from it. We are not free—it is not given to us—to
refuse a destiny that is ours here and now, yet neither the advantages
of modern techniques nor the inevitability of their use are sufficient to
make the balance positive. Besides, we might not be willing to accept
the idea that the ultimate evaluation of technology would depend on a
balance, since the *essence* of technology—Being as granting a particular
way of presencing—does not let itself be submitted to calculation. Is not
the very idea of a value-judgment as based on calculation a symptom
of the technological way of being from which we should be delivered?
In fact, Levinas does not advance his second point in isolation from a
third one, which stresses human responsibility: the parasitic comfort of a
certain rhetoric is harmless unless it betrays ethical indifference. In the
rest of this paper I will concentrate on this third reason, and on a fourth
one which the essay "Secularization and Hunger" presents as a sort of
apology for technology. Let me begin by stating these reasons:

3. Modern science and technology are indispensable conditions for the nourishment of millions of people in the third and fourth world and for the "development" of poorly developed countries. Those who condemn technology without giving an answer to the question of how we shall abolish worldwide poverty reject or ignore their primordial responsibility.

4. As the modern form of secularization, technology has destroyed:

> the pagan gods and their false and cruel transcendence. Therewith, certain gods—rather than God—are dead, certain mysterious powers of the elements in the depths of the World or the Soul now provoke laughter notwithstanding their splendor or secrets—which, for a mystery or a god, is equivalent to death: unchangeable gods of pride and domination, gods of astrologic conjunctions and fate, gods of soil and blood, and the trajectory of the celestial bodies; local gods and gods of the place and landscape of unshakable domains, all those gods "below on the earth or in the waters under the earth," in the still waters of subconsciousness—the worst ones!—reflecting or repeating, in anguish and terror, the visible gods of the heavens. . . . Technology takes their divinity away and, by giving us power over the world, teaches us that these gods belong to the world, that they are things and that things are, after all, no big deal, that there is trickery in their resistance and their objectivity and rubbish in their splendor, and that we must rather laugh in their faces than cry and implore. Through the secularization it achieves, technology participates in the progress of the human spirit, or rather it justifies or defines the very idea of progress and is indispensable for the spirit, even if it is not its final goal. (SF, 107)

As we will see, the ethical argument (3) and Levinas's praise for the secularizing function of technology (4) are intimately related and together explain his fierce attack on Heidegger's perspective in "Heidegger, Gagarin and Us." However, in order to understand the position from which Levinas looks at technology, it is necessary to start from issues more central to his thought, and in particular from the place and meaning which he gives to nature.

Ethical Meta-physics

The key to Levinas's thought is the "concept" of transcendence; that is, the relation of the-one-for-the-Other, as experienced by every human being in everyday life and analyzed again and again in Levinas's many publications. This relation can be characterized by the following properties.

1. *Asymmetry*: the superiority of the human Other, whose face or speech surprises me, coming from "on high," is due not to the Other's talents, skills, deeds, or worth but solely to the existence of the other *as* human Other.

2. Human otherness differs absolutely from the (quasi-)otherness of any nonhuman being, because the former cannot be assimilated or integrated as a moment, part, or function of my consciousness, my knowledge, my plan, or my self-realization.

3. The Other's "height" or "highness" expresses itself through the impossibility of being reduced to a content of my consciousness or to an integral part of my world. But simultaneously and as such it obliges me morally through an originary (or "pre-originary," an-archical) claim which precedes all the possible choices, contracts, or conventions in which the other and I have freely engaged ourselves.

4. The ethical demand revealed to me in the face (or the speech or, in general, the self-presentation) of the Other cannot be separated from the Other's existence. Fact and value cannot be separated here; the answer to the question "What do I encounter when I meet with another human being?" cannot be given without using a normative, or, more precisely, an imperative language. What *is* (what, here and now, faces me, regards me, or speaks to me) *is* a *command*; that which (or the Other who) is there obliges me. Any Other's existence reveals to me that I am responsible for this Other; I am never able to escape from this responsibility, which neither I, nor this Other, nor any other human being has ever chosen.

Since I am essentially and inescapably responsible for any other human person, I must be free. What I ought to do, I can do (*du kannst, denn du sollst*), as Kant already stated. At the same time my free responsibility implies a noncoincidence, an unbridgeable distance or "separation" from the Other for whom I am responsible and whose existence (*not* "whose choice") endows my life with meaning. How is this free responsibility at a distance, this being separated in a relation of transcendence, possible?

At this point nature can be introduced in the form of the natural elements. Earth, water, air, and fire, the whole realm of the senses, appears as the context and the material of the human subject, insofar as it is an "animal," that is, a spontaneously living being using its hands, legs, and head in order to establish itself as something independent, a substance. The vitality of its *conatus essendi* realizes itself in a process of active, corporeal, affective, and hedonistic self-identification. The dynamic constitution of the human identity precedes the levels of consciousness and representation. "To live on . . ." or "to live from" water, fruits, and meat, to breathe the air, to enjoy the light of the sun, etc., are ways of assimilating the elements, modes of centering the world and establishing oneself in it as ego. Starting from this commerce with the elemental, ego establishes itself in a dwelling-place from which it goes out into the world in order to come back with prey. The spontaneous vitality of this living "from" (or "on") the elements is close to a sort of osmosis, although it is also the possibility of a first selfhood: it is the narcissistic selfhood of an adult baby for whom the only meaning of life lies in enjoyment.

The level of an elementary commerce with the world precedes handling implements or tools (neither the elemental nor dwelling is a "ready-at-hand" or *Zuhandenes*), but equipment emerges when human vitality develops into appropriation through hunting and labor. Objectification of the world, however, is not possible as long as ego has not yet acquired the distance that is necessary for the representation of objects in front of a subject. Being in the mode of *Vorhandenes* or objectivity presupposes a distance from one's own narcissism. How can such a distance emerge from narcissism itself? It must be given to this hedonistic subject, but how? Only another can urge me to such a distance by revealing the discrepancy between my spontaneous striving for solitary enjoyment of myself in the world, and the responsibility that drives me out to take care of the Other. Objectification, representation, knowledge, science, and scientific technology presuppose not only needs, but also another's presence, and therewith transcendence with regard to my involvement in a world of impersonal powers, structures, and things.

The Gods of Nature

The elemental is the first apparition of nature in the progressive self-constitution of a free ego. It is there to be enjoyed, a sort of paradise for rational animals who have not yet been awakened to their ethical responsibility. It is the world of irresponsible but already independent children of nature. If this were the whole truth of existence, the elements would be the most real reality. If the reality of the ethical is not discovered in the Other's face, the elements monopolize the universe; they should then be venerated as the mysterious forces that decide about joy and pain, subsistence and decay, and the meaning of life and death. The dimension of the elemental is then the realm of mythical gods; the magic of obscure, supernatural forces would then rule human destiny.

Notwithstanding technological conquests and the various forms of emancipation and secularization that are said to constitute modernity, there is still, in our day, a nostalgia (or at least an intense sympathy) for those pretechnological times in which humanity was familiar with the elemental powers of nature (but also subjected to their whims). In "Heidegger, Gagarin and Us" Levinas draws the following portrait of such a nostalgia in terms that are clearly borrowed from Heidegger's later work:

> To rediscover the world is to rediscover a childhood mysteriously ensconced in the Place, to open oneself up to the light of vast landscapes, to the fascination of nature, to the majestic encampment of the mountains; to walk along a path that twists and curves through the fields, to feel the unity established by a bridge that joins the banks of a river and by the architecture of buildings, the presence of a tree, the twilight of the woods, the mystery of things, of a jug, of the farmer's worn out shoes, and the luminescence of a carafe of wine on a white tablecloth. The very Being of the real manifests itself from behind these privileged experiences which offer and confide themselves to human heeding. And to this grace, man, the guardian of Being, owes his existence and his truth. (DL, 300)

And here is Levinas's judgment about the mode of being and thinking expressed in this portrait: "Here we have the eternal seduction of paganism, beyond the infantilism of idolatry, which has been left behind long ago; *the filtering of the sacred through the world.* . . . The mystery of things is the source of all cruelty with regard to humans" (DL, 301). In "Secularization and Hunger" Levinas shows that this enthusiasm for a new mythology of nature goes back to the Greek roots of European civilization. He sketches how philosophy, starting from a cosmos filled with divinities, progressively freed the world from gods and myths, and he defends the thesis that this secularization is a necessary condition for ethical authenticity.

Through a phenomenological analysis of the mode of being which expresses itself in the religious veneration of the starry sky—that is, through an ontological interpretation of Greek mythology, Plato's *Timaeus,* and Aristotle's theory of the heavens—Levinas identifies the specific form of transcendence that ruled the space in which the Greeks lived. Looking up to an inaccessible firmament, their eyes detached themselves, as it were, from the body with its trivial needs. Awe and wonder, inspired by a secret cosmos, generated the contemplation of visible gods which ruled a firmly established earth at rest. Philosophy concentrated on the admirable hierarchy of a universe, and tried to discover its rational structures and necessities in the light of Being. The gods disappeared; the components of the cosmos became homogeneous and the human desire for knowledge freed itself from allegiance to any particular god or pantheon. This atheism prepared the way for philosophy and modern science; it enabled them to give a universal and ecumenical response to the hunger of human beings, regardless of place or membership in a particular nation or culture. Thus, intellectual contemplation and the practical needs of human life were united in a scientific and technological effort that was directed toward the liberation of humankind from its domination by nature. Prometheus and Messer Gaster (Rabelais's Master Stomach) joined hands and eyes. Messer Gaster became "the first master of arts" (SF, 105–6).

By robbing nature of her divine pretensions, science and technology made man its master for the service of humanity. To return to a sacred cosmos, even if this were possible, would betray the conquest of human autonomy. It would deny the clear and simple truth that another's hunger, the Other's mortality, is more "sacred" than any god or nature.

Gagarin's leaving the earth and its horizons was a symbol of our liberation from inhuman powers. It represented our freedom from being rooted in sacred places, soils, nations, or civilizations. The ultimate meaning of human existence—and therewith, transcendence, ethics, metaphysics, God—is not attached to any place, not even to the fourfold of divine and mortal existence enshrined by heaven and earth. God can be met in the desert, or in a town—with people—and not only in the solitude of woods or fields.

Of course, Heidegger is not naive. When, in the wake of Hölderlin, he reinterprets certain ancient schemas, he knows very well that we cannot convert ourselves to past beliefs. In trying to indicate the dimension of the holy in a transphenomenological way and perhaps to prepare the coming of one or more gods, he too pleads for a transcendence beyond nihilism and "onto-theo-logy" (as he calls his caricature of the philosophical search for God from Plato to Nietzsche). However, he neglects, forgets, or ignores the ethical "moment" of transcendence, with its demands that cannot wait until better times, and this might, indeed, be due to a resacralization of *physis* along the lines of certain Hellenic paradigms.

As long as the world is dominated by mythical powers, human freedom is not fully responsible and human endeavors are, at least partly, vain. Then Moira or the gods decide the outcome of human history; they ordain what will happen to the human way of relating to the world and Being. Neither the Other nor I is simply a part of nature, not even of the second nature which Hegel called "objective spirit." Neither bios, nor art (nor, for that matter, politics) form the ultimate horizon of life and spirit. Neither an aesthetic, nor an exclusively political vision is able to offer an ultimate meaning to human freedom, because the radical exteriority of the Other does not fit within their horizons. Only a relation that is ethically qualified gives an irreducible orientation. The exercise of ego's an-archical responsibility is the only possibility of converting the elements from a pantheistic or polytheistic enthusiasm to the innocence of data that can be presented to another. The spiritualization of matter is not its poetic transformation into sublime works of art; it is a most concrete, corporeal, and material presentation of food and drink, good air and shelter to needy people. In a worldwide market economy, true spirituality is born from the ethical inspiration of human bodies involved in technological processes that are demanded by the urgent needs of the destitute.

In Levinas's published works, nature is thematized from two angles, which together form a unique perspective. As the realm of the elements, nature is a moment of concrete freedom, but its meaning depends on its transformation into a gift by moral responses to the Other's needs. Ethics transforms nature (as well as art, politics, science, philosophy, and technology) into an essential moment of the Good, and therewith into an essential element of religion. According to Levinas, the encounter with God (who is neither "a god," nor "the God") completely coincides with one's relationship to a human Other. Donation is identical with prayer—or is even more originary and important. In any case, it is more important, older than, and very different from the contemplation of Being, the admiration of beauty, or the veneration of sacred powers and places.

Ethics and Aesthetics

It is only fair to recognize that Levinas's publications contain neither a complete philosophy of nature nor an exhaustive consideration of technology. We must even ask whether such a study would be possible within the parameters of his ethical metaphysics. Does his concentration on the hedonic and the moral aspects of human existence permit any relative independence of the properly natural and aesthetic aspects of nature, or are these so completely subordinate to the ethical, social, and anthropocentric aspects of human existence that nature on its own cannot "tell" or reveal anything to us? Would not such a view in the end coincide with a utilitarian and instrumentalistic interpretation of the material universe? Can it do justice to the admirably enigmatic *and* significant wonders of nature's own radiance?

Levinas has formulated a standard for the balance of the good and bad effects of technology, but is it the only one? Does it cover the entire "truth" of technique, matter, energy, nature? The ethical perspective does not necessarily include an aesthetics, but would nihilism have been overcome if humankind enjoyed a just world without hunger and pollution, but which was as ugly as the ugliest parts of contemporary towns? Is not beauty also revealing and significant? Is not the *kalon* essential to meaning and transcendence? If so, it cannot be wholly alien to the good of ethics and metaphysics.

Indeed, not only mystics like Francis of Assisi or John of the Cross, but many philosophers as well, and perhaps all great poets "read" nature as a "book" or hear it as a hymn in which they participate as writers or singers who enjoy the half-revealed, half-hidden meaning of that with which they are cooperating. Their collaboration is already art, although not everybody can show how impressive and "telling" nature is by enhancing it through architecture, music, or dance. Nature's faces and voices make their own suggestions. A technology that listened and responded to them would be aesthetic; it would not necessarily be less technical, but it would not hurt our sensibilities.

Perhaps a certain aesthetic does constitute a part of ethics. Hunger, the Other's suffering and mortality, is certainly so basic that by ignoring or denying it one is a murderer, but to be for Others cannot stop at the satisfaction of basic needs. Education, for instance, involves other concerns. And what if it is impossible to satisfy basic needs because of the situation (a famine or drought, for example) or because the Other is dying from an incurable disease? Peace and even joy are possible with hunger and poverty. Sometimes the latter are more tolerable than a lack of wit or beauty. Heidegger has scandalized many readers of his essay on "Building—Dwelling—Thinking" by stating that the real problem of dwelling in postwar Germany was not the lack of houses, but rather our inability to think the essence of the house and housing.[3] Did he, by this shocking statement, want to awaken us to the insight that the possession of a house does not solve the problem of how it is possible to build, to dwell, and to live in a meaningful or "true" (or "good" or "admirable") way? Even if the technological possibilities of our age are employed in the service of humankind, and not for the benefit of the wealthy and powerful alone, these possibilities have a character, and even a tendency of their own. They do not necessarily respond better to the "sacred needs" of human existence than to the suggestions of nature. Levinas must agree with Heidegger that the *realm* of technology, its ruling "essence," imposes a style of looking, handling, and functioning which threatens the meaningfulness of human existence. From an ethical perspective, too—in the name of responsibility and concern—we must try and hope to become free from any reduction of nature, poiesis, and knowledge to mere systematic functionality within a framework of exploitation.

Technology and Politics

A full thematization of technology in the spirit of Levinas's philosophy should stress its connections with the world of politics. Since the command of technological "means" coincides with the most efficient political power, and since the technological machinery has become closer to a self-governing system by losing the character of a set of tools, it would be naive to simply state that technology has realized human autonomy by freeing it from gods, and that it should be directed to the realization of universal justice.

Levinas's work contains a thorough reflection on the relationship between ethics and politics. This relationship is, in fact, one of the main topics of *Totality and the Infinite*. Starting from the insight that politics, as the incessant attempt to overcome war through compromise, ought to be inspired by morality, but is in fact so full of violence that it "suspends morality" (TeI, IX; TaI, 21), Levinas shows that ethics transcends the state and has a history (a "fecundity") of its own. The demands of ethical transcendence condemn the violence of history. As the history of works and political events, world history has its own mechanisms and concatenations. The micro-ethics of those who put their responsibility for others into practice points in the direction of a peace without violence, although such a peace is not yet possible. The prophetic action of responsible people might itself be caught or hindered by the warlike situation in which they participate, but they have recourse to an eschatological hope which grants them the courage to do justice here and now.[4]

We could apply the schema of this argument to the relationship between the ethical perspective (including the "natural" and the aesthetic one) and the realm of technical mechanisms and structures (including the captains who command them). The inherent violence of technology cannot be overcome by an exclusively technological practice. The micro-ethical practice of persons who are well disposed in regard to Others, nature, and art, notwithstanding the distorting networks in which these people function, can point the way toward better disposed constellations of justice, technological utility, and natural beauty.

This ethical argument must be complemented by an argument that starts from the other side. Just as the responsibility for this and that human individual demands a general order of justice as a condition for its concrete possibilities—and thus also demands political authorities, legal codes, and economic structures which neither exploit nor kill—so, too, ethics calls for the technical and technological conditions without which such a justice would be impossible. According to a sentence from Bergson's book *The Two Sources of Morality and Religion* quoted as the epigraph to "Secularization and Hunger," "mysticism calls for mechanics" (SF, 101). Notwithstanding the dangers of generalization, the Others must *also*, but subordinately, be treated as members of the state, of humanity as a whole, and as individual subjects of human needs. Liberty and equality, politics and technology do not entail fraternity, but neither do they necessarily exclude it. This does not mean that they can be understood as neutral, purely instrumental forces or structures. Left to themselves, they reduce and suppress the Other's uniqueness, and thus also the indispensable inspiration of a human justice. As somehow mediating, however, they belong to the transcendence of ethics.

9

Presentation

Logos and Texts

Discursive language thematizes and arranges the world of beings from the perspective of systematic coherence, in which principles, structures, and horizons play the leading part. Philosophical discourse is the most explicit example of such a systematic language. It gathers beings by showing how they fit into the order of a whole. As a search for foundations, philosophy has a fondness for *archai*, be they source or seed, end or completion, cause or matter. Philosophy is totalitarian and "archaic." As the gathering of reason, it is "logical" and systematic.[1]

As a concatenation of judgments, a *text* has what we could call a "syllogical" or "syllogistic" structure. Its composition tries to outline different wholes as integral parts of a complete totality called "the truth." The idea of such a totality is, however, contested by the fact that every text relies on a host of conditions and other texts whose legitimacy it cannot prove, but inevitably takes for granted. And yet, the idea(l) of the total truth cannot be suppressed altogether, even after we have discovered that truth does not have a direct and immediate rapport with the totality of beings, events, principles, and thoughts. From the perspective of philosophical research, the history of textual oeuvres and successions appears as an endless series of attempts to bring a complete and universal truth into the perspective of the reader.

The *synoptic* and *synchronical* character of a text is manifested in the fact that we can start our reading from many different points: not only from the text's beginning to its end, but equally from the end to the beginning or from the center to both ends, and so on. All the elements of a text are contemporaneous within one space, the space of their being present at once in the form of a book or paper. All reading demands time, but the order of priorities depends, to a great extent, on our choice. Such a choice is not completely arbitrary, since a text has its own tricks to impose a specific order and specific demands on the reader, but the very discovery of such demands presupposes a survey of the text as a limited whole that can and must be deciphered from all sides successively.

The independence of a text from its author seems to be its main distinction, if we compare it to the spoken word. After writing her paper the author leaves it to the reader, who may do with it whatever he wants. Everybody can appropriate it in his own way. Whether this appearance is completely true will be one of the questions to which I would like to return when we reflect upon the peculiarities of speaking and speech. For the moment we may leave the question at the stage where Plato answered it in the *Phaedrus* and his "Seventh Letter" by stating that the text cannot be assisted (helped, defended, developed further) by its author, whereas the spoken word can.[2]

Between being written and being read, a text is as dead as a fossil that, under certain conditions, can still come back to life. As written but not yet read, it is a score before performance. Its kerygmatic character is not noticed; the meaning of its themes and structures has vanished, but it can be brought back to life by a new understanding. A thinking different from that of the author's is needed to transform the original inscriptions into a way of understanding the order of reality. Another voice is needed to change the never-spoken words into an audible message. Left to itself, a text does not mean anything. *Someone* is needed—one who reads aloud or silently, a commentator or apologist (and the author himself may fulfill this second function)—to present the text in another context than the one in which it was written. A new initiative presenting or representing the text is an indispensable condition for the possibility of understanding, explaining, or discussing it and in this sense for "reading" it.

Logos and Evasion

Is it the overwhelming multiplicity of texts and textual procedures in which we find ourselves involved—and almost buried—that has created (or at least has intensified) our feeling that the space of systematic logos is too narrow to be true? From the beginning of European civilization, the "archaic" order of synchronizing and syllogistic reason has been seen as an eminent, but problematic, enterprise. Platonism itself, for instance, developed a double movement of thought: beyond the phenomenal order which was contemplated in the light of its own ideal truth, another orientation, born of desire, pointed toward something nonphenomenal and nonideal to which the ideal and phenomenal order of beings owed its possibility of becoming true, a source of light for the work of logos.

The universe of logical and syllogistic thematization was felt to be too narrow. The whole idea of *embracing* truth has indeed been problematic from the beginning. Neo-platonism and its Christian transformations might be understood as systematic attempts to evade the prison into which philosophy, not only as hedonism or materialism, but even more so as idealism and faith in logos, threatened to force the human search for . . . for what? A desire for transcendence has manifested itself[3] in the Greek, medieval, modern, and contemporary discussions about the limits of philosophical thought and the possibility of a more radical dimension which would not be irrational. Why and how can the logic of a noncaricatured kerygmatic thinking be felt as a narrowing of "what there really is" (to be lived, enjoyed, celebrated, etc.)? Which experiences, adventures of the mind, or events of history do not permit the gathering of logos to enclose them within its horizons?

The main direction in which Western philosophy has sought a possibility for evasion and transcendence was the "up there" (*ekeise*), the "height" or the "*epekeina*" of some One that would not fit into the possibilities of logos, not even as its summit or first and last being, principle, idea, or ground. A careful reading of Plotinus, Augustine, pseudo-Dionysius, Bonaventure, and Kant—to name only a few pillars of Western spirituality—shows that they have never seen the transcendent as the highest of all beings. If the name "ontotheology" is at all applicable to their thoughts, it should not be forgotten nor left unsaid that they dedicated the utmost energy of thinking to showing that the "*theion*" could not be grasped by the patterns of ontology, and that there was infinitely more difference between God and phenomenal being than between a highest being and the rest, just as there was an infinite abyss between God and reason, whereas the highest form of logos, nous, or reason differed only in degree from other forms. However, it is true that the Western attempt to transcend the system of logical discourse by taking the way of ascending toward the divine is a Greek heritage, and it is also true that Christian theology had a lot of trouble trying to prevent its combination of biblical revelation and Greek (onto)logic from degenerating into an absolutization of philosophy. In the best examples of Christian thought, however, like that of Anselm or Bonaventure, philosophy takes a turn or makes a bow by which it changes its kerygmatic language into adoration or gratitude.

Levinas's novelty is that without denying the necessity of attributing "transcendence" to God, he shows: (1) that the circle of philosophical logic is opened up by the fact that all discourses are necessarily addressed to another human, and (2) that the transcendence of God destroys itself if it is separated from the transcendence of the other human. Moreover, the latter transcendence implies a sort of radical descent into the depth of the subject indicated by the words "me" or "I." Neither God, nor the Other, nor I can be thought of in terms of kerygmatic discourse alone.

In order to prepare an interpretation of Levinas's analysis of transcendence, we might reflect on that other attempt to evade philosophy in which Levinas sees a certain affinity with his own way of thought: the skeptical attempt.

Skepticism

Skepticism may be understood as an extreme dissatisfaction with logos in its philosophical form. It tries to evade philosophy, but is there any logos-free space where it could settle in order to maintain itself?

Since skepticism is a historical fact as persistent as philosophy itself, it must have at least some meaning. Its recurrence after every refutation suggests that its logical impossibility does not preclude something else in it from being true or valuable or at least worth meditating upon. Skepticism is a child of philosophy, but is it also a "legitimate child of philosophy"?[4]

As an attempt to state something totally and absolutely negative, skepticism gives short shrift to philosophy as the logic of truth. But is there a realm for thinking outside of philosophy? Where can one find another dimension from which to deliver a total condemnation without falling into the traps of universal logic? Is such a realm outside of philosophy a sort of post- or prephilosophical naivete? Or is it still philosophical? But how, in the latter case, could skepticism save itself from its own condemnation?

The inspiration that prompts the negativities of skepticism looks like an expiration: not only are all the answers given to the important questions of humanity untrue, but there is not even the possibility of true answers. Boredom, fatigue, and the exhaustion of an epoch are fertile soils for such a spirit of negativity, but it can also be expressed in the haughtiness of an acute intelligence that has tested every theory without meeting any that commanded respect. Could skepticism itself be a mask for something else? Can it be the reverse side of some positive orientation or position?

What skepticism says, its thesis or "said," can be formulated in a sentence like the following one: "All (philosophical) theses are false" or "None of the possible theses (in philosophy) are true." We must perhaps distinguish (1) a skepticism that limits itself to a critical judgment about philosophy, from (2) a less careful and more absolute kind of skepticism which condemns all statements, including the extraphilosophical ones. The former limits itself to the universal negation of the possibility of *philosophical* truths, while the latter does not recognize any limit to its negativity, thus absolutely denying all Being and thinking as such.

The classical refutation of philosophical skepticism consists in a simple analysis of the thesis or "said" in which skepticism takes a stand with regard to the universe of all possible theses (or "saids"). If the skeptical said is true, every thesis is false, the skeptical one as much as any other thesis. This falsehood follows from the skeptical said's belonging to the universe of saids that skepticism denies. The difference between the skeptical thesis and the affirmation of its falsehood is the difference between an *explicit* thesis and an *implicit* thesis. It is not a difference of time, at least if we consider a thought that is logically entailed in another thought to be *simultaneous* with the latter. There is, however, a temporal difference between hearing or uttering the explicit thesis and discovering its falsehood. One must think about its implications—and this takes time—in order to see that it refutes itself (if it is applicable to itself). If this analysis is right, skepticism can neither defend itself by pointing out that (1) the indicated contradiction found by the refutation is a misinterpretation of the divergence between its saying and its said, nor by claiming that (2) its main thesis (which according to skepticism is true) *precedes* the thesis that skepticism must on that very premise be false. For (a) the refutation does not uncover an opposition between a saying and a said, but between an *explicit said* and an *implicit* said, and (b) although there may be a temporal difference between the moment in which the skeptical thesis is understood in a global sense and the moment in which it becomes evident that it is a self-contradictory state-ment, the insight that it is self-contradictory destroys it as a philosophical statement. At least *within the realm of philosophy*, it must be considered to be nonsensical.

Could the skeptic defend himself by claiming that his thesis belongs to a metaphilosophical level? The question that he must answer in this case is the following: Where do you find a metaphilosophical level from which you can state some thesis about all philosophical theses, without either becoming yourself hopelessly naive or being refuted by the inner contradiction of your very thesis? Is there place for a logos or thought above or outside of philosophy?

If skepticism is defenseless against its classical refutation, how can we then save the passages in which Levinas claims that the refutation puts the saying and the said of skepticism on the same level and neglects the diachrony by which they are separated?

> The periodic return of skepticism and of its refutation signify a temporality in which the instants refuse memory which recuperates and re-presents. Skepticism, which traverses the rationality or logic of knowledge, is a refusal to synchronize the implicit affirmation contained in saying and the *negation* which this affirmation states in the said. The contradiction is visible to reflection, which refutes it, but skepticism is insensitive to the refutation, as though the affirmation and negation did not resound in the same time. Skepticism then contests the thesis which claims that *between the saying and the said* the *relationship that connects* in synchrony a *condition* with the *conditioned* is repeated. It is as though skepticism were sensitive to the *difference* between *my exposure* without reserve to the other, which is saying, and the exposition or statement of the said in its equilibrium and justice. (AE, 213; OB, 167–68)

Is the diagnosis of skepticism given here correct? It does not seem to be true that skepticism distinguishes itself from all other forms of classical philosophy by contesting the thesis, be it only implicit, that the Saying and the Said must be seen as simultaneous and connected synchronically. Its way of stating and arguing does not differ from the traditional way of philosophy, except in its impossible attempt to be absolutely negative about everything. Its very thesis appeals to everybody's memory in order to gather all possible sentences and systems and to grasp them as a collection of positions which claim to be true. It does not present another alternative than the traditional one of true or false theses and theories. It claims to embrace all possibilities of truth but destroys the representation of this universe immediately. If skepticism is "a refusal to synchronize the implicit *affirmation* contained in saying and the *negation* which this affirmation states in the *said*," then the implicit affirmation itself is not a form of saying, but a said, a said it cannot refuse to affirm because of the absolutist thesis in which this said is contained. The structure of both saids as saids is not different; both are parts of the same logic. If the (implicit) affirmation and the (explicit) negation do not *resound* at the same time, this is due to the fact that a discourse cannot tell all the aspects and moments of a thesis at once, but this is nothing special about skepticism in comparison with other theories. A trained logician, however, hears immediately the simultaneity of the affirmation and the contradictory negation in the statement that "all theses (including this one) are false."

If the skeptical thesis is meant to be a philosophical one, it cannot be saved. If it cannot find a way out, in order to condemn philosophy from a nonphilosophical, nonthetic, and nonsystematic standpoint, it should either give up and die or show the possibility of another form of thought, a metaphilosophy or transformed philosophy in which the logos of traditional philosophy is overcome. This would perhaps convince us that it "traversed the rationality or logic of knowledge" before it launched its presumptuous claim upon all attempts at stating truths.

However, there is another way to interpret the uneasy feeling that remains after the classical refutation of skepticism and the latter's insensitivity to the force of that refutation. There must be some hidden affirmation in the skeptical position. The strength of its logical refutation is exactly the truth (a very formal truth, as a matter of fact) that an absolutely negative statement is impossible. The weakness of skepticism is its incapacity or unwillingness to make explicit the affirmative moments of its position, its positivity. In order to save some sort of skepticism, the positive side of its negation must be recognized. But can it be stated, posited, taken, refined, and located within the archaic and totalizing order of philosophy?

Both Kant and Hegel are exemplary in exploiting hidden possibilities of (a mitigated form of) skepticism. Kant even calls the "skeptical method" indispensable for acquiring access to the most radical questions of philosophy.[5] In order to show the incapacity of experiential and scientific knowledge with regard to the truths of metaphysics and the dimension of transcendence, Kant argues for the necessary destruction of a certain form of philosophy by proving the inevitable simultaneity of contradictory theses about the world as the universe of phenomenal beings. This insight gives access to another dimension and procedure of thought than the traditional one. Skepticism is a good weapon against the dogmatism of traditional metaphysics. A new, positive but very strange dimension of truth, full of negations, limitations, and impossibilities, is opened up for those who dare traverse the contradictions of skepticism. But what shall we call the sort of *Fürwahrhalten* (holding-as-true) which becomes possible after and through the suffered loss?

Hegel follows Kant's example in a less caution way by acknowledging the most radical form of skepticism, while submitting it at the same time to an equally universalistic but positive position. Faithful to the syllogistic framework of Western philosophy, Hegel converts and integrates skepticism by showing that all its explicit and implicit negations are true, except its negation of the unique truth of the absolute itself, which is also the whole. By integrating all those finite negations into correlated affirmations, Hegel imprisons the spirit of negativity by extending the horizons of truth just a little beyond that spirit's range.

The radicalism of skepticism and its affinity with true metaphysics, however, lies in its pointing beyond totality. This is the reason why Levinas writes phrases like the following: "Philosophy is not separable from skepticism" (AE, 213; OB, 168), "Language is already skepticism" (AE, 216; OB, 170), and "The entire history of Western philosophy has been one long refutation of skepticism as much as it has been one long refutation of transcendence."[6] From the standpoint of logic, Hegel argued that such a "beyond" is possible only if the "beyond" (the absolute itself) somehow coincides with the totality of truth in which it unfolds itself by means of a universal and double negation. However, like Plato and Plotinus, but in a different vein, Levinas maintains that the One beyond the whole of being is separated from it.

From Hegel we can learn that truth is infinitely more dramatic than most antiskeptical *and skeptical* philosophers think: the force and width of negation are as universal and *almost* as absolute as the absolute itself. Absolute skepticism, however, is absurd, because in denying whatever is said, it does not say anything and therefore exists as if it did not exist. The skeptical position must be "traversed" because the logos of kerygmatic philosophy is not wide enough. But what comes after both?

Kant's traversal of the skepticism that results from the inevitable antinomies of metaphysical cosmology was an attempt to break out of a well-assured and solid knowledge toward an ambiguous sort of "holding-as-true" which awakened many suspicions because it looked like an illogical faith. Did this sort of relation to the true belong inside or outside of philosophy?

Levinas's appraisal of skepticism, too, seems to be inspired by the search for a dimension beyond the order of well-founded and self-assured logos, a dimension in which the eminence and strangeness of the transcendent expresses itself in the loss of syllogistic certainty and in the preference for words like "perhaps" and "it is as if" or "everything seems to suggest" over the bold statements of conceptual comprehension and kerygmatic language. Levinas's great discovery was finding a way beyond the solidarity of logic and its skeptical denial in the difference between the *Said* and its *Saying.*

The order of the Said—the dimension of the logos and its synoptic structures—refers to the Saying, which can never become an element of it. Levinas sees skepticism as a position in which that difference is recognized more clearly (be it only in the form of a feeling) than it is within the logic of traditional philosophy. His mild and perhaps too positive diagnosis of skepticism becomes illuminating if we read it as a description of his own attempt to think the relation between the logical way of doing philosophy and the beyond which does *not contradict* the dimension of logos and phenomenology, but is *incommensurate* to it.

Before we reflect on the importance of this discovery, however, I would like to come back to the problem of textuality and ask the question that we earlier postponed: Is it altogether true that the author is *absent* from his texts once they are written or after he dies?

Presentation

A writer cannot address himself to us from the shelves of the library where his books are located. He needs at least the assistance of some other instance, a person, group, or tradition, to present his text to us. In this case he is represented and in a way existing behind or even *in* the text, coming from our past but provoking us, here and now, to read his words. At least the echo of his voice is perceptible, even when his name is unknown. Can the voice of an author be silenced completely? Is it true that "in a written text the saying certainly becomes a pure said, a simultaneity of the saying and its conditions"?[7] Perhaps synchrony is not the whole truth of a text, because it only "functions" if it provokes us to understanding, interpretation, or discussion. No text could affect us if it were not brought to our notice by a *presentation*. Is it essential to the meaning of a text that it be addressed to possible readers or listeners? The presentation of a text to me by a third person or by myself not only reminds me of its known or unknown author, but represents and revives the author's position as someone who calls to me.

When we reread Levinas, who saves his texts from fossilization? Who addresses them to us? To what extent is it Levinas himself? Or isn't there any instance in particular responsible for our being provoked by these texts? Are they "interesting" because we decided (or something in us decided) to read them or to make them readable? But how could we take this initiative? Must our initiative not be preceded by an initiative that belongs to the past and is a constituent of it? Does this lead us to an infinite regression?[8]

Even if we were capable of deciding sovereignly to treat texts as ownerless property or free "food for our souls," our treatment would meet with voices and provocations whose absence would kill all meaning. The meaning of a kerygma depends on its being proclaimed *and addressed* by a voice. Reading a text is always responding to a call that summons us, although it is true that the presenting voice comes from the past in which the text was born from its author. Re-presentation is essential to reading. Our discussing "Levinas" presupposes and implies our addressing his writings to one another; when we are doing this, the master's voice is echoing in ours.

If this analysis is acceptable, we should not overemphasize the distance by which a text is separated from its writer. A text is not a tool made by someone before it was given to us, who, in turn, take it into our possession: neither can it be compared to the bread which I will not eat because I give it to someone else. A tool can be understood and handled perfectly without any reference to its maker (except when it is a very original work, but then it is a "poem," not only an artifact). Giving bread is not analogous to offering a text, because I cannot eat or assimilate a text of my own (except, perhaps, later, when I have become different from the writer that I once was); I can only give it away. An author is not a maker, because in presenting his text, he presents *himself.* To utter words is to address and to expose myself to the benevolence or the violence of readers over whom I have no power, but whom I cannot help invoking.

Levinas's analysis of Saying and responsibility can be applied to the necessary presentation of a text. In order to get an idea of this analogy, I would like to turn to the analysis of speaking and spoken words.[9]

Speaking

A kerygma is always addressed to one or more addresees. Saying is a condition of the possibility of all discourse. What is communication insofar as it is not the production of a message but an address to possible listeners?

When I direct myself to someone by saying "Hello!" I enter into a relation with the person who is there, in front of me or at the other end of the line, while I am here, speaking to her. In telling what I have to tell, I count on the Other's memory: she must synchronize the succession of words in which I unfold my narration or my argument. My Saying itself, however, "precedes" that which is told or argued for by my communication. What sort of "precedence" separates the Saying from the Said?

When I say "Good morning!" I am not delivering a message, but through a sort of benediction I am wishing you a happy or successful morning. Here, too, the Saying differs from the story or the discourse that can be unfolded thereafter. If we reserve the Said for the message, then, too, the Saying precedes the Said. Within every Saying, however, we can distinguish between the fact of addressing oneself to another and the wish ("Please . . .") or accusation ("Bastard!") or command ("Come!" or "Away!") worded by it. In his analyses of Saying Levinas concentrates on the moment of addressing. The said indicates primarily the order of kerygmatic language and especially theoretical discourse. There is, thus, still room for other distinctions and elaborations.

The precedence of Saying differs from the precedence by which a writer has a distance from his text. Between a speaker and her speech the unity is closer: she herself actually exists in the proffering of her Said. Nevertheless, there is a sort of interval, a nonsimultaneity, between her Saying and the Said. Not only is a saying possible without kerygma, whereas the reverse needs at least a representative of the original voice, but "Hello" or "Here I am" are not meant to communicate a story or a thesis; they are an appeal to the addressee to pay attention to the presence, here and now, of the speaker, who may deliver a message hereafter. By saying "Good morning" I might be initiating a communication, but it is also possible that nothing else will follow. Saying is a sort of foreword or "preface" to the message that follows. Saying and Said do not coincide perfectly; they are not completely simultaneous: the Said comes from a Saying which takes the initiative, resounds before and stays behind it. The interval between the Saying and the Said is much smaller than the distance between author and text, however. The speaking voice is a much more intense presence than the style, the souvenirs, and the echoes by which a writer is recognizable in his writings.

To speak to someone is not identical to reading a paper or delivering an address. Indeed, it is essential to speaking that the speaker not only directs himself to one or more listeners but also invites and provokes them to a response. To deliver a speech without intending it to be the beginning of a discussion in which my speech will be subjected to other perspectives is a hybrid form of language, halfway between speaking and reading. If we not only want to "read Levinas," but also intend to give his and our saying(s) a chance, we must hear his texts as calls and provocations to which we respond with words of our own.

To sum up the difference between texts and spoken words, the following features might be stressed. The synoptic character of a text is less obvious in speech. Not only does a series of spoken words lack the completeness of a text, whose elements are all present here and now in one pack of paper, but the intention of speaking is also less totalitarian. Spoken words are meant to be fragments of intersubjective chains of exchange and conversation. Normally they do not claim to constitute a well-rounded whole; by scanning the flow of time they trust that there will be more time for speaking in order to respond, correct, augment, and relativize what has been said before.

Since a speaker is present in his words, he thereby addresses *himself* to the listener. The temporal distance and the "diachrony" between an author and his text are more obvious, but even a writer is not altogether absent from her writings. This difference in distance is the reason why Levinas, in some passages of *Totality and the Infinite*, quotes Plato's defense of oral teaching against the pretensions of written texts. Authors cannot defend their message when it is distorted by misunderstandings or attacked by objections, because their presence in the text is a diminished one. Speakers can elucidate, interpret, and correct their words by prolonging or adjusting their discourses.[10]

A spoken word is not a score, like a text before it is read. Speech cannot exist in separation from the speaker. Even a tape-recorded speech differs from a text by (re)presenting the speaker's voice and intonation, which is another form of existence than the style. Speech, however, is not to be compared to writing, but rather to the *reading* of a text: both are the presentation of a message by voices in which the author is present or represented.

Whatever the differences between speaking, writing, and reading may be, all these modes of language present us with a radical difference between the *Said*, whose structure was clarified by the analysis of kerygmatic language, and the *Saying* of it. This difference cannot be reduced to the traditional opposition between an autonomous interiority and its exteriorization, nor can Saying be understood as a complication of a said, and certainly not as an anonymous *saga* or *Sage* coming from the past of our traditions. *Language does not speak*, although everybody recognizes that all our commonplaces and dicta, and even the most original sayings of our history are shaped and marked by different elements of a forceful past.

Against the domination of anonymous powers and mores it is not sufficient (although it may be useful) to stress the originality of a personal style. Through a style of her own, an author shows that her appropriation of the current usages and patterns, stories and discourses is not the simple repetition of everybody's *Gerede*. The more she transforms commonplaces into a said of her own, the more she emerges from anonymity. A personal style is not the most important characteristic of language, however. Above, before, and behind all features of a personality as expressed in style, the *addressing* of the Said to someone is at once the most common and the most radical distinction by which language transcends the whole range of things that can be said.

Sayings and Adhesion

In addressing words to someone, I present and expose myself to that person. This most common event of everybody's daily life realizes the transcendence that philosophy is looking for without finding it in the realm of logos. *Saying* (1) is the condition that precedes every said, all systematic discourse, thematization, and phenomenology; (2) cannot be understood as a modulation or modification of a human or superhuman Said; and (3) cannot be reduced to the act of an autonomous subject or the free initiative of human self-consciousness.

In directing myself to another person, Saying exposes me. What I present cannot be named by summing up my material or spiritual qualities, my words or the phenomenal characteristics by which I can be recognized as this specific person. Through and behind or beyond all my masks and appearances, I am present to the Other as a naked subject whose "essence" is to be given and extradited to the Other. Being present to another in Saying is spoliation and extradition. I am hostage to the other and nobody can replace me in this service, which constitutes me as this unique individual. Subjectivity as the relation of the-one-for-the-Other interrupts and forbids the absolutization of a narcissistic way of life prompted by the spontaneous drives of an isolated ego. The Other's very existence, not her decisions, poses an infinite claim on me: I will never be able to fulfill the obligations contained in this claim, but this does not release me from fulfilling them. The opposition between the Other's claim and my spontaneous narcissism is expressed in the humiliation and injury of my egocentrism. This is the reason why being-offered-to-the-Other implies pain and suffering. Everybody has to suffer for the Other. Suffering and vulnerability are essential to human subjectivity.

A crucial point in the analysis of the relation of the-one-for-the-Other is the impossibility of understanding this relation as the result of a decision, a contract, or a convention based on acts of some human will. Human freedom is not capable of creating its own meaning and orienta-tion. The foundation of ethics cannot be found in the self-determination of one or more wills. If I try to fulfill my obligations, I obey a law that was there before I awoke to consciousness: the law regards me from the eyes of someone who simply by existing deserves esteem. My devotion to others does not begin with dedicating myself to them. It was already there before I became aware of it.

The same must be said of my directing myself to another by *Saying.* My act and my intention, not only my work of exteriorization but the whole dynamism of my inner life, is preceded, caught, and carried on by an already-being-addressed, -given, and -dedicated to the Other. My dedication comes from an immemorial and irretrievable past. I discover what I am when I discover that I have been given to the Other before I could agree to it. My first agreement occurs when I obey the order that constitutes me more radically than does autonomy. It is in obedience that

I get an inkling of what subjectivity or being-human is. Although I never wanted or even accepted to be responsible for another, I cannot escape from this infinite responsibility. My devotion to the Other is a past in which neither my consciousness nor my will has been present, but this past determines all the presents of my life. The core of human subjectivity is the extreme passivity of someone who always comes too late to accept his task and autonomy.

One may, however, ask whether it is not at all possible that a human subject, in the course of a life, approaches the point where free will coincides completely with responsibility and obligations never contracted willingly. Is it not possible and even the basic task of a moral life to learn to agree with our subjectivity *afterwards* and that we assent *progressively* to our having become infinitely responsible before all memorable time? Levinas stresses the interval between my election to responsibility for the Other and the emergence of conscious autonomy; upon awakening, my spontaneous egoism is not ready to agree with the infinite demands of responsibility which took possession of me without my consent and against the desires of my spontaneity. But this excludes neither the possibility of a future agreement with the orders of the Good, nor the perspective of a final peace through full adherence to the law of infinite obligation. Isn't death, after all, the possibility of a full payment of all debts? Even if we are justly aware that the extent and intensity of responsibility are so enormous that they will always exceed our capacity for accomplishing what should be done, a certain peace is ideally possible, on the condition that one also accepts the exact measure of one's destiny or election. Must we not conclude that the two strains of our existence suggest and demand that we consider a certain union of goodness and peace to be the destination and final meaning of an individual's life?

Being exposed to others and being responsible for them is to be animated by a spirit of devotion. It is to have a soul. Every reminiscence of the vulgar opposition between matter and spirit should be banished from our understanding of subjectivity. Human spirituality is a particular position and movement of earthly bodies with regard to other bodies. Inspiration is not a mysterious spell taking place within some inner recess, but rather the extradition of a subject in flesh and blood. It does not leave any private property to a subjective interiority that could extract solitary pleasures from it. By agreeing to the reversal that has taken place before I became conscious of it, I lose all possibilities of isolation and spiritualization.

The transcendence practiced in the most simple acts and gestures of everyday life, such as speaking, suffering, or helping, is not at all heroic in the sense of an ensemble of impressive plans and actions; it is realized as endurance and patience. Instead of an ascension by means of elitist projects and originality, it demands a descent to service and devotion.

Saying, responsibility, goodness, proximity, subjectivity, inspiration, and spirituality do not fit into the horizons of kerygmatic discourse and logical appropriation. My own saying captures me in a movement that started before I could move my will. It takes me away from my attempt at identifying myself as the central or transcendental point of reference. The presentation of myself in my addressing words to someone cannot be welcomed within the system of logos and phenomenology. It cannot be gathered or synchronized within the Said. At the same time, however, the Saying and the Said are united in the very act of speaking in spite of their being "diachronically" related to one another. Their combination in one and the same time is possible because their difference does not produce a contradiction. The Saying and the Said are not contradictory, but incommensurable. If they were related as contradictory terms, skepticism would be inevitable and the only possible defense—a narrow escape!— would be in stressing the temporal precedence of Saying, which would be separated by an interval from the Said. Against the synchrony of the kerygmatic synopsis the duplicity of Saying and Said would have to realize an authentic diachrony without any overlapping.

By taking up once again Levinas's analyses, I have insisted on the presence by which the author, the speaker, and the saying subject present themselves or are (re)presented in their message. I have thereby diminished the importance of the diachrony by which Levinas distinguishes Saying, responsibility, and subjectivity from all possible objects and subjects of logical thematization. That the Saying "precedes" every said, that the obligation in which I discover myself belongs to an immemorial past that precedes my awakening to consciousness, that "He" from whom that obligation comes (and thereby the ultimate meaning of world and history) will have always already passed away—all these references to an irretrievable "before" must be affirmed and meditated upon. Transcendence must be practiced and described as an exodus out of the logical and archaic temporality of Western philosophy, but what sort of time is introduced by pointing to the *before* of God, law, and subjectivity? It is not merely the precedence of civilization, history, and the traditions that support us and our language as *Sage* and *sprechende Sprache*. Which sense is applicable to the "somewhere else" that affects us? In which sense is the "beyond" a *temporal* before?

In a degenerate form of metaphysics, which became a bugbear for giants like Nietzsche, transcendence was understood as a transition from this empirical world to a higher world "behind" this one. The "hinterworld" has lost its spell. As a matter of fact, it never had any attraction for philosophers; they have always known that the image of a *Hinterwelt* is no more than an awkward spatial metaphor and that its value depends exclusively on its capacity to adjust the orientation of our being in a unique world of natural phenomena and human history.

In Levinas's later works the spatial metaphors like "a higher order," "the highest being," "the deepest ground," "the fundamental or basic principle," "that which is behind the phenomenon," and so on, used in the context of old metaphysics, are replaced by adverbs of time, and especially by expressions that indicate the *past*. "An immemorial and irretrievable past," "He, who passed away," "a past that has never been present," "a passivity more passive than all passivity," and similar expressions suppress the metaphorical "behind" and "above."[11] Must we also understand Levinas's *anachrony* in a metaphorical way? What then is the meaning of *temporal metaphors*? They are not absent from the philosophical and theological traditions of Western civilization, in which, e.g., God also was imagined as He who already existed before creation began and as He who will exist when it is completed, but even more so as He, whose presence is the "first principle" (*arche, principium,* "beginning") of all principles. If Levinas's characterization of transcendence by its diachronical structure must be understood as a metaphorical language, the question arises whether temporal metaphors are better suited to a consideration of transcendence and to what extent their power of evocation and suggestion differs from that of spatial metaphors. Could it be that the preference for the quasispatial eminence of the transcendent is connected to a cosmological vision in which the main attention is given to the space of nature, whereas temporality occupies the center of our symbolic language when human history or its elementary and everlasting emergence in intersubjective relationships has become the principal concern?

The Unity of Saying and Said

My conclusion must remain sketchy. I will only suggest a few possibilities that should be tested, rejected, or amended in further meditations.

1. The noncontradictory incommensurability of the Saying and the Said makes their combination, unity, and simultaneity possible, in spite of the "diachronic" primacy of the Saying.

2. At the same time, their difference makes it very difficult to clarify the peculiarity of the Saying, *but also to determine the characteristics of the Said*, which is always a said presented by a saying (or reading).[12]

If the Saying and the Said cannot be isolated from one another, we have to cope with two major difficulties: The first is the classic difficulty of how it is possible to thematize and objectify constitutive *moments* of an object or theme, like, for instance, matter and form or noumenality and phenomenality. If a thing is essentially composed of matter and form, it is obvious that we cannot treat the form as if it were a thing, but how can we treat it, then, as the subject of our predictions? The second difficulty results from the very special essence of the Saying, and the impact it has on the peculiarities of the Said. If every said is necessarily presented by a saying and if there is no saying without any said, their interwovenness must be constitutive for the modes of being characteristic of both of them.

3. The simultaneity of the Said and the Saying, which is not abolished by their difference, must be thought as such. The transition between the two and their belonging together is stated many times, but how can it be thought? This question is even more urgent than the question about the relation between myself and the Other in the separation that does not abolish this belonging together. But in the end both questions coincide.

The alternation of the *dire-dédire-redire* and so on proposed by Levinas does not seem to be the final word on this question. Indeed, to know that we must jump from one dimension (the dimension of logos) to another dimension (the dimension of Saying, exposure, and responsibility) and again to logos, and repeat this jumping back and forth an infinite number of times, implies that we somehow "know" about the secret passage that binds them together. The alternation of "yes" and "no" in our saying-denying-saying-again in a time of repetition (in which, in a sense, "the same" is said and denied again and again) implies at least the repetition of a moment in which the transition from "yes" into "no" and from "no" into the selfsame "yes" testifies to their simultaneity—albeit briefly. That this simultaneity can be *accomplished* is evident; that there is also some secret awareness of it seems to be plausible; but can it be transformed into a part of philosophy? Responsibility is better than reflection, but philosophy cannot give up reflecting upon its extradition to the better. As long as responsibility remains reflexive, it cannot evade philosophy. Repetitive reflection may, however, be a final attempt to avoid the pain of radical passivity.

10

Transcendence

The question of transcendence has been dominant in two philosophical contexts: (1) the epistemological and ontological context of human subjectivity in its theoretical and practical relations to the world, and (2) the context of philosophical theology. Socrates's pointing to the Good, as that which, from "beyond the *ousia*," grants Being, light, and truth, gave orientation to Plotinus, pseudo-Dionysius, and Bonaventure in both areas, and they were not the only ones who were grateful for his suggestions.

In our century, Heidegger and Levinas have drawn inspiration from Socrates's hint, and both of them—though Levinas more than Heidegger—have asked whether and how that hint could be used to translate another, older inspiration about goodness, Being, and truth into philosophy. In this chapter I would like to show how Levinas has retrieved Plato's enigmatic phrase about the Good's goodness beyond Being.

Beyond Being

If the translation of *to agathon* as "the Good" (*le Bien*) and of *epekeina tes ousias* as "beyond Being" (*au-delà de l'essence*) is correct, the paradoxes contained in this phrase are obvious. How can we speak about the Good, or about any *x*, that is neither a being, nor Being itself? Is Being enclosed within the limits of a horizon? Is it separated from another dimension, a beyond? Would this beyond then be and not be at the same time? If the Good were inaccessible to ontology—and, a fortiori, to phenomenology—shouldn't we be silent about it, rather than stammer on in a pseudological manner? The fact that such paradoxes as these and others also threaten the logic of Aristotelian, Thomist, or Heideggerian ontologies cannot console us once we are entangled in the paralogical difficulties of a Platonizing meditation. For some practitioners of philosophy, "metaphysical" paradoxes are reason enough to drop these questions altogether, at least within philosophy; other thinkers, and not insignificant ones, see them as the unavoidable consequences of thinking that approaches the limits of human thought. When human thinking reaches out beyond its own dimensions, it produces contradictions: but this is not a good reason to withdraw to easier terrain. Thinking through and beyond the unfolding of *ousia* and *physis*, meta-physics or meta-ontology, seems to be the task that philosophy must achieve, today as yesterday.

Transcendence and Transgression

While Plato characterized the human relation to the Good-and-Beautiful as an ascent or a "transascendence" (TeI, 5; TaI, 35), modern secularization has leveled the dimensions of heaven, earth, and hell. Still, even in today's enthusiasm for "transgression" we hear echoes of the ancient desire to reach beyond the order of a world ruled by the laws of equivalence, exchange, coherence, and logic. The fact that a certain violence is inherent to all kinds of transgression shows the finite character of its passing beyond the limits, for violence is possible only between limited realities: the Infinite does not compete with anything. As philosophers from Plato to Hegel knew, God is not jealous.

But does transcendence not cause suffering? Yes, but not in a violent way; that is, not at the cost of a loss in human worth or dignity, and not at the price of sickness or slavery. How then must transcendence be lived and thought, if it exceeds the possibilities of human existence without repression or violence? It must be in accordance with or even coincide with the deepest of human desires.

Desire

The first part of *Totality and the Infinite* opens with a chapter on "Metaphysics and Transcendence"; and the first section of this chapter is entitled "Desire for the Invisible" ("*Désir de l'invisible*" (TeI, 3; TaI, 33). Transcendence, as movement toward the Other, is identified here as a desire, and the text seems to start with a phenomenology of *eros* which makes obvious allusion to Plato's metaphysics. I would like to spend a few moments on a careful reading of its first lines.

What does desire for "the invisible" announce? Does Levinas champion a theory of nonempirical, nonphenomenological realities, a kind of *Hinterwelt* from which we thought Marx and Nietzsche had finally delivered us? Or does he, like Heidegger and Nietzsche, aim to show that transcendence leads away from a false reality and thought in order to discover and achieve a truer loyalty to body and earth? All thinking—and not only thinking—is situated; an explanation of any possible thought demands the reconstruction of its context, an interpretation of the material and cultural network, the customs and traditions from which it emerges. However, hermeneutics as (re)contextualization is not enough, because all thinking—and not only thinking—turns to something or someone which is completely new, and which cannot be contained in the text or context that is already there. Thinking addresses some Other that is elsewhere and different, some Other than the parts or elements of a context or an economy in which the thinker feels at home. To think is to leave the familiarity of one's home country for a foreign place, which is "elsewhere" (*ailleurs*), *alibi*, "there" (*là-bas*), as Levinas, alluding to Plato, writes.[1] By abandoning the closure of "being-at-home-with-oneself" (*Beisichselbstsein*), one enters a dangerous kind of existence. Unrest, but also passion, are the consequences of a desire which precedes all choices and decisions.

The urgency of an exodus manifests the post- or meta-physical character of human existence. This does not lead to the heights of heaven or the depths of a netherworld; it is not even a synthesis of ascent (*anabasis*) and descent (*katabasis*), as Plato's *Politeia* would have it. Exodus leads to Others who share the earth with me. For "we are in the world." This world is more than a space to dwell in and more than the general condition of a common ethos; as universe it embraces all possibilities of exodus and wandering. The only way to leave the world is to die, and all attempts to get in touch with gods or God are earthly modulations of worldly possibilities. And yet "true life is absent," as Rimbaud declares in Levinas's quote from *A Season in Hell*.[2] Of course, in a secularized world hell is no longer below or out there; it is an infernal mode of existence whose description is given in the outcry "What a life! The true life is absent. We are not in the world." In this complaint, a certain form of existence—or, in fact, a form of coexistence (the coexistence of Verlaine and Rimbaud)—is revealed as inhuman, devilish, extramundane. Desire is frustrated. But can it be satisfied? Does the desired Other open a possibility of escape from suffering, boredom, violence?

The Other awakens us to new possibilities, but how can we wake up if we are not already moved by a desire for the surprising new? Exteriority and otherness do not destroy all elements of *anamnesis*, but they respond to what we already are before we know it. Desire is oriented before one can discover it. In trying to say what and how we desire, we thus try to reach back to that which precedes our consciousness.

Economy

In prevailing interpretations, human praxis is caught in a web of needs, desires, values, the rational use of means toward chosen ends, exchanges on the basis of calculated equivalence, etc., that is, as an *economy*. The law (*nomos*) of the house (*oikos*), the law of being at home in the world, is constituted by a combination of natural needs and rational choices. Human beings are rational, i.e., reasoning and choosing, animals, looking for satisfaction. Since isolated individuals cannot satisfy their own needs, they group together, creating social, political, and cultural conventions to achieve their ends, the "norms and values" of their communities. Sociality rests on individual hunger and fear, although reason implies the possibility of distance, choice, delay, and the preference for some "values" or "satisfactions" over others. The most popular explanation of the ethos that belongs to this economy is utilitarian. By distinguishing quantitative and qualitative differences of satisfaction and dimensions of satisfaction, such an explanation tries to maintain all human ends and actions within the limits of an economy. Not only entertainment, but also science, art, philosophy, and religion are seen as values, and the fulfillment of these values has a place on the overall scale of human contentment and happiness.

The global picture given here shows the decadence of a long philosophical tradition: the Aristotelian tradition of *eudaimonia,* perfection, and self-realization, which is much more respectable than both its trivialized caricature in eighteenth-century *Glückseligkeitslehre* and twentieth-century utilitarianism. All these doctrines share a common presupposition, however. Like Plato and Aristotle, they understand the fundamental desire to be a lack, a privation, a want that must be filled or fulfilled. All behavior, including all choice, is motivated by a felt emptiness that urges the feeling subject to search for fulfillment. All action is self-realization; all feeling is, in the end, self-affection; and all consciousness is self-consciousness. The elsewhere and all otherness are forms of a return of the self to itself. Beauty, the Good, truth, the gods, and God are valuable only insofar as they promise someone's satisfaction. All kinds of want and desire, then, fit perfectly into the structure of intentionality, as defined by Husserl: the dynamic emptiness of the "erotic" intention is the exact correlate *in negativo* of the desired satisfaction. Both have the same width and identity. "True life" might still be absent, but the measurement of desire reveals the exact contours of the desired and beloved who would still our hunger. It is then obvious that the beloved cannot be infinite, unless the depth of our heart is as infinite as the beloved. In any case, the first principle of ethics, according to this interpretation of human *economy*, is: "Fulfill, accomplish, realize what you are!"

Levinas does not deny the importance of human needs and the part they necessarily and rightly play in politics, culture, and history; but his interpretation of their economy differs from the prevailing theories. *First*, Levinas grounds the economy of needs in a wider and more elementary phenomenology of human life as spontaneous assimilation and enjoyment (TeI, 82–90; TaI, 110–117). *Second*, this phenomenology permits him to see all human activity, including art, science, philosophy, and religion, as an attempt to enjoy the world's wealth. *Third*—and this is the most decisive move—Levinas reinterprets the characteristics of economy as emerging from Being itself. In *Otherwise than Being*, the connections between economy and Being are analyzed through a phenomenological ontology in which Levinas explicitly expresses his debt to Heidegger (AE, 49 n. 28; OB, 189 n. 28).

Whereas the chapter on "Interiority and Economy" in *Totality and the Infinite* reinterprets our being-in-the-world as the vital enjoyment of a dwelling place and nourishment on an earth bathed in water, air, and light, *Otherwise than Being* deepens those analyses by showing that Being itself has an economical (or "pre-economical") character. Levinas's phenomenology of Being describes the way of Being's being—its mode of happening, arriving, and coming to the fore, its behavior and its course ("*la geste d'être*")—as an active and transitive "essence" (*essance* in the sense of Heidegger's *Wesen und Walten*) which is essentially interested— an "inter-essence," or a being-linked of all entities, whose interrelations are determined by each being's endeavor to maintain and expand its own existence. *Esse* is *interesse*; *essence* is being-interested, "inter-est-ing," *inter-essence*. Levinas appeals to Spinoza's *conatus essendi* and Pascal's analysis of *concupiscence*[3] as key elements of his phenomenology of Being, and his entire effort is oriented by the desire to transcend[4] the realm of general interestedness without exception, that is, by the desire to escape Being as such.

This explains why Levinas can think of the Good only as surpassing the limits of Being. Yet, is his phenomenology of Being really an ontology, or does it show only a *mode* of Being? Do not goodness, generosity, giving, and substitution exist? Are they not other faces or powers of Being? Hasn't Levinas made his task too difficult by separating the Good from Being?

He is not at all convinced of the generosity that other thinkers hear in "*Es gibt,*" and prefers to stress the dark, threatening, and chaotic side of the indeterminate *il y a*: But how can there be a place for goodness if Being fills all the gaps? And if it does not need a place, how can it have its time?

Desire and Need

In *Totality and the Infinite*, Levinas's phenomenological critique of economy starts with a radical distinction between needs (*besoins*) and desire (*désir*); in *Otherwise than Being*, the ontological structure of economical existence is analyzed. Desire, thematized in the beginning of the first book, transcends economy, just as the Good, in the second, is shown to transcend ontology. Desire is not interested in satisfaction or exchange; it does not assimilate or integrate, because it is not oriented toward enrichment or expansion. As desire for the Other, it accords with the surprising strangeness and distance without which there would be no otherness, and thus no relation between the Other and the Same. Proximity does not diminish, but rather intensifies, desire. If it is a hunger, this hunger grows by coming into contact with the desired one.

The formal analysis of desire with which *Totality and the Infinite* begins does not immediately focus on a concrete figure of the Other. Shortly thereafter, however, Levinas does declare that, in desire, the otherness of the desired one is "understood as otherness of the human other (*autrui*) *and* as otherness of the Most High" (TeI, 4; TaI, 34, my emphasis). The remainder of the book concentrates on the other human's face. In later publications, the difference between *autrui* and God is thematized, but the affirmation that the encounter with another human coincides with one's relation to God remains constant in his work. *How* do they coincide, since it is obvious that God and *autrui* are neither wholly nor partially identical?

Desire transcends economy by desiring the Other—not for satisfaction or consolation, not as a partner in love, but as the one whose face orients my life and thereby grants it significance. In desire I discover that I am not enclosed within myself, because I am "always already" to and for the Other: responsible, hostage, substitute.

Transcendence surpasses and sacrifices but also presupposes the economy of enjoyment, for how could I give without having experienced the pleasure of fulfillment? How could I live for Others (which also involves—at least some—dying for them) without myself enjoying the goods of the earth I want them to enjoy? Levinas is not a preacher of austerity; transcendence does not condemn the joys of life, but it prevents them from becoming absolute; it despises idolatry.

Transcendence, responsibility, substitution are there before we discover them. Consciousness and self-consciousness, the possibility of initiatives and choices comes afterwards. I am "always already" dedicated to the Other, chosen before I can agree or accept what I desire, transcend—and *am*! My own transcendence has started before my time, in a strange sort of "before," in a strange quasitime that does not belong to human history. Levinas calls it the diachrony or the anachrony by which an immemorial past is inserted into the time of history. "A past that was never present," a past more and otherwise past than any preceding time period—should we degrade these expressions by calling them "mere metaphors" for a timeless eternity? Are we, then, able to think of such an eternity without narrowing it down to a kind of presence without past or future, which would then constitute a finite presence? And what shall we propose as a nonmetaphysical translation of the "before" by which our always-already-being-responsible has become an inescapable "given"? Perhaps the temporal "metaphors" of "before," "past," the "pre-original," "diachrony," and "anachrony" can be neither translated nor dropped when we try to speak about transcendence—no more than the spatial metaphors of height and depth more frequently used in classical philosophy.

In any case, transcendence constitutes our ultimate passivity. Not being able to choose or reject my responsibility, I am therefore not free either to be or not to be responsible. The Good that chose me created me as already oriented, listening, looking up to the Other, obedient to the "law" of substitution. In this sense everybody begins by already being good. Of course, when I become conscious of the enormous burden responsibility puts on me, I can decide to refuse further obedience. The passivity and the patience of responsibility demands and presupposes the freedom of decision and initiative, as celebrated in modern philosophy, but it rejects the arrogance of an autonomy that begins with itself. Freedom cannot be originary in the strongest sense of the word; it is released by the "pre-original" compassion that comes from the anachronic Good.

Indeed, passivity is a passion. The subject's being possessed and obsessed by transcendence is concrete in sensibility and affection. Levinas breaks with a long tradition according to which what is ethical and truly human stems from an immaterial spirit that conquers or saves or informs the natural tendencies of corporeality. To be for the Other is neither a fight of the spirit against temptations of the body, nor obedience to a purely formal law of reason in ordering the chaotic material of emotions and drives. The human subject is first of all an animated and inspired body, the incarnate, affective spirituality of a passion for the Other.

Subjectivity is being sensitive, being touched, affected, already wounded by the Other's proximity. It is passion and affection, vulnerability and suffering. The classical duality of spirit and matter has been replaced by the duality of two affective modes of existence. Economy and transcendence, enjoyment and living for the Other need one another to be human, but the passion of responsibility governs their ethical concretization.

Passion is more than passivity; it is also suffering. Levinas's ethics does not promote heroic actions or loudly celebrated tragedies. The transcendence of "pre-original" passivity is lived in the humility of a devotion that is not planned but undergone. It both burdens and wears one out. The life of a hostage is tiresome and exhausting; one grows old by obedience. To live for Others is to suffer, and even to suffer gratuitously, without meaning, for nothing, because only such a passion unquestioningly realizes the nonchosen, entirely disinterested character of transcendent passivity.

The figure of the silent "servant of God" thus emerges from Levinas's phenomenology of sensibility and affection. That is the other possibility of human existence, over against the satisfied and boasting ego, whose sin is not hedonism but the attempted infinity of a monopoly.

Transcendence is no longer the ascent to a heaven of the ideal or the sublime, but the humble endurance of everyday life, touched, affected, burdened, wounded, obsessed, and exhausted. A human subject is an inspired body. It is moved by a breath that comes from an immemorial past. As respiration between this inspiration and the expiration of tiredness, old age, and death, a human life is breathing for Others, the repetition of obedience to the Good's command. The Good itself can neither be chosen nor contemplated, but only loved by accepting the responsibility for goodness in the world. This is at least a partial answer to the question asked above: How does my relation to *autrui* coincide with my relation to the Good?

This answer becomes more complex, however, when we bring in Levinas's distinction between the immediate Other (*you*) and the third (*they*). You and I are related through a double asymmetry, in which you are the highest for me, while I am the highest for you.[5] At the same time, all Others are present with and among you and me, as those to and with whom we ought to achieve justice in reciprocity. The triad of you, me, and the third, contains the human universe *in nucleo*. It could and should be developed in a theory of the intertwinings of intersubjectivity and sociality in ethics, politics, and history. For theology, Levinas's indications about the diachronic past that was never present and about the trace in which we live are precious but difficult. He uses many words which traditionally were reserved for God to describe the human Other. Terms like "invisible," "absolute," "absolution," "epiphany," "revelation," "separation," "liturgy," "height," and "highness" name the transcendent "character" of *autrui* and his/her proximity to God. For God, not much more than "*Il*" or "*ille*" is left over, but the abyss that separates God's "glory" from all powers of anonymity is immense. The Name is never pronounced, but always remembered. As inspired by the Good, we are in the trace of its passage. To love this inspiration is spirituality.

11

Passages

I f God is invisible, there is no phenomenology of God. We are told
"Do not make images of God!"; and yet we read "He made them in
his image." And what do the mystics mean when they describe their
experience of union with God through the symbols of fire, water, and
love? What do the psalms mean when they name Him Light, Fire, Rock,
Lord, Love?

There is a phenomenology of religion—there are even many, if we
include texts from the spiritual and mystic traditions among the phenomenological documentation of humanity's experience of its relation
to God. But God is never given. There has been no experience of Him, if
"experience" were to mean that He has presented Himself as the element
of a context or as a being surrounded by a horizon. God does not appear,
because He belongs to no context. He is neither a being Himself, nor a
text or context, nor even—in the phenomenological sense—a horizon.
God absolves Himself from all image, from all text and all ensemble or
chain of texts and contexts, from all "world" and even from the universe of
all possible worlds and languages. All forms of textuality—and all forms
of consciousness or language in general—are incapable of containing
Him. But where—and how—can we encounter Him?

Those voices are rare, and have always been rare, which know how
to speak of God in a way which is not only credible and tolerable, but
seriously sincere. Between the solemn language droning out the usual
predicates, and the hatred of everything greater than human freedom,
what word is pure enough to reply to the most urgent and radical of all
questions?

The voice of Emmanuel Levinas surprised us, coming as it does from
a past which is both philosophical and prophetic, and which still traverses
the theisms and atheisms of the European tradition from Plato to Hegel,
and from Spinoza to Nietzsche and their descendants. In interpreting
contemporaneity as the consequence of the long project of reason in its
Western form, this voice has awakened us to a more radical fidelity than

that of philosophy (and therefore also than that of theology). This fidelity is more ancient and less elitist, but also more present and urgent, as the recent manifestations of a widespread worry regarding the needs of the third and fourth world have shown. No romanticism nor verbal magic disturb the persistent purity of this voice which makes heard the vocation of a radical rectitude.

If an experience of God is impossible, if God is not the noema of a "religious" intention, then we cannot meet Him through the route of phenomenology. Still, it may be that this path leads to a point where God surprises the traveler, or comes to mind. Certainly human beings are drawn through desire and hope toward something ultimate and absolute. But however long we may aspire to an ultimate accomplishment and plenitude, something other than God always shows itself: a human figure as full or perfect as it can be. God can neither be a means, a part, nor the summit of human self-realization. Though it includes a free and vital plenitude, Glory is not identical with this. But must we therefore think the meaning of human reality as an ecstasy or exodus which liberates the human from itself? If concern with the self is replaced by concentration on a more originary orientation, wouldn't this change the desire for perfection into an effort to follow the movement of excess which, instead of filling the human essence, wears it down and empties it? If life culminates in plenitude, this can be due only to a profusion which is neither acquired nor deserved. Could it be that the only way to get into contact with God is a form of grace? But how could this be integrated into or appropriated by the human essence?

The first and ultimate desire is that Glory shines forth and spreads. To desire God is to love Him for Himself, to bless Him because He is God, because of his own Glory. And if the Glory comprises peace, freedom and life, that is admirable, a reason to give Him grace.

The desire for the absolute cannot be satisfied, because it intensifies and empties in the same measure to which it approaches the desired. The impossibility of repose, the essential restlessness comes perhaps from the fact that the loved itself is desirous and without rest. As incessant restlessness, desire delivers me from endless reflexivity without ultimate satisfaction. It sends me toward the Other which is outside and absolute. Desire orients me to the Other and carries me to Him. Concretely, that means that the existence of a human ego, by itself, has already begun to dedicate itself or to give—that is, to be good.

To desire is thus to tend toward that which we neither know how to produce nor to appropriate; it is to be ready to receive a meaning from that which has already destined the desirer, before even surprising her. Through desire we have always related to the absolutely Other (and in this sense been close to it), and waited to be surprised, shocked, amazed or criticized, accused, condemned, or pardoned. In coming to me without my ever having asked, the fact of the Other fills me with an ever-increasing hunger. Through a total commitment, which is independent of any acceptance, this fact creates me as a passivity which will continue to the point of suffering with no imaginable motive, or with a motive that seems pointless. Is useless suffering necessary so that the only meaning of an existence which is distinguished by its being-for-the-other-as-for-the-absolute may emerge?

The human Other is the surprise for which we can live and die without losing the meaning of existence. It is possible to suffer for Others without falling into a kind of masochism. Through transcendence toward the Other, life and suffering can have meaning, even if, taken separately as experiences or adventures of a solitary ego, they prove themselves useless. By imposing itself as a total exigency, the Other signifies deliverance from an obstruction, and thus becomes the guarantor of radical significance. The existence of Others reveals myself to myself as forever embarked—since a past which has never begun—on an endless exodus. The Other opens a future to me, in awakening me to a task too limitless to be accomplished. Death will end the possibility of obeying this demand, but will not rob the task of its meaning. To die for the Other holds the same significance as that of living for the Other: the being-for which makes humans right and good.

The Other who imposes itself on me has no more chosen this imposition than have I. Neither she nor I were present at any moment when the demands were born, before the commencement. We are bound by a commitment older than our own freedom or that of our ancestors (since they too came too late to participate in the origin of these demands). I never wanted that which started me out, and if I want it now or when I accept suffering, it is not through any initiative but is in response: the contrary reaction—a refusal—would destroy me as human. Inasmuch as it has meaning, human or spiritual, my life is older than I am. It is inspired. I am preceded by an election, by a call or a vocation which has made me human, that is, concern for the Other. Devotion moves me even before I have had time to wonder what I want to do or be. It outstrips and exhausts me; it thus ages me.

Responsibility, commitment, vocation, and election come only from the Other or from myself: they surprise me in the trace of a past which never appeared, a past which does not belong to the history of philosophers or historians. When the Other concerns me here and now, then, its presence confronts me with a command which is older than the existence of humans and their world—an injunction or vocation which precedes creation. This injunction is not a position or an element, nor a consequence of the human essence—of the Other or of me. On the contrary, it precedes the human essence. Does it not constitute alterity itself, the absoluteness itself of the Other? But in that case, would not the alterity of the Other consist in an ancientness before its existence and mine, before all human existence? The "presence" of the Other in the face which looks at me here and now, its arrival from a "time" before all time, is "at the same time" the absolute of a future more future than all futures. It is radically impossible to satisfy the demands of the command which speaks to me, arising from this face. The meaning of human existence precedes it by a past before history, and exceeds it by the future of an *eschaton* which cannot realize itself in the form of a now in the future. Here then is a "temporality" which refutes all theories according to which the real universe consists, in the final analysis, of substances which bear accidents. Here also is the beginning of a thought which lends justice to an inspiration exceeding the limits of historical "time."

That which regards me "in," "by," "through," "as," and "in the form of" a face or speech has preceded us, while presenting itself as a marvel which has never stopped taking place. Through the face and the word of the Other, God looks at me without becoming visible, in dedicating me to the service of the Other and in delivering me from the circle in which reflection confines me. It destines me to a work of justice where all that which seems to be valid will be consumed. My possessions and powers, my entire being, is put at the disposition of the Other by the passage of a past which no memory can revoke; a past which still traverses the entire time of human history in order to accomplish me. It comes to where I find myself, "come into the world" as sent and elected to speak, act, suffer, and die, living in a unique time, unable to rid myself of concern for the Other to whom I find myself compelled. God looks at me without showing Himself, but the unavoidable presence of the "pre-historic" demand which makes me human makes me "know" Him as the nonviolent initiator. He is revealed in the nudity of a vulnerable face, in the nonthreatening cry of those who, forgotten by the history of the world, pay the price of the great monuments, and of the grand actions perpetrated by a few heros in whom are concentrated political, ecclesiastical, and religious or quasireligious power. The enigmatic order or disorder of this God is the most serious, but also the least solemn and triumphant, the most humble and gentle that is. Its only sanction is the shame which flows from preferring a retreat into the self of an indifferent me. It is not a God of vengeance which has elected the me, because His "punishment" consists of my own betrayal of that which makes me human.

As a living body in the world I take possession of everything which concerns me up to the moment where the emergence of a face or a word refutes my solipsism by rendering it shameful. I discover my body—mouth and hands, eyes and legs, brain and heart—devoted to service. But does an existentiell (or even existential) contradiction not follow if it is true that I am constituted as a double adherence: active self-identification of an independent self *and* servant belonging to Others?

In implying that all that I am and possess should be put at the disposition of the Other, the concern for the Other seems to exclude the economy of an egocentric implantation. Emmanuel Levinas has shown that without this, we could neither think the independence of the self, the separation of the Other, nor transcendence. How am I capable of a generous proximity without fusion if I do not identify myself as an autonomous subject and agent of my own life? A certain hedonism— the joy of a world of my own—seems necessary in order that I am not completely absorbed into the world of others. Transcendence is structured like a separation in asymmetry, through which I lose my life more and more—"to what point"?

Hospitality is a clear example of the consent which makes my being-for-the-Other concrete, especially if the Other is unknown to me, a stranger, or if the Other is not liked by me, an enemy. But does this way of welcoming go far enough? Does it achieve the seriousness of the desired response which is suggested in an "after you"? If the demand revealed by the encounter is unlimited, it seems to condemn me to extreme poverty. Should we not give *everything*, house and clothes included, if Others need them? This would come down to displacing the poverty of the third and fourth world to the rich nations, instead of abolishing their deprivation, or diminishing it by uniting forces. In the name of reasonable justice, Hegel attacked the contradiction implicit in the custom of alms-giving: in helping the poor by gestures of charity we impoverish other people who, until then, had been doing well. Here is a substitution confined to the Hegelian framework of reasonable universality. Can it be solved without turning reason into a pure and simple enemy?

If substitution is the secret core of the self, should I not in fact prefer to be poor myself than to leave the poor in their condition? Is the accumulation of riches in order to benefit those who have less than oneself, or the capitalization of profits in order to distribute to the deprived, an economy which expresses the enigma of transcendence? Is that where the invisibly concerned Regard takes place?

If the self is "defined" by the *for* of the for-the-Other, we no longer have a world, nor even part of a world for ourselves; the self can reserve neither space nor time for itself. Everything in the self is offered, given; everything in it exhausts itself.

In order to give or to be given in a human way, we must not only have goods and provisions, but also education, feelings, so that we can encourage or console, humor, joy, etc. For how could we make Others happy or good if we were stripped of all that? And how could we not be stripped of it if we found no pleasure in participation in the life of the world? This is not egocentric hedonism, but rather the accomplishment of my being for the other. Should I not feel at home in the world and at peace with myself if I want to make another feel happy? But am I not expelled from my world by the Other's existence?

Can I ever feel at peace with myself? If I am defined as a devotion-to-the-Other, I encounter myself as a me which imposes itself on my capacity for initiative, on my freedom, on myself as will and free choice. I am thus an Other for myself. What I am obliges me, or rather "me" obliges my "I." Am I an Other for myself in a way comparable to the alterity of the Other? Am I for myself *as* ("an") other? Have I been entrusted to myself so that I must treat myself with respect, maybe even with a certain veneration? Did not a similar "experience" give rise to the conviction within traditional morality that there are "duties to oneself"? But do we not destroy all the Levinasian analyses of the relation to the infinity of the Other, and of the self as a hostage removed from the center, if we put the Other and myself on the same level, declaring that "we" are "both" subjects who have comparable or even equal rights? Does this not take us back to the social philosophy of a tradition which submits all singularities to the universality of general reason, by abolishing all reference to a transcendent Infinite or in conceiving it as (the) mere guarantor of universality?

If I am an Other for myself, this does not mean that my alterity is as important as that of Others, for this would contradict the asymmetry which reveals itself in the distance between that which I can demand of myself and that which I can impose on Others. It does not follow either that the dedication to the task which I am for myself would have more or less value or urgency than that which concerns Others. The dimension of alterity, which is that of the Infinite, does not allow such calculations; furthermore, the two directions of the dedication coincide, because the me which I must obey *is* the me which has always been devoted to Others. Conscience enjoins me not only to live and to suffer for the Other, but by this very enjoinder reveals to me that I must concern myself with the meaning of my own existence: this demand, then, relates also to me. I am entrusted to myself, not by myself, nor by the Other, but by a "past" before my birth, by a "choice" or a "vocation" which must coincide with the creation of my existence. I must love myself as I must love Others, though not quite in the same way.

The relation to myself we are discussing here is radically different from that which ties me to myself in the vital joy by which I place myself in the center of a hedonist economy. The terms of the two relations which tie my freedom to "myself" are not the same. In saying that I must respect or even love myself, I say that it is the "I" of the economy of pleasure which must serve the "me" which is like the Other for it, in that it gives it an ethical and therefore human sense. The "me-as-Other" resembles the Other without, however, being equal to it. "Me" reveals itself in a very different way, because it shows me no face and does not speak to me, except in a very metaphorical sense. The spontaneously egoist ego, which manifests its essence by constituting the world in the context of appropriation and power, the I which is the "subject" of "economic" autonomy, has not yet been awoken to the dimension of alterity. Its slumber prevents it from being surprised by the "me" in it; it does not yet have a human conscience. The "me" as Other for the economic I is the command to realize a meaning which comes from elsewhere, "through the door"; it is not found in the dimension of life, and cannot reduce itself to a vital element or aspect. As Other for myself, the devoted "me" in me surprises me and compels me. "I" am tied to "myself" by a relation of asymmetry: the accomplishment of the task (or obligation) that I am for myself is not the same as the self-realization of a spontaneous life which has not yet awoken to morality.

I have "always" been entrusted to myself, and this reveals a "voice" and a strange sort of "look" to me. The commitment to myself, in which I discover myself, is like a sending; already embarked, already en route, led by a concern which precedes me, oriented by the alterity which concerns me always and everywhere.

The parenthesis which I am closing here cannot be defended within the horizon of the Levinasian opus unless we can show that it is possible and necessary to love oneself as really Other, in a profoundly different way than the egoistic concern for myself—in a *disinterested*, and in that sense "unselfish," way. Such a love of the self entrusted to me is no less pure, and no less demanding than the true love of one's neighbor, for it should detach me from all self-love which is not obedience and offering. How can we avoid betraying or wounding the self, inasmuch as it is the presence of infinite compassion among humans? No one can think oneself possessor of such compassion, but it is not necessarily arrogant to think oneself called to the work and suffering which is inseparable from this compassion. When Saint Francis asked pardon of "brother body" for having mistreated it, was he aware of a lack of love toward the "self" which had been granted him for the glory of a free creation? If an unselfish self-love is possible, all kinds of having and power are measured by a kind of obedience: by a listening which hears what was said before birth. The me discovers a promise, or even the beginning of saintliness, in the echo of a voice ringing out from a past which has not resounded in any present.

But *how* must I be for the Other; what must I give or do for him? How can the (non)principle of an-archic responsibility unfold in an ethic which can guide human conduct?

As Levinas has underlined several times, it would be immoral to spurn the most elementary needs of Others in the name of an extravagant spiritualism. The structure of the one-for-the-Other would merely be an inconsequential abstraction, if it were not corporeal: to give, is to have hands. Substitution leads to suffering, when there is a shortage of terrestrial nourishment, and Others than the self are still able to partake. Concern for Others does not stop there, however; it extends at least as far as the meaning of their existence. This implies that we participate in their maturation toward freedom and responsibility for Others. Is this not the beginning of paternity, or of a fraternity which is as much "spiritual" (or ethical) as corporeal?

If the meaning of human existence comes from a goodness which precedes the human being, the heart of the human heart cannot be egoistic. As soon as we open our mouths to speak, we are vulnerable and available in the face of an infinite demand, the historical realization of which can only be expected from a timeless inspiration not bound to any present, past, or future. Even if selfishness perverts the Saying through which we put ourselves in the trace of a history more radical than the history of human works, we are still, by this Saying, open and devoted to Others. From beneath self-concern, a prophetic and indestructible testimony emerges. Is this the "image of God"? An invisible image, because it emerges from a meaning before all meaning; a donation before any giving has been desired or consented to? Then goodness—and gratitude as well as hope—would precede evil; it would prove stronger than it. Complete isolation would be impossible, since we discover ourselves as always already greeting the Other. The originary Good does not lie in good will or obedience, and this might explain why all moralistic admonitions ring so false. Just like obedience, crimes are preceded, borne and supported by a goodness older than all human initiative—a goodness not destroyed by any evil, and thus more futural than the historical battle between good and evil. Gratitude returns, beyond actions and works, to that which precedes their origin in a yesteryear without evil, where all good began. In admitting that hatred is not strong enough to conquer this anachronic good, we celebrate the creative origin. Even the most pointless suffering cannot kill hope, because hope is stronger than the alternation between life and death.

12

Becoming Other

For Emmanuel Levinas at his seventieth birthday

I

Self-evidence in the form of fulfillment by corporeal presence is no longer the supreme criterion of truth. Through temporality, the thing eludes us and we elude ourselves. Henceforth we can no longer count on a unifying regard that here and now gathers the past and the future to tell us what the true essence of this or that is *sub specie aeternitatis*.

Beneath those intentions that present or represent things to us, we discover other intentions or pre-intentions: other modes of contact, of approach, of submission, of attachment. The world holds us through these modes, and we cannot dominate it by a light that we master. We cannot escape the world, but the things of the world escape us. I elude myself, therefore: encumbered as I am by the massiveness of the world, the part of me that is constituted by pre-apparent attachments escapes me. These attachments are transmitted by a collective and private history formed by linguistic facts and traditional or revolutionary evaluations, by judgments that I did not invent or choose: and I cannot control the inexorable unfolding of this history.

The concretization of our concepts is no longer the sovereign synthesis of a luminous knowledge that redeems and sublimates shapeless matter by transforming it into a house of the self. The concept now comports too many uncontrollable and irretrievable "moments": all sorts of ways of belonging to time prevent us removing ourselves from the risks of an uncertain existence that lacks self-confident consciousness. If we accept the risks of an existence aware of its lack of self-possession, it is still possible that we gain some certitudes or quasicertitudes, not by way of our conquests or productions, but as if—after a long effort of thinking and seeking—they settle in on their own, come, in a way, from nowhere. A question of training, habit, fatigue? A lack of skeptical courage? Or—at least in certain cases and under certain conditions—implantation and rootedness coming from a depth more deep than that of a reasonable consciousness in search of a foundation?

Inasmuch as philosophy is the search for truth, it can no longer pave a royal path with conquests established once and for all. Nor, of course, can it employ negative triumphs, such as that of pointing out, in sovereign fashion, the presuppositions and structural obsessions of others, or that of unmasking others' ideologies from a marginal or removed perspective. Philosophy has become too mistrustful of itself to find redemption of some sort by accusing other consciousnesses that it might be in a position to judge. It feels too distracted by stories and histories, too dominated by the commotion of unconscious motives, and too inclined to a variety of lies, even in the course of the unmasking that it performs—especially when it enjoys the debunking. Philosophy knows that it is moved by many factors, at least some of which cannot be converted into "reasons," or even into givens of consciousness. It does not know, however, the extent of the influence these factors exert on consciousness and its power of decision. We could suppose that its action and thought are determined by still other elements than those detected by psychoanalysis, history, sociology and phenomenology. However, philosophical consciousness does not see these factors as pure obstacles which contradict freedom, but rather as an obscure dimension, from which it feeds. To philosophical consciousness, the very problem that opposes a suprasensible freedom to the determinisms in which it is caught, and the conception of the human economy as a conflict of intentions between two powerful finalities seem suspect. Instead of a combative dualism, it advocates an ethics according to which the main part of "spiritual" activity happens in a manner of admitting, supporting, modeling, and fashioning what comes to it from below or what happens to it through its corporeality and history.

The philosophical search for truth is rooted then in an existence that has always been tangled up, and for which contemplative retreat to an observation deck is impossible. Existence acts without entirely understanding itself, but its consciousness illuminates a surface of its own night. Through thought, life attempts to roll out the dawn, and, since the core of obscurity remains impenetrable, it tries in particular to discover how it must behave in relation to the obscurities and semi-obscurities of the world and of existence itself. In the end, then, even while not knowing what dominates my thoughts and my decisions, I can and I must ask myself what I will do with them. This remains the case even if a good response were to affirm that the value of my behavior is greater to the degree in which it is accompanied by the knowledge of its inevitability. Even then, my characterization of how things are issues from my own contribution: my effort to know who I am, what I am, and what the meaning of my existence is.

In order to say what philosophy is, therefore, it is necessary to indicate the ways in which different philosophers exist and what positions they take toward their own being-in-the-world. One theory of philosophical work presupposes an analysis of existence on the level of positions held, a level that we can call—in a very wide sense, as large as the concept of behavior—the "ethical" level. What are we saying here: the ontic comes before ontology? Should we pay attention to specific ways of existing before asking the question of the essence of being such as it is seen, thought, felt, or said by existing philosophers? Are we suggesting the primacy of a certain anthropology, the primacy of an existential concern: the concern of human existence whose own existence is the issue?

The mode in which existence lives is the discovery of a way (*hodos*). Moved by desire, it aims at knowledge, which is also self-knowledge, and thus knowledge of that which makes existence desiring.

Existence tries itself. What is at stake in its experimentation? Itself? Something else to which it can dedicate itself? The certainty of desiring is a nonknowledge of that which provokes it. If at this stage we speak of a desire for the absolute, the word "absolute" has no meaning unless it indicates the most desired, the extremely desirable, the absolutely desired, the supreme or the summit. But can we be sure that there is or there can be a compelling end that pushes us onto a path we cannot refuse to take? Is desire nothing more than an endless repetition of satisfactions which—while going beyond what was already attained—show themselves to be as little absolute as those which preceded them? What can put an end to the romanticism of nostalgic voyages? Is desire nothing more than fundamental discontent?

A phenomenology of existence seems possible as a description and analysis of "figures," manners, or "stages" that existence can go through in the course of its self-discovery. It would then be a theory of routes to take; a guide to the adventure of meaning.

If philosophy is the lighting which illuminates existence by lateral reflection, its essence is said only in a metatheory of this thought of the paths of existence. It is said in a "met-hodo-logy" reflecting on the partial self-consciousness through which existence is illuminated to itself along the way, and on the relations that this self-consciousness maintains with the non-conscious that it lives without encompassing. Philosophy as methodology would thus be the attempt to recover, by a second reflection, a part of the wisdom that is the result of the experiences and failures of the living and thinking subject.

If "methodology" cannot be separated from an elucidation of the paths with which existence becomes involved or can become involved, then it cannot neglect the diversity of concrete ways in which subjects live their belonging to the world.

The attempt to detect the modes of the subject beneath its con- sciousness and its involvements cannot reach an absolutely precultural layer preceding all language and all history. One reason that I elude myself is that the ways in which I perceive, sense, appreciate, and live the world, are impregnated with the molding that the traditions of my family and my community have given me, and with the history that I have already lived. I do not know everything that has happened by me and in me, nor everything that is at play in my ways of feeling, perceiving, desiring; I do know, however, that my past and the past of those who have formed me continue to live in my way of living. I desire to know what this past is and to consciously assimilate what makes me say, feel, want, in such a way.

A phenomenology of existence is therefore only possible as a *hermeneutic* of the historical concretization of the living and thinking subject. The ex- egesis of texts in which the summits of history and thought are crystallized is not sufficient, because such an exegesis does not capture the ways in which the individual reader here and now receives and assimilates texts. It neglects the originality of life and individual thought. Such an exegesis must be grafted onto an existential hermeneutic of strictly individual progression: but how to express "haecceity" other than by describing a large variety of real and possible situations, attitudes, specific paths, and perspectives?

As for the hermeneutic of traditions, such as these appear in our documents and monuments, the need that we feel to turn our attention to them does not necessarily mean that these are living traditions. As long as we continue them in a (re)creative way, they are self-evident, and the problem of their (re)actualization does not even arise. Once the power of traditions has diminished, and the community rooted in them begins to consider them as a framework and as values that it *must* live, then it seems that the community feels the need to rescue them from imminent drought and death: it returns to the source from where formerly issued the desirable spring. Certain hermeneutics are perhaps symptoms of the dying agony of a religion or of a long philosophical history. A return to the past is a promise only if it succeeds in giving new life to what was said and done formerly, or if it creates something new from the past. But something new that is not just fashion presupposes a creative power, a breath to animate dry bones.

Again, ethics appears as a condition of all quests for truth. To give (back) the voices of truth to ancient texts, the reader must already be qualified for the work of truth. In this wide sense, ethics precedes the hearing of language.

But from where can a spirit come to us, a spirit that would not only lend the reader the necessary quality, but would at the same time give meaning to texts? What is it that orients and inspires good reading? Is it not the same thing that orients existence: "the Good" that directs the progression of life if this life is good?

"The Good" guides us without us being certain of it, however. The subject that loves it can control neither her own access to the Good, nor the rules or the conditions of possibility of this access. Therefore, progression toward the Good—and, in philosophy, the search for truth through which the Good reveals itself to thought—is characterized by a certain modesty.

Methodology cannot master what it is that orients existence and thought before all reflection on the essence and possibility of these. Good taste in philosophy is expressed by humility. We can never prove that we are on the good path; belonging to the history of the good is expressed not by the evidence of some views or truths, but by a nonilluminated tranquility that affirms: "Thus it is as it should be."

II

The first stage that the soul goes through in search of the Good is that of egoism and pleasure. This is not a simple attitude that we can embrace or conquer, but an ontological structure constituting the subject in its substantiality and separation.[1] It is therefore in a certain way the support and condition of all the subsequent stages that existence can live. The subject is not itself capable of stopping the circular movement of concern for its own growth to plenitude. Its needs push it toward a natural union of absorption and abandon. Satisfaction is a fulfillment of time, but when the echoes no longer resonate, repetition takes over: pleasure of life, joy in presence, fulfillment and repose of the self-evident.

The world of technique and technology can be understood as an immense reproduction of nature in function of our needs. To consume, produce, work, dominate, organize, study, forecast, plan—all this chain of activity makes of the world a framework and a system of satisfactions. Sometimes we oppose art and contemplation to this setup. Still, understood as ways of letting the essence of things, works, landscapes, or sentiments be, contemplation and art are also figures of the joy that the subject takes in laying out the world around itself and in making the world its natural milieu.

The methodology that reflects pleasure as it becomes philosophical is content with the evidence of a shadowless noon and uses the schema of a time that joins, by the arch of a great becoming, an absolute and primitive beginning to an absolute and ideal end. The motto "become what you are" is reflected in its method by the demand for a teleological recovery of all the pre-evident past that an archeology would have to search through. Even while recognizing that the subject eludes us through language, the unconscious and history, we continue to hope and work for a full self-possession, including the clarity of a concrete self-consciousness.

Few philosophers now think that absolute knowledge is an historical possibility. Still, the postponement of the end of history does not really change the fundamental presupposition of a provisional opacity that we are to clarify by progressive illumination without end. In this perspective, postmodern writers who bring to light the ways in which the subject is linked and constrained only complicate the modern schema of an I that is equal to itself and for which life consists of self-realization in autonomous unfolding. By the detour of its concentration on a written past, this hermeneutic of existence restores forgotten or distorted meanings. Desire remains nostalgia. It is lived as a radical and sublime need for plenitude. Thought is, in Hegelian language, a belly,[2] and all conquest is compensation.

The Other halts the movement through which the I tries to unfold. Ethics is not the search for happiness, even a sublime and generous happiness. The fact that the I cannot be equal to itself is not due to the endless postponement of its concrete identity with itself; it is due to a more radical impossibility. The attempt to unfold all of my potentialities is contested by another ontological structure more ethical than that of initial egoism. I do not belong to myself and I elude myself, not because of preconscious opacities or because of a historical burden that I have to integrate positively, but because my essence consists in a being *toward* and *for the Other*. From the very beginning, I am decentered from myself, passive by a more profound passivity than the simple opposite of activity. I carry the Other in me and discover myself as related by a profound inequality. I am carried away by time and animated by an inspiration that I will never be able to recapture. This makes me aware of a "not-enough" and of a "more!" inscribed in me without my having chosen it.

The Other commands me without oppressing me. But he makes me suffer by urging me to endlessly detach myself from the desire to return to myself as ravenous center of the universe, avidly utilitarian, artistic, and practical. The sudden appearance of the Other changes everything, even the project of my voyage toward the truth—a project that is revealed to the extent that my thought turns toward the Good. Henceforth the Good is revealed as that which shines and commands in the face of the Other. If I refuse the responsibility by which the Good directs me, I go around in circles without ever being able to break the cycle of egological repetition. Why and how would I still want to make progress? What sense is there now in speaking about different stages of the history of a soul, different levels or degrees, of voyages through deserts and nights toward a promised land, of ascensions that—through horrible anxieties—would lead to the silence of God? Here and now is the place. Here is the opportunity to be what I am good at. The absolute is attained by an endless devotion, not by admiration of the Good in itself nor by jubilation before the ocean of the Beautiful. The only progress, the only thing that remains to be desired, seems to be the continuation of this humanism of the Other.

What does this reversal mean for the "method" of thought that my exodus here tries to clarify? The subject can no longer trust the evidence that gives her the feeling of being at home in a consistent vision. She is in her place, in her natural setting, inasmuch as she accepts to be concerned for an Other instead of concentrating on the fulfillment of her self. The Good clears a path for truth when the subject does not revolt against the passivity by which she precedes her own consciousness.

Is this passivity an experience? It precedes all forms of presence that can satisfy the subject by a full meaning measurable and enjoyable by this same subject.

The value of this new implantation is no longer measured by fidelity to the promise that we have always been, nor by the degree of accomplishment we have attained. The desire for full presence, hidden beneath a thought eager to establish the unity of archeology and teleology, is stopped by a *here and now* that has its meaning in itself. It no longer seems necessary to look behind the horizons of a future that will not take place. The sublime worry of *eros* makes room for the effort to be here and now what I have been since the immemorial time before my birth: "yours" and "at your service." To become what I am, I have only to accept this "to you" which co-constitutes my self. Instead of great achievements, I have only hands to offer you bread for today.

In concerning myself with what fits (and thus benefits) the Other, my thought is no longer limited to the search for my own truth. The Other needs meaning as much as bread. Philosophy is called to become a thought that is offered to the Other in order that she discover meaning. Philosophic discourse is ministry.

When I think for the Other, I raise myself above my rational subjectivity in order to produce a certain form of universality, without, however, skimming over all human beings with a form of speech that is valid for all. Sincerity confines me to the limits within which I can see, feel, want, and say; the fact of directing myself toward this Other individualizes the word that I offer. The concrete universality of my speaking can rid my ministry of ever-threatening imperialism. My words are rhetorical, in that they cannot abstract from the one or ones to whom they are addressed. Instead of a brilliant lesson explaining (the) all, my words do not transcend the space between my interlocutor and myself, but the interval of this proximity is infinitely wider than grand views on the union of heaven and earth.

The responsibility of a word, in addressing itself to someone, is not said into empty space: it can do good or harm. The art of the philosopher comports an exact mixture of nonviolent force and liberating modesty.

The Other provides my existence with meaning. The radicality of being-toward-the-Other breaks the monotony of pleasurable repetition. Is the discovery of this meaning—the discovery of what "really" is at stake in existing humanly—a new experience? Is it a new kind of accomplishment or completion? Can we interpret the ethical attitude as a stage in which human desire has become a desire for the true good that not only commands, but promises? *Or* must we reject the schemas of a genetic phenomenology as still too dependent on a teleology of the I?

The fact that existence is characterized by two ontological structures that seem to be contradictory suggests a dialectical language. The anarchic passivity of the for-the-Other does not dispel the profound egoism that dominates the subject even up to its irrepressible thirst for salvation. How can I live these two temporalities at the same time?[3] Should I divide my life into two times: one time for blossoming and for joy, and another time for the dedication that makes me suffer by the diminishment of my own importance? Half-way egoism? Terrible alternative: either I am guilty of absconding—even if only provisionally—from the goodness that constitutes my subjectivity, or I can have pleasure only when I am alone.

A synthesis by subordination seems impossible, since a hedonism that would merely be a condition or instrument of ethical responsibility would have to empty itself of everything that makes it desirable for itself. Such an asceticism seems deceptive. Pleasure as such would be evil par excellence, or else I should restrain the ethical demands that constitute my self and give me meaning.

The only way out of this aporia seems to be through the possibility of a salvation that is no longer feverishly concentrated on the self, but which instead renounces the self to the exact extent that concern for the self prevents the *Fürsorge* for the Other.

Outside the framework of an asceticism centered on my own growth or harmony there can be no prohibition against joy other than that which flows from the law obliging me to live for the Other. If I take this obligation seriously, will I have any time or energy or concentration left?

Is a *particular* concern for one's own salvation perhaps compatible with an *absolute* attention to the well-being of the Other? It seems that there is at least one "experience" in which the "salvation" of the Other and a certain "salvation" of oneself are identical: the joy that a subject experiences because of the well-being of the Other. "I am happy that things are going well for you." Happiness because of another's happiness: "I'm pleased about your being fine." Is it possible and nonegoist to embrace in this spirit what the Other needs and desires? Can her well-being coincide with mine? If recognition, hope, gratitude, and joy arise for me from my neighbor's good and happy life, that does not seem to exclude my being "fulfilled" at the same time and because of the Other's "success." If my pains contribute to your well-being, I do not feel mutilated by a law of self-centered ascetism. There can even be contentment in my sacrifice.

An interpretation that would understand dedication as a means or as a stage on the way to my own happiness would lead us back to the hedonism—be it noble or sublime—of circular concern. But the exodus to which I am called does not absolutely forbid entry to a land of milk and honey. We can always deflect the promise from its altruistic meaning by displacing the attention due to others to the singularity of our own concerns. This ambiguity of the promise comes perhaps from the fact that an individual's *true* salvation coincides with the salvation of the Other. This statement can only be affirmed by someone who loves, however.

To live for the Other—to live for after my death and thus to overcome the extreme anxiety concerning my existence—makes me escape vain repetition by the sacrifice of a *specific kind of* concern for myself.

But the concern to do what should be done, to achieve what I am for, and the happiness that comes from being in my place, in the place that is assigned to me by that which beckons me in the face of the Other, do not seem to oppose themselves to the being-for-the-Other that makes me *unique*, and makes me *one*. If I carry the Other in me in such a way that his suffering pains me and that his joy fills me with joy, then there arises an identity of perspective and desire that does not comprise the equalizing overview. In identifying myself with the radical inequality that refers me to the Other, I identify myself with that which is (the) good for him. If he is lucky enough to be happy, I am happy. If he must suffer, I endure it with him. If I have to suffer for him—and, as denucleated, I am necessarily sacrificed—I am content. It is precisely that which gives me the opportunity to realize my meaning.

The Law does not forbid me to be happy nor even to be happy because of my happiness, but it forbids me from demanding happiness (my happiness is always something that comes to me as a grace) and from concentrating my attention, my tension, and my concern on my own joy. Why? Because in centering myself around my own existence, I steal time and attention from the other person. The law does not promise me the plenitude of fulfillment, but it gives me a meaning and even an implantation— on condition, however, that I do not become attached to it.

To live in the observance of the Law is worth it, but this worth, which makes me content, is not constituted by this contentment. According to Eckhart, love is much more a recompense than an obligation. For through love, I rejoice in what the other receives, does or lives, despite the harm that makes me suffer. Still, the reason for love is not in the joy that it procures; this is only a sign of its abundance.[4]

To offer bread or money to the Other presupposes that I take from what is my own. "The bread of one is the death of another," and vice versa. With separation, conflict is inevitable: one must share. However, if I offer a word, a thought, or a book to help the Other discover what "all that" is good for, to find a meaning in life, suffering, or history, the difference between my wording and the Other's understanding does not prevent the establishment of communication, thanks to a single meaning that unites our versions of this meaning. The master of thought who addresses himself to his visitor with benevolence, or the person who, distressed by the unhappiness of the Other, tries to comfort her with some light, cannot satisfy the need for bread that the Other feels. This is not possible just with thoughts or friendship. But neither can anyone be content with the satisfaction only of alimentary needs. Far from being too spiritual, the dimension of typically human meanings that opens from this is absolutely necessary for human being. The question arises, however: What must I look for and offer my neighbor to really help her? The gesture of the offer is not enough to make her happy, nor is all content which she merely *needs*. What is the end or the meaning of her desire that I must take to heart? Just to repeat to her what I have discovered for myself ("You also, you must live for the Other") is not enough, because then the question arises for her again: What should I hope and do for my neighbor after giving her what he needs? What is the dimension toward which the desire of the Other leads the ethical subject? Does responsibility oblige us to prolong our exodus toward a subsequent end that does not abolish but confirms and preserves the absoluteness of ethics?

III

For humans, the human is absolute but not the supreme. The manner in which the Other arises before the one, and in which the one approaches the Other, effectuates transcendence. The "tone" or the "color" of concrete behavior reveals by what "force" this behavior is moved and by what "spirit" it is animated. Inspiration testifies to that from which we live or to the one by whom we are obsessed.

A prophetic word that summarizes many others translates radical responsibility in the following terms: "Love your enemies, pray for your persecutors; thus will you be the son of your Father who is in heaven, because He makes His sun rise on the wicked and the good, and He makes the rain fall on the just and the unjust. . . . You therefore, you will be perfect as your celestial father is perfect."[5] A more developed parallel of this text replaces the word "perfect" (*teleios*) with "compassionate" (*oiktirmon*): "Love your enemies, do good and give without expecting anything in return. . . . You will be the son of the Most High, for He is good to the ungrateful and the wicked. Show compassion, as your father is compassionate."[6]

Perfection is not in the full unfolding of a subject who progresses toward the realization of his own possibilities. It is rather in the goodness that, without regard to what is good for me, asks itself and gives what is necessary to the other person, without asking what it can mean for me, even if the Other's concrete life damages or diminishes me. Through compassion, we are what we should be; we are what in the end we always are; we are "like God."

A certain master says: The highest work that God has carried out in all his creatures, is compassion [*Barmherzigkeit*]. . . . In all that God has

ever done, the first eruption [*der erste Ausbruch*] is compassion; not
the compassion that consists in forgiving sins, or in someone pitying
another; the master means rather: the *highest* work that God carries out
is compassion. . . . The work of compassion is so intimately allied to the
essence of God, that—although truth, abundance and goodness name
God . . . —the *highest* work of God is compassion. This means that God
puts the soul in the highest and the purest that it can receive: in the
expanse, the sea, an unfathomable sea; there the compassion of God is
carried out.[7]

The beginning and the deepest depth of all creation is therefore
a compassion that precedes all sin, deeper even than the abundance of
goodness that cannot be contained and that has been characterized by
the expression *diffusivum sui*. Compassion is not only emanation nor even
giving, but donation-despite-everything: *grace*. God created us through
compassion . . . a strange manner to act, that contrasts sharply with the
heroism of great lives and the aristocracy of a harmonious humanity—
humble incognito through which "the heavens" prove to be completely
terrestrial. To live and suffer humanly with and for the Other, this is how
God realizes fidelity to the unique world of human being. To the extent
to which humans act in this way, God is alive.

To live in the trace of God, and even "like" God, could this somehow be
the life of God on earth? Could He live in the *manner* in which certain
human lives shine? Is it thinkable that a certain way of fulfilling existence,
a humanism of the human Other, not only testifies to an immemorial past
out of which all true people are born, but also expresses and realizes an
even more profound union and communion? Could we risk the thought
that the life of just persons ultimately coincides with that of God in the
history of the world?

Yet, how can we avoid being pushed by this mystical communion to
fall back into magical forms of participation? The submersion of human
beings, along with trees, animals, and stars in the ocean of the divine,
would surely kill the core of all ethics. How can we respect both the
separation of the ethical relation and the no less certain truth that desire
terminates neither in me, nor in any other finite being, nor even in the
"more" without end of moral responsibility? Is there a way of sympathizing
with the texts of the mystics that does not diminish the absoluteness of
the human Other, but honors him as "son of God"?

Long before Spinoza, Eckhart said that life wants nothing more than to
live, to be what it is. It does not aim at becoming, because it has no need,

no concern, not even with itself. It is pure abundance, fire, goodness *without reasons* or end: "If someone, for a thousand years, asked Life: 'Why do you live?' if it could reply, it would say nothing other than this: 'I live *because* I live.' This comes from the fact that Life lives from its own ground and flows from what is proper to it; that is why it lives without why [*ohne Warum*]." In the same way, the person who lives the true Life acts without why: "If someone asked a true person, for whom action arises from its own ground: 'Why do you do your works?' if this person replied correctly, he would say nothing other than: 'I act because I act.' "[8] In acting in the way of the Father, humans live in truth. Egoistic concern is forgotten by a nonsentimental and disinterested compassion. The cycle of return upon itself is broken by a straight and direct line that links me to the Other.

Is the exteriority of the Other opposed to another interiority than that of the egological universe? According to Eckhart, the just person depends on nothing exterior, for she no longer has any interest. She does only what she is since always, since before her birth. Her motivations no longer come from outside, nor even from what she was able to discover or choose. Can we still speak here of a will? Even the thirst for God, the desire to attain him or to rejoice in his presence no longer plays a role:

> When humans procure or take something from outside themselves, it is not good. We should not grasp and conceive of God as being outside of ourselves, but as my own and as what is *in* my self. Furthermore, we should not serve for some why, neither for God's sake nor for our own honor, nor for the sake of something exterior to my self, but uniquely for that which is my own being and my own life.[9]

> Here, the ground of God is my ground and my ground is God's ground. I live from what is proper to me, as God lives from what is proper to him. . . . Out of this innermost ground, you must do all your works without why. I tell you in truth: so long as you do your works for the kingdom of heaven or for God or for your eternal salvation—i.e., for something exterior—you are not really doing well.[10]

> The supreme and extreme thing that man can renounce, is that he renounces God for God's sake. Saint Paul renounced God for the sake of God; he renounced everything that he could take from God and . . . everything that God could give him. . . . . When he renounced, he renounced God for God's sake, and God *stayed* with him in the way in which God is in himself, not in the mode in which he is received or conquered, but as the essence that God is in himself."[11]

In being disinterested in her own needs, the subject's desire overcomes the teleological project by the affirmation of a freedom in which she no longer identifies herself with *anything*. Henceforth, she no longer clings to any reality or figure, language, history, or symbol. No manner of being can capture her love, not even the sublime modes under which the absolute reveals itself "because God is in no way either this or that."[12] Eckhart does not hesitate to say that such a person is "equal to nothing": "Only those who are equal to nothing, are equal to God."[13] Without this equality to anything, without this emptiness of self, God cannot act, for God is without modes.

> There where the image of some creature enters (in you), God and his entire God-head must go. There where this image goes, God enters. God desires so much that you get out of yourself according to your creatural mode of being, it is as if all His happiness consisted in that. And so, dear friend, how can it harm you if you allow God that God be God in you? Get completely out of yourself for God's sake; then God gets completely out of himself for your sake. When the two get out of themselves, what remains is a simple one.[14]

Thus the end of self-attachment, consequence of the right turn toward the Other, would be—thank God—the grace of an intimacy more profound than the rejoicing of a reflective consciousness: the tenderness of someone who prays.

While remaining a creature, without fusion or confusion, the subject does not transcend his relations with the Other, the Others, God. He rather exerts these relations in the (com)passion of the "as God" that animates him, without flaunting itself before his eyes. The part of the light or glow which falls to him surfaces as an excess of wisdom. One of the conditions that this wisdom demands—and here is a consequence for "methodology" as "science of the way"—is that thought holds itself in the attitude of one whose regard, instead of dominating the entire universe, turns toward the One who connects without us knowing how. Hope and gratitude henceforth orient and tune philosophy. Thinking has then fallen in love with a wisdom that befalls as grace. Or: to think and to pray are not that different.

Il y a and the Other:
Levinas vis-à-vis Hegel and Kant

Although Levinas's work almost constantly quotes or alludes to Heidegger's thought, it is obvious that Hegel's philosophy, more than Heidegger's, is a paradigmatic case of the "totalitarian" philosophy that Levinas attacks in *Totality and the Infinite* and elsewhere. Another of the philosophical classics who seems to be present in the background is Kant, whose conception of the good and of the human essence as an "end in itself" shows affinities with Levinas's descriptions of the Other's highness. Thorough confrontations of Levinas' work with those of Kant and Hegel are desiderata that have not yet been fulfilled.

This chapter offers a few hints for such a project. In the first section, I compare Levinas's understanding of Being, as expressed in his analysis of *il y a*, with Hegel's analysis of Being and nature, while the second section shows to what extent the nonphenomenality of Levinas's "Other" and Kant's conception of human dignity are similar and different. In a short epilogue, I reflect on the difference between Levinas, on one side, Kant and Hegel, on the other, with regard to the relations between ethics and politics.

Hegel's Being and Nature

For Hegel, "Being" is the minimal determination of thought and (because thought and reality are one and the same) of all reality. No thing, either actual or possible, can be conceived of or be what and how it is, if it has not the (onto)-logical structure of a being. Being is, thus, the most universal ontological category. It is almost nothing; it is certainly no thing, because a thing presupposes many other determinations as well. Being is as much as nothing: it is not any one of all the predicates that can be attributed to a subject. Concerning all realities and possibilities, however, we must say that they "are . . . ," for example, that they "are" a reality or a possibility. The copula affirms this "is" or "are"; it covers all beings—but a being is already more than the determination *Being* through which it is. Because of its extreme abstractness, "Being" is empty and therefore open to all possible determinations. It is the quasidetermination of indeterminateness, of pure transparency, of the nothingness of an abstract openness in which all varieties of things and nonthings can manifest what they are. Being can be conceived of neither as a predicate nor as the subject of a sentence. As copula it cannot exist except in something else (a nonbeing) in which it is united to (other) determinations. It includes, therefore, that which it is not: *non-Being* is its necessary complement. In order to be freed from its (almost) nothingness, Being needs a determination that is an anti-(quasi)determination: its opposite. Of course, non-Being is also not able to be what it is (a "non-is"), unless it relies on its opposite (Being), of which it is the inseparable complement. Being and non-Being cannot be (and not be) what they are (and are not) unless they pass continuously into one another. The unity of Being and non-Being is their ceaseless changing into their opposite: an endless movement of *becoming*, which—just as Aristotle's *dynamis*—is the ontological core and secret of movement and materiality. Nothing can escape from the texture woven by Being and non-Being as they become what they are not and therefore become what they are. There is no other dimension and no other "stuff" of which a being could be made. If the universe has meaning, it *must* be found somewhere within this texture or in the whole of it. Nothing is, unless it can be developed from this fundamental text.

Hegel's logic is the attempt to show that the universe of thought and Being (in which "thought" and "Being" are two names of one and the same idea) is nothing but the complete unfolding of a minimal thought. The movement through which Being starts its transformation into its opposite and its adventures following from this first negation could not take place if Being were not animated by a life that is virtually as wide and strong as the universe. Being is the first mark and mask of an inspiration, which, as Hegel wants to show, is the absolute. Being is the first incognito of absolute spirit, which, in its full development, reveals itself to be the fully self-conscious insight into the structures and contents of the totality of beings. The texture of Being and non-Being is the neutral light in which the spirit presents and understands all finite beings as moments of its own appearance. This light produces its own shadows by negating its own blinding positivity, in order to reflect and enjoy itself in the darker exterior of a perfect mirror. The first, still very indeterminate determination of thought produces the horizon within which everything becomes an object of circumscription and definition, whereas every definition and delimitation passes immediately into its opposite, until the horizon of totality is reached by a complete unfolding of all possible determinations, which are . . . and are not . . . and move . . .

The Infinite itself—the breath of inspiration—appears within *and as* the horizon. In fact, it appears twice: once as a being that is not finite but is the ground, the source, the substance, the essence, the telos, and the idea of all finite beings; and a second time as the union of all finite beings with that first infinite which, if it were isolated from the finite, would itself be a finite being. The light of the ultimate horizon coincides with the appearance of the totality of all beings manifesting the Infinite as their ground and subject. The infinite manifests itself as the spirit's throwing light upon its mirror and upon itself and contemplating its own face in this circularly reflecting light. The concrete Infinite knows that the onto-logical totality is identical with its own inner life. The triumph of knowledge is the full expression of the idea, which is the core and secret of the totality. As thought, in which thought and Being are conceptually one, the idea contains all realities and all the lights and shadows of which they are composed. It is the womb in which everything breathes and moves according to the rhythms of its categorical diversifications. There is no elsewhere, nor any margin from which the idea could be looked at; according to its own universal law of self-negation, the idea must transcend the level of the onto-logical and realize itself concretely as exteriority.

The exteriority of the idea is *nature.* The passage from the onto-logical realm to the level of its most elementary concretization constitutes the first form of concrete phenomenality. What the idea gains by this self-expression it pays for by a loss of coherence and light: natural exteriority is the dark and scattered side of the idea, the side of its not-being what it is, the chaos of its almost-death. Although the light and the life of the idea are strong enough to submit and "sublate" its own chaotic night, its nightside must affirm, strengthen, and organize itself in order to give the idea its possibility of a mirroring and self-conquering autonomy.

The most primitive level of nature is pure exteriority, without any interiority. The ongoing drama of the Infinite's self-realization separates the extremes of its pure, ideal light from the restless darkness of a faceless "prime matter," unidentifiable because of its ever-changing (non-)nature.

Il y a

When Levinas considers Being under the name of *il y a*,[1] he does not think of an abstract categorical structure, as thematized in the beginning of Hegel's (onto-)logic, but of the most elementary form of being real or being there, which resembles the lowest level of Hegel's "nature." The *il y a* precedes the formation and appearance by which nature organizes and manifests itself. Even space and time, insofar as they include certain rules of figuration, are still hidden in this most primitive "stirring" (*grouillement*) and "rumbling" (*bruissement*). The phrase *there is* points to the dimension of a completely contourless and dangerous protoworld, the anonymous underworld of faceless monstrosity, a chaos in which there are no facts, no data, no givens, a neuter without any giving, the contrary of generosity. The *il y a* burdens and bothers us, but at the same time it seduces us by the magic of its invitations to self-abandonment and dispersion. Its dangers cannot be mastered completely, but we build a wall against its irruption by pursuing the fulfillment of our needs through the enjoyment of the (more determinate) elements (TeI, 82–142; TaI, 110–68).

The Being that Levinas describes—in a gesture that reminds us more of Sartre's *être* than of Heidegger's *Es gibt*—is rather similar to Hegel's concept of *nature* as pure exteriority, which is exterior even to itself. As the first concretization of the interplay of abstract Being and non-Being passing ceaselessly into each other, Hegel's "nature" accepts and rejects all the contours of all beings, having no form of its own. As a sort of prime matter in movement without end, it is certainly not a totality, but rather pure dispersion or materiality.

The allusions to the formless *tohu wa bohu* of Genesis 1 are apparent, but not inappropriately Levinas also uses the Greek *apeiron* to characterize its unbounded indeterminacy. Levinas's phenomenology of the *il y a* does not constitute a complete philosophy of nature, not even of materiality as such. Nature, vitality, and matter pre-suppose more determinacy than the formless and limitless anonymity of "Being's" *il y a*; they belong to the realm of the natural elements which can be enjoyed because of their enjoyable qualities and determinate suggestions. Water invites us to drinking or swimming; fire illuminates and warms; the earth permits us to stand, walk, build, and dwell; the air elicits breathing, and so on. The elements can also harm or threaten us, however. Nature is ambiguous.

The dimension of the elemental gets form and figure in myths about beneficial and threatening gods and demons. The threat of primordial dispersion cannot be entirely overcome in the economy of elementary satisfaction; the laws that rule this economy are still too ambiguous, too mythical, too enthusiastic (i.e., too full of gods). A sober, unambiguous orientation is needed for determining the human meaning of nature.

What Levinas must reject most of all in Hegel's theory of Being and nature is the thesis that the Infinite reveals itself within and as the realm of the anonymous in which Leviathans are at home. As the dimension of magic forces, mythic gods, and delightful enthusiasms, nature cannot reveal the Infinite, since this does not exist as an idea or spirit whose exteriority realizes the oscillation between Being and non-Being. Levinas's rejection of Hegel's conception of the relationship between the finite and the Infinite is clearly expressed in his attack on Heidegger's attempt at resuscitating the gods of Greece through a retrieval of Hölderlin's evocations. It is easy to adapt Levinas's criticism of Heidegger to Hegel's way of looking at nature and culture as the expressions of a spirit that unfolds its life through the hierarchy of stones and stars, plants, animals, and people, states and history.[2]

Can we defend Hegel against this criticism? According to his system, the natural exteriority of the idea should not be isolated from its interior light; if it were isolated, nature would indeed be an ungodly, monsterly chaos without any meaning, structure, value, and light, but isolation is one of the greatest mistakes you can make in philosophy. Could Hegel not object that Levinas does not avoid a dualistic view, according to which Being or *il y a*, as stuff of which the world is made, is essentially unholy and unredeemable.

Levinas might respond that we are not obliged, nor are we able to have an answer to every question—or even that we are not allowed to ask every possible question. But such a response would make him weak in the eyes of any thinker who cannot help reflecting on all answers that seem to imply a contradiction or a gap. A more philosophical answer would be that Being, in the sense of "there is," can indeed be redeemed from its chaotic character—and Levinas has shown how; but it is not altogether certain that he thereby fully answer's Hegel's question (which does not necessarily mean that his partial answer is bad, because it is not certain that Hegel's question is a perfect one). Approached from the perspective of our economic and hedonic existence, the anonymous stirring of "prime matter" comes to the fore in the contours of various elements capable of satisfying human needs. The *there is* receives a meaning from our involvement in the elemental. Chaos has then changed into a medium which we enjoy by bathing in it, possessing it, and transforming it through labor into a human world full of homes, tables and tools (cf. TeI, 100–25; TaI, 127–51). An existence exclusively devoted to needs is ambiguous, however; it may bow to the gods of nature, but it can also follow another, more spiritual orientation. Instead of an inspiration from within, organizing by its breath the living totality of one "great animal,"[3] another inspiration is possible, coming from outside nature and its play of Being and non-Being: the breath of the Other—a silent whisper—shakes the foundations of a world based upon the needs of nature. The meaning of Being remains undecided, as long as that whisper is not heard. The orientation of a natural life must be subordinated to our relationship with some Other, which cannot be located in the dimension of Being and non-Being.

Levinas's answer to Hegel's question implies that Being and nature do not possess their meaning in themselves. They cannot be isolated from human existence and history as oriented by a certain transcendence. The meaning that saves them from absurdity lies in morality.

The Other According to Levinas and Kant

The orientation brought into being by the emergence of the human Other, the Other's self-presentation which is not just "being there," cannot be described, defined, or known as one of the many phenomena within nature, world, or history. The Other cannot be arranged among, and connected with, other sorts of phenomena, nor is it a new sort of light within which the phenomena would appear. The "being there" of another is not a horizon which permits us to synthesize all other beings. Such a horizon would still presuppose that the ego takes advantage of it in order to collect and comprehend all other beings for an overarching perspective. The Other would then be the source of transparency within which everything can be what it is. The Other would take the place and function of Being, and the ego would remain the center of an enlightened universe, the hero of a theory. But this is not the way in which the Other's epiphany is produced. It is not a source of light, throwing beams and shadows, but an inexhaustible and incomprehensible claim. The Other obliges me to give a straightforward answer different from knowledge. I "know" where to go and how to behave, I have an "idea" of the demands put on me, but I do not have an insight into the infinite claim that directs me, because the Infinite is neither an object nor a noema of my consciousness. The answer to our questions about the meaning of Being and history and the "end" of our desire can be discovered only through a moral and *pretheoretical* relationship with the Infinite.

The structure of our relationship to the Other reminds us of the way in which Kant reopened and "saved" the dimension of metaphysics through morality. The spatiotemporal order of phenomena permits us to acquire knowledge of them but we do not *know* what and how things and persons in themselves are. However, we have access to the dimension of "being-in-itself" through respect for human autonomy as it reveals itself in the Other and in our own existence. What Kant calls a "fact of reason" resembles the epiphany of the Other's face and speech as Levinas describes it. However, whereas Kant stresses the universality and fundamental equality of being human manifested in that "fact," Levinas describes the encounter with the human Other more truthfully as an asymmetric relationship. Both Kant and Levinas refuse to call the revelation of the Other's respectability an "experience" (*Erfahrung, expérience*), because it cannot be understood as a perception ruled by the conditions of empirical schematism or phenomenological fulfillment, but for both thinkers that revelation is an exceptional sort of awareness, from which all philosophy should start, although all attempts at objectifying it necessarily betray it.

In the encounter with another, the ego of *I think* discovers itself as an *I am obliged.* Kant translated and betrayed the discovery of this submission or "subjection" by formulating it in terms borrowed from the structure of theoretical reasoning. He described it as a universal law, to which the individual must submit its particular inclinations, thus preparing Hegel's synthesis in which morality is only a formal moment of *Sittlichkeit.* But behind this betrayal, the structure of a receptive subject is still legible: I must obey an orientation not chosen by me, but "choosing" me as a reasonable, that is, human being; my being human commands me to respect humanness in every human being as an end in itself; my life is being-for-this-end from which I cannot escape; morally relevant behavior is based on radical passivity.

Levinas opposes the idea that humanness can be defined by autonomy, because this term easily suggests the idea of a *causa sui*—a suggestion transformed into a bold thesis by Sartre's exaggerated claim that human existence is condemned to choose its own essence. The Other reveals to me that the "essence" of the self is to be a subject in the accusative: not *I think, I see, I will, I want, I can*, but *me voici* (*see me here*). However, Kant knew very well that autonomy does not exclude all heteronomy: I am not able to establish the law of pure reason by which I am ruled independently from any wish or choice or decision of mine. Do Levinas's images of a self (*soi*) "more passive than all possible passivity" (cf. AE, 65–72, 132–46; OB, 51–56, 104–15) and those of a hostage, a servant, and a victim (cf. AE, 114–51; OB, 113–18) not all hint at a similar nonobjectifiable truth? Once again the highest (the ruler of human existence) and the lowest (the hostage and servant) coincide in a being that cannot be defined as an object, but must be described through the use of opposite metaphors. Kant's idea of transcendental self-determination and Levinas's emphatic being-for-the-Other of someone who no longer belongs to herself seem to point to the same orientation: a "being-for" that includes a nonphenomenal and unknowable but practical awareness of an absolute orientation. True, Kant has not made explicit the asymmetry characteristic of duty and respect, but a meditation on the connections between the Other and the third, as seen by Levinas, can show that this difference between him and Kant is somewhat smaller than it may appear at first sight, as I will try to show below.

A classical objection against Kant's practical philosophy states that its dialectical part reintroduces the concept of happiness as a fundamental one, on which our belief in God and an afterlife relies. This objection can be reinforced from the perspective of Levinas' sharp distinction between *desire* and *need* (TeI, 3–10; TaI, 33–40). If it is the *good* we desire, and not *satisfaction* or fulfillment, the separation between *ethics* and *economics*, in the wide sense of the Levinasian word "*économie,*" seems clear. But in defense of Kant it may be said, *first,* that an absolute separation between the human desire for the good and our needs seems even more difficult to make than a sharp separation between the chaotic darkness of primitive "being" and the "economy" of enjoyment, on the one hand, and the service of the Other, on the other. No philosopher can be satisfied with the duality of two unconnected levels that thus comes to the fore. *Second,* Kant does not say that we must postulate an afterlife because *we* cannot do without happiness, but because a universe in which goodness and happiness remain forever separated or even partly opposed would not agree with the necessary presuppositions and demands of reason: it would be an unreasonable and absurd, unjust, unfair, immoral universe. In such a universe morality and justice would not be accepted as a dominating perspective; it would be ruled by blind fate or a cruel God. Kant's claim is much less narcissistic and more disinterested than is often said. The basic postulate of his philosophy is his faith in the radical justice of the existing universe.

From Levinas's perspective, the satisfaction of human needs is necessarily associated with the fulfillment of our obligations because I cannot serve the Other concretely without offering the Other a meal, safety, a house, work, education, and sympathy. Being-for is being a body, having hands as well as a heart: it is building a home in which warmth and meals are available, and so on. I cannot be for-the-Other if I do not enjoy the world. But also, the Other cannot be served unless I know her needs and at least try to provide food and clothes, etc. Ethical life is associated with a practical interpretation of messianism in the name of this other and all other others whom I meet. Contentment cannot be separated from morality.

The Other and the Third

This brings us to a consideration of the relationships between the Other and the third(s).[4]

The "fact" of the Other is the revelation of the Infinite because it breaks the economic totality in urging me to accord my behavior to my ethical orientation, an orientation which coincides with my desire for the absolute. Since the Other would not be fully Other if he or she were my parent, husband or wife, son or daughter, sister or brother or friend, the Other is represented as a stranger. Because of the Other's infinity, my life no longer belongs to me: this claim is absolute. The kind of love thus demanded from me is unjust, however, if it excludes my living for other Others than the one who confronts me here and now. I am responsible for *all* Others, but I cannot love all of them with the same exclusive intimacy. From the exceptional perspective of my relationship with this Other here and now follow the obligations of universal fraternity, and this cannot be realized without the organization of our being together through universal laws, social technology, planning, objective knowledge, and so on. Love orients me toward *universality*: I must overcome the perspective of "you and me" by somehow combining it with the perspective of universal rights and equality.

Has Levinas thus not justified (but also subordinated) the principle of Kant's and Hegel's metaphysics of duties and rights, and, on a more popular level, the principle of universal human rights? By adopting the perspective of reason, we adopt the claim of universal justice and condemn every ego's tendency to prefer his or her own well-being over that of Others. As Levinas admits, equality and symmetry are the criteria for a society in which the just claims of all Others are taken seriously. Levinas agrees with Hegel when he affirms strongly that the existence of others whom I do not know obliges me to uphold more than good will, moral intentions, and individual behavior. No third can be safe unless (s)he has become a member of a well-organized society in which the war of general egoism is suppressed by the concrete universality of collective institutions and customs. Morality, therefore, includes participation in the good functioning of the economic and political organization of a community, insofar as this is the never-ending attempt to counter violence and war.

Levinas accepts and welcomes the order of inevitable counterviolence-against-violence in the name of universal justice. But the dimension of immediate encounter and discourse cannot be reduced to any form of universality. Hegel, too, reserved a particular place and function for personal relationships. A family, for example, is not only a necessary element in a well-ordered society; it is based on the private intimacy of *people* who happen to love one another. As such, the family mediates between the perspective of individual morality and the demands of society as a whole. Hegel recognizes the necessity of love between husbands and wives, parents and children, brothers and sisters; he has a place for help to the poor, and for religious fraternity. Private life is not banned from ethics, but the real question lies elsewhere. The meaning of justice, laws, social and political organization, war and peace, etc., depends on the perspective from which they are accepted as necessary. Whereas Hegel regards the individual, the moral subject, and the perspective of morality as mere moments of a concept that triumphs in the concrete universality of the state, Levinas interprets the state as a necessary, morally conditioned, but general system of equality and justice, intermediate (and in a sense mediating) between goodness and war. The difference between the perspectives of morality and general justice explains why Levinas holds that true peace cannot come from the state and that the dialectic of violence must be overcome and redirected by a voice that "comes from the outside, 'through the door' [*thurathen*],"[5] whereas Hegel, from his "totalitarian" perspective, defends the state as the highest guarantor of peace, outside of which no *practical* reconciliation is possible. World history, as the history of social, economic, and political life, is unable to put an end to war, because the sovereignty of states hinders their sublation into a wider whole. On the level of moral and political life, no final reconciliation can be found. The bloody madness of history ("a slaughterhouse," as Hegel calls it) forces us to console ourselves through the artistic, religious, and philosophical contemplation of its tragedies. Knowledge enables us to see and feel and enjoy that the Infinite-in-us realizes itself in spite of *and on account of* its continuous corruption throughout world history. To the philosopher the terrible drama of existence is only a reflection of the eternal *clair-obscur*, which is the finite way of being of the eternal spirit.[6]

In rejecting the pseudoreligious satisfaction of a final vision, Levinas places the unpredictability of time above eternity; but does he dispose of a place from which he can pronounce his preference for morality over history? He proclaims the primacy of the moral perspective over the Hegelian (pseudo)concept of a judgment pronounced by history,[7] but how can he take enough distance from the life and history in which he is involved? The only distance given to him is the separatedness which the I, in awakening, discovers between the Other, as coming from elsewhere, and "me." There is no space from which I can have a view on the duality of my being involved in the moral relationship with this Other here and now *and* my being involved as one of the many moments of world history. If both dimensions are dimensions of one and the same subject, we cannot but somehow "think" their unity, yet this thought remains formal and abstract; it cannot become a synthetic knowledge, in the style of Hegel's concept. The margin from which Levinas projects a hierarchy between morality and history is minimal; it is no more than a line without any volume, a nonplace (*non-lieu*)[8] in which there is only a little breath, a whisper that can be recognized as enigmatic voice, or not.

We can neither master nor "know" our own orientation and the meaning of human life, because we cannot have a vision of it. We cannot know what history is doing and where it goes. But we can and must receive the stranger. The texts of our synthetic judgments and nicely coherent papers have to be unwoven, because they change into fossils as soon as we consider them to express the truth. No alchemy can extract life from the inscription of history; they come to life, however, when touched by the breath of a simple speech interrupting the coherence of a synchronizable time. The "rigorously calculated strategies" in which other writers have put their hope for a radical transformation of the languages in which we live are new expressions of the old desire to gain mastership by imitating the gestures of a demiurge. Infinity demands more modesty.

My attempt at comparing some elements of Levinas's text with some thoughts of Kant and Hegel may have underscored the differences separating them. The nonphenomenality of the face, the difference between Levinas's approach and the customary methods of philosophy, and especially the irreducibility of Saying (*le Dire*) to the Said (*le Dit*) are discoveries that oblige philosophy to make a new beginning. But within the discourse of philosophy to be born, classical elements of the modern tradition can be recaptured and transformed into legitimate parts of a text that denies, not only to them but also to itself, the right to function as a highest perspective. The Other, our idea of the Infinite, the meaning of desire, the most radical orientation of our behavior can only be formulated in a language that betrays them immediately. This betrayal makes them look like the concepts and oppositions of a Kantian or Hegelian dialectic. Yet, we might approach the truth if we do not venerate the text but try to overcome it by an extreme attention to the inconceivable Saying, to which all texts, including those of philosophy, refer the listener as to something more originary than anything that can be said.

Perhaps I am not Jew enough and too much of a Germanic intellectual, full of reverence for the heroes of late Greece and their modern heirs. Perhaps the love for a motherly tradition in which one can feel at home prevents me from a more audacious exodus. It seems, however, worthwhile—and Levinas gives us an example of it—to meditate on what unites us with the heritage of our Greece-inspired modernity and to plunder it as much as we can before we leave it behind—before we are renewed by the arid sufferings of a desert.

On Levinas's Criticism of Heidegger

As we have seen in chapter 4, Emmanuel Levinas was first known as a rather Heideggerian interpreter of Husserl and Heidegger.[1] Beginning with his essay "On Evasion" (1935), he also added modest criticisms to his expositions, but his criticisms gradually became more radical, especially after the end of World War II. The title of the small book published in 1947 even called for a reversal of Heidegger's orientation: *De l'existence à l'existant* (*From Existence to Existents*) is indeed the translation into French of the German phrase "*Vom Sein zum Seienden*" ("From Being to beings"), which polemically turns Heidegger's program upside-down. Levinas's criticism of Heidegger reaches its summit in *Totality and the Infinite* (1961), which can be read as Levinas's anti–*Being and Time*. *Otherwise than Being or Beyond the Essence* (1974) rarely mentions Heidegger, but his thought is even more present than before. However, Levinas's increasing hostility does not prevent him from considering his former master to be the greatest philosopher of our century or from praising *Being and Time* as the most important book since Hegel's *Phenomenology of Spirit* (see, e.g., EI, 27–34). The style of Levinas's work remains marked by Heidegger's mode of thinking, although Levinas, after *Totality and the Infinite*, tried more and more to avoid a language that suggests the primacy of Being. Nevertheless, even *Otherwise than Being* presents ontology as a thought that must be integrated as well as overcome, as we have seen in chapter 6.

After 1935, Levinas's critique is rooted in the conviction that Heidegger collaborated with the Nazis not only as rector of the University of Freiburg, but also as a thinker who came close to their inspiration and mentality. If it is true that philosophy cannot be separated from the prephilosophical elements of a particular form of life and the understanding implied in it, it is appropriate and even indispensable to ask how Heidegger's thought was related to his position on Nazi politics. The methodological approach expressed in this question presupposes that the distinction between the existential and the existentiell ultimately cannot be upheld, since thinking, if it is serious, "always already" testifies to an existentiell position. As we will see, this also implies that every philosophy expresses a particular ethos and a morally qualified attitude.

For Levinas, Heidegger's philosophy is the clear expression of a paganism that ignores the essential demands of morality and does not resist Nazi ruthlessness but rather is prone to collaborating with and even promoting it. This thesis, which might be somewhat overstated here, must be proved by purely philosophical (i.e., phenomenological) means, and thus not in a theological or ideological way. To this end Levinas reads and criticizes Heidegger's philosophy as the expression of a view which is not true to the ethical phenomena as they present themselves, since it submits them to a certain ontological schema. This failure to recognize the ethical phenomena for what they are not only leads to a neglect of philosophical ethics (in which case it could be amended); Levinas sees it as symptomatic of a way of thinking (in accordance with most European philosophy) that distorts the truth of God, (wo)man, and world by degrading their moral aspects to a secondary concern. According to Levinas, the very suspension or *epoche* of the ethical, the seemingly neutral decision to postpone philosophical ethics until the foundational questions of philosophy have been treated, testifies to a false understanding of reality.

This reproach does not imply that Levinas favors a reversal of the relationship between "first philosophy" and "philosophical ethics" or wants to replace the former with the latter. Thoughtful exposition and analysis of the basic moments of the ethical do not form a special discipline apart from the other disciplines of philosophy. Rather, they are constitutive components of first philosophy, which *Totality and the Infinite*, in its polemic against Heidegger, calls "metaphysics."

The greatest difficulty of a confrontation between Heidegger and Levinas is that they do not give two answers to one and the same question, but ask two different yet kindred questions, as is always the case when radical thinkers approach the origins of reality and thought. Both philosophers try to give a diagnosis of our time, of the history of European philosophy, and of Western civilization as a whole. By dedicating themselves to unfolding a new *philosophia prima*, both want to overcome so-called Platonism, objectifying thought, every kind of dualism, and all celebrations of a world behind the phenomenal one. Both are convinced that our conception of politics and morality cannot be renewed unless the traditional practice of philosophy is radically transformed. However, their oeuvres express two deeply different convictions about life; to greatly simplify this difference, we could call the one "Greek" and the other "Jewish" in a particular sense of the word, although both Heidegger and Levinas, as philosophers, express themselves in modern translations of a Greco-Roman-Germanic conceptual language that died long ago.

The confrontation of these two thinkers will not be fruitful unless we understand, in and through the texts in which they express themselves, the different inspirations that animate their work. Thus, while it would be possible at times to parry Levinas's attacks on Heidegger with quotations from the latter's texts, those attacks are still justified as criticisms of the spirit (or, as Levinas sometimes says, the "climate") of Heidegger's thought.

The two questions from which Heidegger and Levinas start can be formulated provisionally as: (1) the question of the meaning (*Sinn*), the essence (*Wesen*), and the truth of *Being*; and (2) the question of the *Other*, which gives meaning (*sens/signification*) to the existence of men and women in the world and its history. The relevance of and the difference between these questions can be elucidated only by unfolding both philosophies.

In this chapter, I will focus mainly on the question of how Levinas's thought relates to Heidegger's political and ethical theory (and perhaps also to his practice). How is it possible to criticize Heidegger's moral and political philosophy if these hardly exist? One could answer that the presupposition of this question is wrong. Although in *Being and Time* Heidegger firmly states that he is not concerned with ethics, it could still be argued that this book contains at least an implicit foundation of ethics, since it places itself at a point before the split between theory and practice. In his later work, as well, Heidegger gives at least basic hints for an ethics when he writes about ethos as the fundamental way of appropriation, dwelling, orientation, belonging, etc. Thus, a critique of Heideggerian ethics and politics should highlight the particular ethos that Heidegger seems (at least implicitly) to prefer in those writings, and should evaluate this ethos and the theoretical and practical consequences that follow from it.

A second element that must be emphasized in a critique is the place and function to be granted to Heidegger's practical philosophy. When ethics is explicitly excluded from the fundamental ontology to be unfolded in *Being and Time*, this does not mean that ethical questions are merely postponed or not stated at all. The apparent neutrality that separates all moral moments from the all-preceding thinking about Being, truth, and meaning is in fact already a decision that is full of consequences: ethics is declared to be a secondary and nonfundamental concern of philosophy. In this decision, Heidegger follows an old tradition of European thought, which in modern philosophy has led to the progressive degeneration of ethics into a discipline that can be postponed until the philosophical groundwork is finished, or even into an appendix to the uniquely fundamental and deep philosophy to be found in logic, epistemology, ontology, and perhaps a fundamental anthropology. The modern dogma of the separation between "is" and "ought" is not a discovery of Hume's, but a symptom of the specific mode of European philosophizing, at least in its modern form. The thesis defended by Levinas insists that every true philosophy, i.e., every philosophy that is true to authentic experience, must be ethical from the outset, and that it is totally impossible to think seriously and fundamentally if the moral perspective is placed in parentheses, even if only provisionally. First philosophy ipso facto avails itself of ethical categories from the very beginning. This is the reason why the thought of Being or ontology cannot claim to coincide with first philosophy if it is not at the same time an ethical theory. Because first philosophy is simultaneously a fundamental ethics, it is a "meta-physics." As such it testifies that reality is more or otherwise than a morally indifferent and fateful *physis*. Thus, Levinas does not say (as some interpreters attribute to him) that metaphysics ought to be based on ethics, as if moral philosophy as such, in distinction from ontology or a non-normative metaphysics, were the basic discipline of philosophy on which the others should be built. First philosophy must show that "is" and "ought," the theoretical and the practical, are not originally distinguishable, and thus that "the Good" is another name for the very source.

The Other

A correct understanding of Levinas's critique of Heidegger requires that we understand Levinas's starting point. It is neither the Husserlian nor the Cartesian *cogito*, nor a pre-understanding of Being, but a relationship that both distinguishes between and connects "the Other" (i.e., the human Other) and me. There are two sides from which to approach the phenomenology of this relationship: from the side of the I or the self, by analyzing "my" desire for what is absolutely Other, or from the side of the Other, who coconstitutes the existence of "me" by revealing him- or herself to me as unintegratably foreign. The connection between the Other and me is a complex one, since it includes both the separation and the inseparability of the Other from me. Without separation (*séparation*) we would fuse into each other or be caught up into a dialectical unity in which the absolute difference between us vanishes. However, the Other and I are also inseparable, since our relationship constitutes both the Other's identity and my own. The most fundamental intersubjective relationship, however, is not one of similarity or symmetry. It is characterized by a radical *asymmetry*. The Other originally appears *not* as one who is similar to me; she is not primarily another instance of the same humanity that is concretized in my individuality, as Kant, for example, understands our "humanness" (*Menschheit*). The Other reveals herself as "high"; otherness means "height" or "highness" (*hauteur*). As a stranger, the Other comes from afar and from an "absolute," "infinite" height. Her arrival disrupts my life insofar as I attempt primarily to maintain myself and absorb everything foreign into me. The Other forbids me to stick to my *conatus essendi* as the highest norm and guide for life. The prohibition revealed in the emergence of the Other ("You should not kill me by depriving me of space to live or other conditions for my life") is the reverse side of a positive command: "You shall admit me into your space, world, and house; you shall feed me, clothe me, serve me, etc."

If I disregard the factical existence of the Other—even if only in a preliminary and entirely theoretical abstraction—I am merely an activity that appropriates and integrates everything "other" into my own self-identification. This is natural and necessary if I am to be an independent I at all. Such a self-identification by assimilation is carried out in enjoyment: I enjoy the world, arranging it for myself so that I can dwell, eat, work, perceive in it; I consider all phenomena to be there *for me*. However, the mere existence of others indicates to me that subordinating all beings to my own self-unfolding cannot be the final goal of my life. The authentic meaning of my existence is not the consummation of a *conatus essendi*. *Before* all exteriorizations of the will and before any possibility of recognition, agreement, or convention, another's factual existence requires me to admit him into my dwelling and world; he obliges my respect, service, and responsibility for the success, the happiness, and the meaning of his life. "*Being-(responsible)-for-the-Other*" is the basic definition of "me." It is the beginning of philosophy and cannot be grasped as a moment of a higher synthesis.

In *Totality and the Infinite* Levinas criticizes Heidegger in the name of an otherness that does not allow itself to be integrated into a totality; in *Otherwise than Being* he attempts to show that thinking must go "beyond Being" (or "beyond essence") in order to gain access to an "otherwise than Being." Heidegger's thought of Being should be replaced by a thinking that does not reduce the Other to Being. However, before we ask to what extent this criticism actually suits Heidegger, I would like to pose the more simple question of whether Heidegger has correctly described the way of being of the "phenomenon" of the Other.

The answer to the latter question is a clear "no." Heidegger's entire oeuvre includes only a few pages about Others. The essential passage is found in sections 25–27 of *Being and Time,* where intersubjectivity is emphasized as an existential of *Dasein* only insofar as it is a constitutive moment of being-in-the-world and thus (just as the authenticity of the self) is a condition of the possibility of falling into the "they" (*das Man*). The Other is introduced as a moment of an original being-with that coconstitutes *Dasein* (which is always my own). The Other is thus understood from the beginning as a moment of a being-together in the form of a "we." He is not (or hardly) discussed as an opponent with whom I struggle, whom I hate or love, admire or fear. Although Heidegger analyzes the essence of solicitude, the relation this points to is represented as a modification of a more originary *Dasein-with* (*Mitdasein*). The Other's appearance causes no break with the preceding description of solitary being-in-the-world. Although the Cartesian beginning, the *cogito,* is fundamentally modified, the framework is maintained of a self-related being there that finds itself within a total and anonymous horizon. The lateral position of the Other who finds himself next to me and is connected with me does nothing to alter Heidegger's question in an essential way; it remains concentrated on the being of the *Dasein* that is always mine, and through this on Being in general. As Heidegger's later work also shows, the problematic of the Other and the peculiarity of the relations between human beings have played no decisive role within the development of his thinking.

Totality

The title of *Totality and the Infinite* is programmatic: it formulates the opposition between the two radical motives that have characterized Western philosophizing and Western civilization in general. The absolutizing of an all-comprehending totality by most representatives of modern ontology must be countered by an apology for the Infinite that does not allow itself to be enclosed within a universal horizon. As the greatest thinker since Hegel, Heidegger is at the same time a clear representative of the combatted manner of thinking which Levinas calls "ontology." Does this mean that, according to Levinas, Heidegger's thinking is totalizing and totalitarian, like the thinking of Spinoza or Hegel? Insofar as Heidegger thematizes the Other as merely a coconstituting moment of the *Dasein* that is always mine, and carries out this thematization only within the horizon of Being in general, we can say that for him, too, totality reduces the Other's particularity to the status of an instance or moment. In any case, the question of the Other is subordinated to the question of Being as such and in general. That leads to the supremacy of an anonymous neuter, thus preventing the "absolute" or "infinite" "height" (*hauteur*) of an other than Being from coming to the fore. The preeminence of the question of Being thus not only prevents the dignity of the Other from becoming manifest, but also obstructs the possibility of placing the universe of beings under the demands of justice. If "Being" is the first and last word, there is no place for the infinite "dignity" (*Würde*, as Kant calls it) of the Other's existence. Ontology implies the impossibility of an ethics.

Against the reproach that Heidegger's thought of Being is a totalizing way of thinking, we could object that while he does in fact think of Being as an encompassing horizon, he does not conceive of it as a totality or a whole. The ontological difference distinguishes between Being itself and the totality of beings that owe their being to Being. Being itself is neither a totality nor a property of a totality, but "that which gives" (*es gibt*) the universe its being.

Nevertheless, as it may become clear in the following considerations, Heidegger's work might be susceptible to the reproach that was mentioned above.

Heidegger's emphasis on the *whole* of care as the structural whole of *Dasein* and on the *authentic possibility for being a whole* (SZ, sec. 45), combined with the subordination of being-with and solicitude under that whole, seems to confirm the thesis that the *Dasein* of Others is acknowledged only insofar as it plays a role within the prevailing self-actualization that belongs to being myself.

The *world*, like *Dasein*, has the character of a whole, as is clear from the following quotations:

> The "how" of *Dasein*'s existence [is] its relation to beings and to itself taken in its totality. The human mode of existing is to determine oneself in and from the whole [*in und aus dem Ganzen*]. The being-in-the-world of *Dasein* means: being in the whole (*im Ganzen sein*), namely concerning the "how." (GA 26, 233)

The comprehension of the world somehow has "the character of wholeness" (*Ganzheit*):

> As primarily characterized by the "for-the-sake-of-which," the world is the originary whole of that which *Dasein* as free gives itself to understand. . . . In the projection of the "for-the-sake-of-which" as such, *Dasein* gives itself its original *commitment* [*Bindung*]. . . . The whole [*das Ganze*] of the commitment that lies in the for-the-sake-of-which is the world." (GA 26, 247)

The world, as the whole of the essential inner possibilities of *Dasein* as transcendent, *exceeds* the totality of actual beings [*alles wirklich Seiende*]. This [totality] always reveals itself only as a limitation, as a possible actualization of the possible, as the insufficiency out of a surplus of possibilities in which *Dasein* always already holds itself as a free project. (GA 26, 248)

It seems obvious from what follows in Heidegger's text that these passages do not represent a provisional description of being-in-the-world as preliminary mode of being that should be renewed by or integrated into the perspective of a being-with-and-for-others:

The whole of the commitment that lies in the for-the-sake-of-which is the world. According to this commitment *Dasein* commits itself to a possibility of being [*ein Seinkönnen*] towards itself as possibility of being with others in the possibility of being with that which is at hand [*das Vorhandene*]. Selfhood is the free engagement [*Verbindlichkeit*] for and towards oneself. (GA 26, 247)

When we combine the passages cited above with the following one, the contrast to Levinas's thesis is immediately apparent.

Only because *Dasein* can be on its own, thanks to its transcendence, can it also be in the world with another self *qua* thou. The I-thou relationship [*die Ich-Du-Beziehung*] is not yet itself the relationship of transcendence, but rather is founded on the transcendence of *Dasein*. It is a mistake to think that the I-thou relationship is as such primarily constitutive for the possible discovery of the world. (GA 25, 315)

The last few lines are probably directed at Martin Buber and other philosophers of dialogue. They do not apply directly to Levinas, who emphasizes the asymmetry of the intersubjective relationship and the Other's height, which cannot be indicated by the familiar form *Du*. Nevertheless, we can read in these words a rather clear formulation of the contrast between Heidegger and Levinas. Even if Heidegger's Being is not to be thought of as a whole (but how should we characterize the being of "the whole of beings" [*das Ganze des Seinden*] or of "being as a whole" [*das Seinde im Ganzen*] if we may not call it "total" or "whole"?), he describes "*Dasein*," "world," and "being-in-the-world" as modes of being that are wholes, and the interpersonal relationship (which for Levinas is the authentic and radical "transcendence") is to be seen, according to Heidegger, as a subordinate element within *Dasein*'s relation to itself.

The originary relationship is the self-reference of care; responsibility for Others is a subordinate moment within this.

Being

If neither is "Being" to be understood as a totality nor is the horizon of the question of Being to be taken as something comprehensive, but rather as *Ereignis* or as an originary "it" (*es*) that "gives" (*gibt*), then we can reconstruct Levinas's objection in the following way.

If we seek, in abstraction from Others and from the self that I always am, to describe the "*il y a*" that precedes all phenomena, what we find is not at all a generous and illuminating origin, but rather the anonymity of a dark, chaotic, and directionless rumbling without any structure or shape. Light and order proceed not from this "Being," but from something else: from the Other, the stranger who comes from afar, from an unreachable unknown, whose visage illuminates the world. The human Other's look is the origin of all meaning, the absolute that answers my desire for meaning without ever satisfying it as if that desire were a lack that could be filled. The obligation under which the Other's arrival places me, the responsibility for others that his or her existence makes certain to me, reveals the truth of what I fundamentally am, the truth of the world from which I live. The Other's existence obligates me to be responsible for her (this is the first truth of consciousness, the certainty of which is therefore ipso facto certain); this means that she is in the trace of the infinite good. In this sense we can say that we are here in order to serve "the Good." The "idea of the Good" exceeds the totality of beings; it prevails "beyond Being;" it is the origin that precedes the I or the world.

According to Levinas, Heidegger's Being is a philosophical name for the anonymous powers that constitute and rule the world, as long as we still have not discovered any face, but only nourishing or threatening elements and phenomena without eyes or voice. If these powers are not subordinated to the intersubjective relationship and the moral laws it reveals, they turn out to be the finite gods of ancient and modern mythology. The enthusiasm these gods arouse is murderous, since it has no regard for the absolute otherness of the Infinite that is revealed not in divine forms but in the faces of other humans. The adoration of the gods goes hand in hand with a politics of inconsiderate self-preservation and scorns the everydayness of moral respect. However, a rehabilitation of ethics requires that thinking be sobered by the look of the Other, thus replacing the intoxication of enthusiasm with the prosaic fulfillment of everyday responsibility.

In *Otherwise than Being* (1974), the main criticism no longer targets *totality*, but *Being*. Here (as already in *From Existence to Existents*) Being is to be equated with the "it" (*es*) of the "it gives" (*es gibt*) that is translated by the French "*il y a*," and the essence and effect of Being is to be characterized as an "*inter-esse.*" It seems impossible to escape this essence, since outside of Being there is (*gibt es*) nothing. Is all transcendence beyond Being impossible? Is the Platonic idea of a "beyond Being" absurd? The other alternative is to choose between atheism and a theology that locates what is high in a second world behind the phenomenally given universe. How would it be possible to rise beyond the realm of Being without falling into some such superstition?

The essence of Being (*l'essence*, or, as some French authors write it in order to emphasize the verbal and transitive sense of Heidegger's Being, *l'essance*) is characterized as an *inter-esse* that interests beings in their own being and by this means interests them in each other. The concept of totality also plays a role here, insofar as Being "weaves beings and worlds—however different and incomparable they may be—together into a common fate" (AE, 4; OB, 4).

The "*inter-esse*" by which beings exist is evident in their *conatus essendi*, in their urge to be and maintain themselves and to unfold their own possibilities. This urge relates beings to each other, since their egoism causes them, on the one hand, to be allergic to and struggle with each other but, on the other hand, to need one another, since they cannot satisfy their interests as isolated beings. As Heraclitus had already said, the gathering of beings is a war. The *inter-esse* is a confrontation that brings about a polemical unity. The rational structures of society, calculation, negotiation, political organization, and dialectical theory constitute a kind of peace: they reconcile beings with each other, since they limit the claims of every egoism. This peace gathers together the combatting moments in the presence of its harmony. It assumes that beings can be made present either by immediate perception or representation or by memory and history. Synthesis and synchrony, presence and what is physically there are basic concepts of ontology.

After *Otherwise than Being*, Levinas further developed his characterization of ontological thinking, for example in a summary essay whose programmatic title reads: "The Thought of Being and the Question of the Other."[2] Its argument proceeds in the following way.

As we have learned from Heidegger, Being is inseparable from appearance. Since the beginning of the history of Greek-Western culture, reality has been understood as a universe of phenomena, the essence and coherence of which must be revealed by thinking. This thinking begins with a seeing that brings the phenomena to consciousness, so that it can define, grasp, and comprehend them. The concept that philosophical thinking desires is a grasp that identifies beings and fixes them in their identity. The mode of being, its essence and effect (*Wesen und Walten*) that thereby comes to the fore in the phenomena, determines the meaning of the Greek manner of knowledge and science, which our history has developed into the "wisdom of the nations." As the intentional correlate of this manner of knowledge, Being is a noema that presents, posits, and emphasizes itself: it is a "bodily" given that provokes experience and gives rise to assertoric judgments. The assertoric identification of beings by a universal and transcendental consciousness presupposes that beings are suited to the stability of resting on the earth. All beings have their specific place in the totality of a hierarchically constructed architectonic. For such a way of thinking, intelligibility means the fundamental and founding character of its constitutive statements. The spirit of this thinking is at home within the sphere of a science in which the circle of the Same encompasses the circle of the Other, as Plato puts it in the *Timaeus* (35ab). The collection of beings forms a closed cosmos, in which, since Copernicus, the dimension of height has been abolished. Under a firm heaven, the solid world offers mortals the leisure to remain, build, and dwell. Everything strange that cannot be domesticated is worked on or thought about so that it can fit into the structure of Being and of transcendental thinking. In the moment of truth, there is nothing in the world that can evade the shining of the noonday sun. Intentionality, in which the noema and the noesis are absolutely commensurable, allows no irreducible otherness. What is actual manifests itself in the evidence of presence or is brought into the present by being represented in memory. Presence and representation secure the evidence of our experience. Since Being rules, we can rely upon the truth of a world in which beings let themselves be identified, gathered, and comprehended. The adequation of Being and thinking is the secret of this world.

However, what escapes this adequation is what cannot be reduced to the noema of an intention of consciousness, since it is much more puzzling than a phenomenon "is." The look of another human reveals something that can be neither perceived as a bodily presence nor established by a conceptual definition. It "is" in such a different way that it bursts all the boundaries of the manner of thinking sketched above. In this sense it reveals an "Infinite." For the subject in search of meaning, the existence of this otherness means that consciousness cannot be what is ultimate or initial, even if its transcendental character is increased to the utmost. An all-comprehending intentionality gives way to a more radical relation that precedes the thinking in search of an *arche*, a beginning, a ground. Since this relation understands that an absolute beginning is impossible for consciousness, we could call it "an-archical." While it acknowledges Being's Other, an-archical thinking testifies to a difference that is not ontological: an absolute nonindifference (*non-indifférence*) in which the ego simultaneously respects the Other and recognizes its own inability to be absolutely dominant.

The Other's visage arouses the ego to its infinite responsibility, and this provocation reveals to the ego its originary passivity or receptivity, which must not be thought of as the contrary of activity since it precedes any dialectic of passivity and activity. Originary passivity is to be shocked or affected by the riddle that is not a phenomenon and in this sense is "invisible": another's look or glance, which reveals me ipso facto as the one who is responsible for her. The uneasiness this causes in me is that I have a "bad" conscience as long as the infinite and ever-increasing duty of responsibility is not fulfilled. The true transcendence is evident in this uneasiness, in which the Other's arrival shakes up the ego.

The critique sketched here does not mean that Levinas would simply dismiss ontology or every thought of Being. The constellation of beings, their gathering in the truth, the essence and effect of Being, and the technical, aesthetic, political, and theoretical modes of existence that belong to it are unavoidable and legitimate; they receive their radical meaning, however, from something different from Being, i.e., from transcendence toward the Good, which (in Plato's words) gives beings their being and truth. Politics, art, and theory are no more the absolute than Being itself is; they derive their worth from a right relationship to Others.

Practice

The question of how these seemingly speculative statements can get a concrete meaning with respect to Heidegger's view of practice is answered in a text of barely four pages that gives the sharpest expression of Levinas's critique. It is found in an essay that Levinas wrote after the first voyage to outer space: "Heidegger, Gagarin and Us."[3]

Present-day technique and technology, along with contemporary industrial and scientific-technical society in general, harbors a great danger—the world could explode—but its greatness is that it is intimately linked to the great endeavors of human liberation that characterize contemporary humanity. Release from the hardships of ancient civilization (with its regional customs, worn-out words, and dead particularisms) and hope for a new, secular, and free way of existing with regard to race, blood, and soil is *not* brought about by modern technology (which is rather the effect of this emancipation), but technology still provides invaluable possibilities for liberation.

What is the motivation for Heidegger's critique of the "essence" of modern technology? Levinas understands it as a protest against the objectifying, calculating, and planning exploitation of nature and humans, which reduces us to factors of a utilitarian(istic) industry. The root of this protest is a self-understanding that could be characterized in the following way.

In opposition to the subjection of all beings to the force of objectification and planning, we must rediscover the world. We have lost ourselves, since we have lost Being itself, *physis*, nature, and our place within it.[4]

> To rediscover the world is to rediscover a childhood mysteriously snuggled up inside the Place, to open up to the light of great landscapes, the fascination of nature, and the majestic display of the mountains. It is to walk a path that winds through fields, to feel the unity established by the bridge that joins the two banks of a river and by the architecture of buildings, the presence of a tree, the twilight of the forests, the mystery of things, of a jug, of a peasant-woman's worn-down shoes, the beaming carafe of wine on a white tablecloth. The very *Being* of the real is said to reveal itself from behind these privileged experiences, giving and trusting itself to humans' care; and humans, the guardians of Being, derive their existence and truth from this grace.
>
> This doctrine is subtle and new. Everything that, for centuries, seemed to us to be added to nature by humans would already have been shining forth in the splendors of the world. A work of art is the bloom of Being and not a human intervention; it makes that pre-human splendor shine forth. Myths speak in nature itself. Nature is implanted in this first language which hails us only to found human language. Humans must be capable of listening and understanding and responding. But to hear and respond to this language is not the same as to engage in logical thoughts raised into a system of knowledge; rather it is to inhabit the place, to be there. Being rooted [*enracinement*]. One would like to take up this term; but the plant is not enough of a plant to define an intimacy with the world. A little humanity is said to distance us from nature, while a great deal of humanity would bring us back to it. The way in which humans inhabit the earth is more radical than that of the plant, which only takes nourishing sap from it. The fable spoken by the first language of the world presupposes more subtle, numerous and profound connections. (DL, 300–301)

This summary characterization has prepared Levinas's verdict on the spirit of this worldview: after all kinds of infantilism and idolatry have been surmounted, it has rehabilitated paganism, revering the world and the place as holy abodes.

> The mystery of things is the source of all cruelty toward humans. The implantation in a landscape, the attachment to the *Place* without which the universe would become meaningless and would hardly exist: that is the very scission of humankind into natives and strangers. From this perspective technique is less dangerous than the ghosts of the *Place*. (DL, 301)

The attachment to the place (Heidegger's *Ort*) within a sacred world in which art and political power rather than respect and justice play the chief roles has too much affinity with the Nazi glorification of soil and blood. The much-maligned technology is a great opportunity, since it delivers us from "the Heideggerian world and the superstition of the place." Through technology we can discover human beings outside the borders of common dwelling-places and allow the light of their faces to come to the fore in their nakedness. Freed from all holy abodes, we can discover the authentic meaning of the human way of being-in-the-world: we are here in order to provide food and shelter for the Others. Dis-enchanting nature and demystifying the world are the reverse side of existing for the Infinite that exceeds all horizons.

Dialogue with Edith Wyschogrod

T his last chapter is a response to Edith Wyschogrod's extensive and important work on Emmanuel Levinas.[1] But before I focus on her interpretations, I would like to underscore her description of the world as contained in her *Spirit in Ashes: Hegel, Heidegger, and Man-made Mass Death* (Yale University Press, 1985), as well as one aspect of her groundbreaking and courageous *Saints and Postmodernism: Revisioning Moral Philosophy* (University of Chicago Press, 1990). Both books testify to a profound experience of radical anxiety caused by the actual state of our world and history, but they also express hope. Wyschogrod's thinking is inspired by an emotion which is as profound as life itself.

Mass Murder

Spirit in Ashes describes the historical reality of mass murder as a summary and symbol of our civilization's being marked by an inherent threat. That this civilization is not evil through and through is shown by the fact that Wyschogrod, like Nietzsche, Heidegger, and Levinas, is able to write a critique of our times. There is, however, a paralyzing force in the recurrence of massive killing which has almost become a "normal" component of everyday news and social life. The extermination of Jews and gypsies in the German concentration camps, the starvation of dissidents in the Gulag archipelago, the genocide of the Kurds, the slaughtering of Vietnamese and Cambodians by their pseudosaviors, and the everydayness of torture and murder as widely accepted functions of national and world politics form a pattern that cannot be ignored in a theory of the social systems that characterize the actual state of world politics. We need a thorough analysis of this situation in order to know where, how and who we are and what we might expect or do. Whoever ignores or hides today's enterprise of mass-murderous strategy will never be able to thoughtfully analyze the social reality. Such blindness would exclude any chance of discovering what it means to be civilized and historical now.

As a paradigm of contemporary evil, "the death event" is characterized in Wyschogrod's book by the following traits: as the thoughtless killing of innumerable and uncounted humans, mass murder disregards human individuality. Annihilation is here the negation of the victims' faces, an effacement which reduces human singularities to elements of an anonymous mass or material. The recognition of human universality has taken a perverse form in the reduction of individuals to the generality of their flesh and bones. In this dimension, too, the technological character of our century expresses itself in the absolute homogeneity of the human substance and the arithmetics of its manipulation. Men, women, children are numbers, their lives a biochemical substance used to systematically abolish their humanity. Intersubjective differentiation disturbs the economy of their dissolution.

The antivital character of this economy is manifested in its uselessness. Even the meticulously regulated labor of the death camps is not so much really productive as meant to induce exhaustion: the camps are symbols of sovereign hatred and perfect nihilism. The victims are stripped of all cultural reference and significance; even moral behavior is hardly possible. Their lives are reduced to being bodies without grace or culture, with no other meaning than survival for a while longer. Who knows why they live? Their meaning seems exhausted by the master's enjoyment of power over life and death.

Since the homogeneity of the victims makes them replaceable by others, who come from a seemingly inexhaustible reserve, Wyschogrod points out that the logic of the death camps has a Zenonian structure. The human mass is infinitely divisible: there will never be a shortage in human material. The main task is to sort out that which must be disposed of immediately from that which must be kept for a while.

The description of artificial mass death as a normal function of our civilization, which for the first time in history is becoming a world civilization, shows the extent to which we "media vita in morte sumus": in the middle of life we are surrounded by death. Not the plague, but peoples and tyrants are now the murderers of humankind. Confronted with this situation, Wyschogrod searches for a possibility of hope not in the direction of a political plan of action, an innovative strategy, or a new social theory, but rather in a postmodern form of saintliness. Leaving behind the ashes of a spirit which, after its monumental history, ultimately displayed its fundamental weakness, she turns to the saint as paradigm for another way of existence, another way of relating and behaving. It is understandable, then, that the philosophy of Emmanuel Levinas has been of the utmost importance for her own thought, for there seems to be no other post-Hegelian, post-Nietzschean thinker who writes about saintliness with the same radical and courageous insight as Levinas. Perhaps it is therefore not too bold to assume that Wyschogrod's publications on Levinas, written before the two books mentioned above, were at least partially motivated by the same deep concern for the necessity of mobilization against the horrors inherent in our culture. In the various deserts of the twentieth century, and through the manifold exoduses which were our fate, amidst the realm of death and abuse, there is perhaps no other hope than the defenseless figure of someone who practices compassion without calculating costs. Across religious denominations, cultures, nations, places, and times, and notwithstanding the technological network of political economy and communication, it is still possible to respond to massive killing and contempt by a certain form of abnegation which is neither masochistic nor proud. If this is true, how then must we understand human existence? What makes humanity capable of peace? How does the mortality within human lives carry meaning?

Levinas's Philosophy of the Saint

In 1974, the year in which Levinas published his *Otherwise than Being or Beyond Essence*, Wyschogrod published *Emmanuel Levinas: The Problem of Ethical Metaphysics*, an achievement which is even more remarkable since it was one of the first books on Levinas, preceding most of his publications that belong to the period of *Otherwise than Being*.[2] After 1974, Wyschogrod published many other excellent papers in which she explained or elaborated on Levinas's thoughts, and in all her publications a certain affinity with his thought is noticeable.

I will here neither summarize Wyschogrod's interpretations, nor discuss those rare passages to which I would perhaps propose some amendments; I would like rather to participate in "the conversation we are" by succinctly discussing a few topics which Wyschogrod treats, in the hope that we do indeed converge in our interpretation, and are able to discuss the remaining divergences in a fruitful manner. These topics are: (1) Face and Speech, (2) Ethics and/or First Philosophy?, (3) Is a Phenomenology of the Face possible?, (4) Infinity, (5) Reason and Violence, and (6) Naming and Gratitude.

Face and Speech

In *Totality and the Infinite*, Levinas focuses on the Other's face or speech. The face regards me. Its eyes are looking eyes; not "a look" in the sense of Heidegger's *eidos* or *idea*, but a "speaking" face: *Le visage parle*. "Speech," too, expresses the Other's active and surprising speaking rather than the message, the text, or the content of the Other's language. *Otherwise than Being* analyzes the relationship between the Other and "me" from the perspective of "my" subjectivity. Instead of the Other's facing me and speaking to me, Levinas now focuses on my speaking or "Saying" as distinguished from the Said. Saying here is the new name for "speech" or speaking (*discours, parole*); the visual aspects are not stressed as much as they were in *Totality and the Infinite*. Both the face (or speech) and the Saying "*precede*" any specific word; the "metaphysical" relationship, which would be impossible without language, and which thus necessitates the semantic and syntactic structures by which a language is constituted, does not simply coincide with them. It has a distance from our being-in-the-world; its time is another time than worldly or linguistic temporality.

Wyschogrod's interpretations most often concentrate on language. She shows that Heidegger's meditations on language have a very different orientation than those of Levinas. Although Heidegger quotes Hölderlin's phrase "that we are a conversation" (*daß ein Gespräch wir sind*), and although he is fascinated by the evocative force of the word that permits things and worlds, and sometimes gods, to shine forth, he never pays attention to persons, nor does he thematize the communicative act of speaking or of addressing words to someone else. Seeing the poet, in his commerce with a world of spaces, times, things, and gods, as the speaker par excellence, Heidegger is full of admiration for singing and celebration: but there is no "you" in his oeuvre. Wyschogrod points out that the structure of *Mitsein* neither implies nor permits the derivation of the structure of the-one-for-the-Other. Gods and things are apparently more obvious for Heidegger than singular faces. Does his philosophy hold the means to prevent or to heal or simply to protest against the blindness for faces and the deafness for voices upon which the organization of mass murder is built?

Ethics and/or First Philosophy?

Does Levinas propose ethics as a foundation of metaphysics? Are "ethics" and "metaphysics" two names for the same enterprise? What does he mean by "ethics *as* first philosophy"?

The face is the simultaneity of a fact and a command. Therefore, Levinas can claim that its epiphany precedes the split between the theoretical and the practical. It precedes the distinction between "is" and "ought"; or it is both in the originary, or "pre-originary," sense of a "first."

A philosophy that does not point toward such a pretheoretical and prepractical origin or first is not radical enough to show that ethics is at least as originary as Aristotle's first philosophy or Plato's dialectic.

A fact which is at the same time and indistinctly a command, is not new in philosophy. Plato's *idea*, as the identity of essence and ideal, Aristotle's *physis* as the identity of *arche* and telos, and even Kant's "fact of reason" as the revelation of an ought which is at the same time the core of human freedom, are other versions of such an origin.

If ethics is a philosophical meditation on the essence and origin of conscience, obligation, ethos, and morality, Levinas's analysis of the face or of Saying is necessarily a theory of the commanding fact these bring to the fore. One could object that ethics should only pay attention to normative aspects, whereas the observable factuality of things and minds should be treated in some theoretical discipline of philosophy. However, these two sides cannot be separated, for—and this is the Levinasian specificity—the fact of the face can neither be described without recourse to the normative terminology of ethics, nor observed in a purely neutral, nonmoral or not-yet-moral perception. The face "*is*" and "shows" its imperative, obligating character. The answer to the question "What *is* the face?" (or: "What does it disclose?") is: "The face obligates me; it reveals that I am already devoted to the one who looks at me; I am responsible for you."

If radical ethics indeed cannot be distinguished from the theoretical consideration of face, speech, Saying, subjectivity, responsibility, etc., and if Levinas can show that the face or the Saying is prior to and more originary than being-in-the-world and Being as such, then his radical ethics coincides with *prote philosophia*. As a theory of that which lies beyond and before the *physis*, it can also be characterized as a *meta-physics*.

The affirmation that Levinas has given us "an ethics of ethics" is unclear to me. If we take the second term "ethics" to mean a theory of moral norms, virtues, obligations, etc., everybody will agree that Levinas does something much more fundamental or originary. If we could use the word "foundation" without immediately becoming conscious of its inadequacy with regard to the "*pre*-original" or "an-archic" character of Levinas's main concepts, we could maintain that his philosophy is a philosophical "foundation" of ethics, or a "fundamental" ethics, not so very unlike Kant's *Critique of Practical Reason*. This "foundation" itself—for example, its initial description of Saying and facing—contains moral elements, but this is not sufficient reason to identify it as an "ethics."

True, to "perceive" what happens and surprises me in a face which looks at me or in my addressing words to you, I must open myself and respond in a certain, more or less well-disposed or even benevolent way, but such moral conditions for truthful perception, feeling, or insight, play a role in all genuine thinking.

Although Levinas himself sometimes calls his "first philosophy" an ethics—for example, in his paper entitled "Ethics as First Philosophy"[3]— he does not deny that it is at the same time a metaphysics, and he calls it that more than once. Like Plato's thought, Levinas's philosophy is a metaphysical ethics or an ethical metaphysics. Surprisingly, and in spite of many radical differences, his use of "ethics" is rather similar to Spinoza's concept of ethics in his *Ethica*, which is as much an unfolding of the way to *beatitudo* as a metaphysics.

Is a Phenomenology of the Face Possible?

The face and the Saying do not fit into the dimension opened up by phenomenology. Levinas wrote many pages on the difference between what, in ontological terms, could be called the face's mode of being (its epiphany or revelation) and the modes of being of anything else (the modes of being and manifestation of the phenomena).

The Other, speaking, transcendence, the "metaphysical relation," subjectivity, etc., can be neither treated as intentions or intentional correlates within the horizon of Husserl's phenomenological analysis, nor as beings or elements or modes of being within Heidegger's "world." Their nonphenomenological character, which is neither ontic nor ontological, resists any objectification; they disappear as soon as one talks of, writes about, or thematizes them. Thus, it is not possible to describe, analyze, or systematize them. All of Levinas's writings therefore change and distort the very truth of what they try to say. The Said of their Saying cannot contain the Saying itself. The visage is invisible.

The impossibility of an adequate language, and the attempt to point out how its unavoidable distortions relate to the nonphenomenological, have posed a problem within philosophy since its beginning with Parmenides. This impossibility has not stopped thinking from developing, and has not prevented philosophy from reflecting on the necessary transcendence beyond the limits of the thinkable. The stammering to which the difficulty leads has not then been considered a good reason for not starting to think. On the contrary, the desire for a passage beyond the finite has become more intense with the attempt to pass through the order of finite phenomena in order to reach the extreme borderline from which one can point to the Infinite. Levinas, too, affirms that one cannot get in touch with the Infinite unless one engages and passes through the world of phenomenality and intentional analysis. One cannot "throw away the ladder," but phenomenology, ontology, and philosophy remain inadequate to explain transcendence and otherness.

Yet, there is a language in which transcendence can express itself without distorting the "invisible" face and the soundless speech. In *addressing* myself *to* another, I can respond to you whom I encounter, without reducing you to a theme. This possibility leaves you intact, but it cannot be a part of reflective discourse. In greeting you or listening to you, I respect your infinity, but I cannot theorize about it at the same time.

Infinity

In one of the first pages of *Totality and the Infinite* Levinas declares that "The Other [*l'Autre*] is *Autrui* and the Most-High [*le Très-Haut*]" (TeI, 4; TaI, 34). The "*and*" here is mysterious. Later on, after having quoted Descartes's analysis of "the idea of the Infinite," Levinas identifies the idea of the Infinite with the metaphysical relationship between the Other in the sense of *Autrui* and me (TeI, 19–23; TaI, 48–52). *Autrui* is thus infinite. Infinite here is the equivalent of nonphenomenological (but still "real" and "perceivable"), invisible, enigmatic, nonthematizable, not belonging to the "world," not fitting into any totality, beyond the universe and yet, thanks to the proximity of my unchosen responsibility, very close. As a substitute or a mother I carry the Other in me. The Other is the absolute toward which I transcend.

However, the infinity of *Autrui* is profoundly different from the infinity of God. The "most-high" Infinite is not only invisible in the enigmatic sense of a nonphenomenon who looks at me and to whom I speak, but He or She or It is also invisible and unthematizable in a different way than any other enigma.

Since there is no *Hinterwelt*, no backstage behind the theater of human temporality, it is difficult to speak at all about God's transphenom-enal and transenigmatic infinity. Wyschogrod has compared Levinas's thinking about God with the tradition of negative theology. Levinas himself does not want to be called a theologian, not even a negative one, because the term reminds him too much of the onto-theo-logical approach. To follow that route would be to turn his back on the exceptional rupture which otherness executes in the circle of Being. Yet, there are similarities between pseudo-Dionysus, etc., and Levinas. If we want to examine the resemblance, we must clarify how negations and negativity operate in Levinas's writing about God's always already having passed from an immemorial past "older" than all possible pasts. The denial of "His" belonging to any extasis of temporality, either to the present or to an extremely old or early past, or again to the farthest future, includes a positive element. It points to a transtemporal and thus metaphorical "before," which cannot be captured in any thought, but which still can be imagined and addressed as having passed in the proximity of the Other here and now. A comparison of this relationship to the relationship between you and me would necessitate careful consideration of the Jewish and Christian treatises on analogical imagination and thought written between Greek and modern philosophy, that is, during the fifteen hundred years of the most profound meditations on language ever.

Reason and Violence

According to Levinas, both Hegel's totality of systematic reason and Heidegger's thinking on essence or difference are clear expressions of the ontological tradition. Levinas accuses them of doing not justice but violence to the Other's absoluteness and of ignoring transcendence. Does this mean that ontology, and even the Said of discursivity as such, is necessarily violent? I do not think that this is Levinas's thesis. Violence is rather the effect of the absolutization of ontology. Within its own, limited horizon, ontology is innocent; in the dimension of philosophy, it is the expression of a necessary condition for a politics of general peace and justice. Levinas not only rewrites ontology when he describes the world of enjoyment or the interwovenness of Being and (inter)essence; he also derives the order of ontology, universality, and reason from the relationship to the Other via "the third." The limited validity of ontology as an integral part of his plea for justice and peace must be shown as a subordinate but stringent demand of the Infinite. Without transcendence, separated or absolved from the Infinite, the order of essence and interessence forsakes the pre-originary enigma of otherness, and the same must be said of world, nature, and art. The call of the Other disrupts *and rules* the order of Being.

Is this call itself a violent one? The command is certainly surprising, and even shocking. To be impressed, touched, affected by the Other is a kind of wound: the wound of love; but to consider obligation a form of violence is to not accept one's own subjectivity. Acquiescence to the ethical is the rejection of murder. This might lead to the torture or sacrifice of the one held hostage to the ethical; but abnegation differs from masochism, if it is obedience to what the subject always already "is."

The saint is a hostage who lives the passivity of suffering and death as the unavoidable flip-side of transcendence. *Fürsorge*, being sacrificed for Others, and subjectivity are one and the same in a being that is a being-for-the-Other.

Naming and Gratitude

The only way for us to posthumously honor the victims of mass-murderous death camps and politics is to save their names. That's why *Otherwise than Being* opens with an epitaph for Levinas's murdered family and for all those who were the victims of similar hatred. As Wyschogrod beautifully writes, remembrance or *anamnesis* is first of all the creation of an abode for the deceased by inwardization. It is the only way for them to escape the anonymity of a monumental and victorious history. Perhaps we could develop this thought into an ethical analysis of the tradition, insofar as it is the history of generations whose acceptance and legacy is made possible by the fact that, like Moses, human subjects in some sense live for the benefit of those who survive these subjects' death. To endure the sufferings of a mortal life for the sake of a just future in which one cannot participate seems to be the definition of devotion. The subject's vulnerability is a condition for its inspiration.

Wyschogrod stresses the purity of such an inspiration by underlining that authenticity is only possible by enduring an extreme passivity: "The one who works does not seek a personal soteriological goal." Appealing to Levinas himself she adds: "Work for the Other demands that the Other be ungrateful, for gratitude would reverse the movement of the same to the other by returning what was given to the self from which it derives."

This is certainly faithful to Levinas's text; it is an emphatic, perhaps even hyperbolic, expression of Levinas's concern that the Other's height or infinity, the asymmetry of the metaphysical relation and the nonegocentric character of subjectivity, not be blurred by a leveling reciprocity. However, I would like to distinguish between symmetry and reciprocity. Since I cannot avoid knowing that I am perceived by you as an Other who commands you, the asymmetry is necessarily a double one: a chiastic and reciprocal esteem and devotion, in which you and I are simultaneously hostage and divine for one another.

Since recognition, esteem, and gratitude are as urgent as bread, the refusal to offer them to the Other is a form of cruelty. The cross formed by an asymmetric but double devotion is the normal kind of intersubjectivity in a peaceful society. It does not exclude the purest forms of altruism, *if* gratitude is not received as a reward for endurance or donation. In seeking or accepting gratitude as gratification, the subject shows that it is not disinterested, and that its donation was thus not a pure gift. Factual gratitude is a sign of hope, however, and the response to it cannot be guilt, fear or rejection, but only gratitude for its grace. By treating authentic gratitude as if it were a reward, we would pervert its character; but such a perversion would show the greedy receiver's, not the grateful person's, impurity. Patience, sacrifice, and dedication are difficult, since hypocrisy is everywhere. The existence of saints, however—or should I say, the belief that saints are possible?—bears witness to the wonder of gratuitous donation. Such purity seems to be an answer. Even in the midst of death there is giving.

Notes

Chapter 1, Emmanuel Levinas

1. See, for the biographical facts recorded here, François Poirié, *Emmanuel Levinas: Qui êtes-vous?* (Lyon: La Manufacture, 1987); Emmanuel Levinas, *Ethique et Infini: Dialogues avec Philippe Nemo* (Paris: Fayard-France Culture, 1982); and Levinas, "Signature," in DL, 373–79, translated as "Signature" by Mary Ellen Petrisko and annotated by Adriaan Peperzak in *Research in Phenomenology* 8 (1978), 175–89.

2. Since "Infinity" might suggest a sort of essence or property, I prefer to translate "l'Infini," which the book's title opposes to "Totality," by "the Infinite," thus trying to avoid that it be understood as an ontological category. "L'Infini" is neither a property nor an essence of God or of the Other's face. The main thesis of *Totality and the Infinite* states that the Infinite transcends the dimension of essences and properties. Cf. also, *To the Other*, 109 n. 53.

Chapter 2, Jewish Existence and Philosophy

1. M. Heidegger, "Bauen, Wohnen, Denken," in *Vorträge und Aufsätze* (Pfullingen: Neske, 1954), 145–62; cf. M. Heidegger, *Basic Writings*, ed. D. Krell (New York: Harper and Row, 1977), 239.

2. *La philosophie et l'idée de l'Infini*. Cf. EDHH, 165–78, and *To the Other*, 38–119.

3. Cf. TeI, 129–49, 187–208; TaI, 156–74, 212–32; and "Le moi et la totalité," in *Entre Nous*, 25–52 (CP, 25–46).

4. I. Kant, *Grundlegung zur Metaphysik der Sitten* (Riga, 1785), 77–80.

5. EI, 108 and 105 (where Levinas uses "coupables" instead of "responsables").

6. The expression "*me voici*" differs from "here I am," insofar as it points at "me" in the accusative, thus rendering more clearly the primordial passivity of a subject burdened with an infinite responsibility *before* it can accept this responsibility. Of course, "*me voici*" alludes also to the answers given by Samuel and Isaiah to the epiphany of God in Samuel 3, 4.6.8.16 and Isaiah 6, 8.

Chapter 3, Judaism According to Levinas

1. DL, 32–34, 209; AV, 144–45, 152–54 (Nom de Dieu); 161, 176–77 (Révélation).

2. Here lies a radical difference between Levinas and Heidegger. Cf. the latter's *Brief über den Humanismus*, in *Wegmarken*, GA 9, 338 (169), and 351–52 (181–82).

3. DL, 29. Cf. DL, 19–20, 23, 44, 72, 135, 280–81; AV, 172 (Révélation).

4. Matthew 25, 31–46; James 1, 27.

5. DL, 214; cf. 277, 288, 290, 112–13. Cf. also "De Sheylock à Swann," *Les Nouveaux Cahiers* 2 (1966), 48.

6. DL, 335 and the dedication of AE. Cf. also, AE, 221–33; DL, 360–61.

7. DL, 209. The quote at the end is from Jeremiah 22, 16.

8. AV, 211–12. Cf. *Kierkegaard vivant* (Paris: Gallimard, 1966), 286–88.

9. See here chapter 6, section 6, 104–8.

10. This is the subtitle of TeI.

11. M. Heidegger, *Wegmarken*, GA 9, pp. 338–339 (169) and 351–352 (181–182).

12. TeI, 275: "La dernière philosophie de Heidegger devient ce matérialisme honteux." In TaI, 299 ("becomes this faint materialism"), the translation seems to use a euphemism for "*honteux*" ("shameful").

13. Cf. PP and the preface of TI.

Chapter 4, From Phenomenology through Ontology to Metaphysics: Levinas's Perspective on Husserl and Heidegger from 1927 to 1950

1. Cf. "Signature," in DL, 373–79; *Research in Phenomenology* 8 (1978), 175–89.

2. "Sur les *Ideen* de M.E. Husserl," first published in *Revue Philosophique de la France et de l'Etranger* 54 (1929), 230–65, reprinted in IH, 45–93; *La théorie de l'intuition dans la phénoménologie de Husserl* (Paris: Alcan, 1930, 1970) (*The Theory of Intuition in Husserl's Phenomenology*, trans. André Orianne [Evanston: Northwestern University Press, 1973]); "L'oeuvre d' Edmond Husserl," *Revue Philosophique de la France et de l'Etranger* 65 (1940), 33–85 (reprinted in EDHH, 7–52).

3. "Martin Heidegger et l'ontologie," in *Revue Philosophique de la France et de l'Etranger* 57 (1932), 395–431 (reprinted in EDHH, 53–76); "L'ontologie dans le temporel," written in 1940, but first published in EDHH (1949), 77–89 (a Spanish version had been published in *Sur* 167 (1948), 50–64); "De la description à l'existence," in EDHH, 91–107; "L'ontologie est-elle fondamentale?" *Revue de Métaphysique et de Morale* 56 (1951), 88–98 (reprinted in EN, 13–24).

4. "De l'évasion," *Recherches Philosophiques* 5 (1935–36), 373–92; "La réalité et son ombre," *Les Temps Modernes* 4 (1948), 771–89; "La transcendance des mots," *Les Temps Modernes* 4 (1949), 1090–95; *De l'existence à l'existant* (Paris, 1947 [reprinted several times, with a new preface, by Vrin since 1978]); "Le temps

et l'autre," in *Le choix-le monde-l'existence* (Paris, 1947), 125–96 (reprinted as an independent book, *Le temps et l'autre* [with a new preface], by Fata Morgana in 1979 and in 1983 by Quadrige/PUF, Paris).

5. See note 2. I will quote from the French text; translations are mine, unless indicated otherwise.

6. TIH, 98–100, 135–41, 190–92. Levinas refers to Husserl's *Ideen* on 243, 227, 228, 241.

7. DL, 374 ("Signature"); *Research in Phenomenology* 8 (1978), 178–79.

8. TIH, 222. "Husserl se donne la liberté de la théorie comme il se donne la théorie."

9. DL, 374; *Research in Phenomenology* 8 (1978), 179.

10. I quote here from André Orianne's translation of TIH, 119.

11. See especially EDHH, 48–49, 51–52.

12. "L'oeuvre d'Edmond Husserl," 33–85; EDHH 7–52. I quote from the text of EDHH.

13. EDHH, 23–24. The same critical interpretation is also clearly expressed in TeI, 95–97; TaI, 122–25.

14. At least since "L'évasion" (1935–36), Levinas had already begun a systematic search for the possibility of departing from Being (*sortir de l'être*), a search that presupposes a critical distance from Heidegger's ontology.

15. *Die Krisis der Europäischen Wissenschaften und die transzendentale Phänomenologie: Eine Einleitung in die phänomenologische Philosophie*, HU 6, 2d ed. (1954), 84.

16. DL, 374–75; *Research in Phenomenology* 8 (1978), 180.

17. Besides the articles mentioned in this study, Levinas published a short, but very sharp criticism of Heidegger's philosophy under the title "Heidegger, Gagarine et nous," *Information Juive* 13 (1961), 1–2 (reprinted in DL, 299–303). See here chapters 8 and 14.

18. In *Totalité et Infini* (1961), Heidegger is quoted very often; in *Autrement qu'être* (1974), he is quoted very seldom, but the discussion with him goes on.

19. In *Revue Philosophique de la France et de l'Etranger* 57 (1932), 395–431. A modified version of it is printed in EDHH, 53–76. I quote from the *first* version, because we are interested here in the evolution of Levinas's criticism of Heidegger.

20. See the note on 396, and other remarks in the text (for instance, the one on 430).

21. *Revue Philosophique* 57, 396. According to a letter of Levinas to me, dated 1 November 1981, he abandoned this plan shortly after the publication of his article. The notes Levinas collected at that time were used in his article, "L'ontologie dans le temporel" (1940).

22. Compare 395 of the *Revue Philosophique* (1932) with EDHH, 53.

23. According to the *Avant-propos* of the first edition of EDHH, the text (EDHH, 77–89) had been presented in 1940.

24. Levinas always translates Heidegger's *Verstehen* and *Verständnis* by "*comprendre*" and "*compréhension*," which are more easy to associate with the idea of totality than "understand" or "*entendre*."

25. EDHH, 89: "En posant le problème de l'ontologie . . . il a subordonné la vérité antique[,] celle qui se dirige sur l'autre[,] à la question ontologique qui se pose au sein du Même, de ce soi-même qui, par son existence[,] a une relation avec l'être qui est son être." Cf. Plato, *Sophistes*, 254e. The Identical or Selfsame (*tauton*) is here identified with the Self or the I itself (*le moi*).

26. *Revue de Métaphysique et de Morale* 56 (1951), 88–98; reprinted in *EN* 13–24.

27. Not for the first time without restriction. In his own systematic work, for example in *Le temps et l'Autre*, Levinas had already expressed this answer.

Chapter 5, From Intentionality to Responsibility: On Levinas's Philosophy of Language

1. Since this chapter pays attention to some affinities and differences between Levinas and Heidegger, it may be good to remember that for Heidegger also meditation on the status and meaning of intentionality was a major path from the tradition to a new origin, as can be seen, for example, from his course of the summer semester of 1925 on the history of the concept of time: *Prolegomena zur Geschichte des Zeitbegriffs* (GA 20). Certain elements of Levinas's critique of Husserl have a striking resemblance to critical remarks made by Heidegger in that course (see GA 20, 61) and the one of summer 1928 (GA 26, 169). Both courses point out that Husserl privileged the theoretical intentionality and considered it to be the most fundamental of all intentionalities. In his critique of Heidegger, Levinas addresses a similar accusation to Husserl's work and also to Heidegger's thought of Being and truth. See chapter 4.

2. E. Husserl, *Ideen zu einer reinen Phänomenologie und phänomenologischen Philosophie*, vol. 1 (HU 3) (The Hague: M. Nijhoff 1976), 52–53 (my translation).

3. Cf. E. Husserl, *Zur Phänomenologie des inneren Zeitbewußtseins (1893–1917)* (HU 10), 29ff.

4. Cf. Heidegger, SZ, secs. 31–34, especially pp. 198–200 (GA 2, 149–51). Levinas's analysis of identification can be compared to Heidegger's analysis in GA 20, 69–70. There, too, *intentionality* is interpreted as implying *identification* and "evidence" is defined as "covering identification" (*deckende Identifizierung*), whereas *identification* is explained as "showing that which is meant in the intuited" (*Ausweisung des Vermeinten am Angeschauten*). Levinas himself refers, with some reservation, to Heidegger's analysis of the "as-structure," when he writes: "'Quelque chose en tant que quelque chose'—la formule est heideggerienne" (EDHH 219; CP 111).

5. The second meaning is close to the meaning of "*vouloir dire*," by which Jacques Derrida translated Husserl's *Meinen*. See "La forme et le vouloir-dire," in J. Derrida, *Marges de la Philosophie* (Paris: Minuit, 1972), 185–207; "Form and Meaning: A Note on the Phenomenology of Language," in *Margins of Philosophy*, trans. Alan Bass (Chicago: University of Chicago Press, 1982), 155–73.

6. AE, 44, 46, 54, 56, 73; OB, 34, 36, 42, 43, 56. Lingis translates "fable" as "tale."

7. AE, 45–46; OB, 35–36. It is possible that Levinas, in using the words "narration," "*récit*," "epos," and "fable" (EDHH, 217–18; CP, 109–10; AE, 46, 54; OB, 34, 42) and also "*kérygme*" (*vide infra*), wants to allude to Heidegger's consideration of language as *Sage*. Compare Heidegger, "Der Ursprung des Kunstwerkes," in *Holzwege* (GA 5, 61); and *Vorträge und Aufsätze* (Pfullingen: Neske, 1959), 212–18.

8. For the following, see AE, 43–53; OB, 34–41. In Heidegger's course of the summer semester 1925 (GA 20), cited in note 1, we find the same series of concepts: "identification" (69ff.), "proclamation" (*Kundgeben*, 75–76), and "denomination" (*Nennung, Nominalisierung*, defined as "the form in which we seize thematically a *Sachverhalt*," 88–89).

9. SZ, 218: "Imgleichen erfolgt die Gegenrede als Antwort zunächst direkt aus dem Verstehen des im Mitsein schon 'geteilten' Worüber der Rede."

10. "Die Sprache," in *Unterwegs zur Sprache* (GA 12, 30): "Die Sprache spricht. Der Mensch spricht, insofern er der Sprache entspricht. Das Entsprechen ist Hören. Es hört, insofern es dem Geheiss der Stille gehört."

11. The idea of "unlimited responsibility," which I am explicating here, is constantly present in Levinas's work. See especially AE, 12, 60, 172–74; OB, 10, 47, 135–36. My responsibility for myself is not emphasized, however.

12. Compare SZ, 52–62 (GA 2, 71–84), 87 (116), 113 (152), 131 (174), 137 (182), 152 (202), 180–81 (240), 181 (241), 184 (245), 191 (253–54), 192 (256), 196 (260). See also GA 26, 233, 234, 236, 237, 247, where Heidegger affirms very explicity that totality (*Ganzheit*) is essential to "world."

13. In *Totalité et Infini* (e.g., TeI, xiv, xvi, xvii, 4, 10, 22, 33, 35, 37, 39; TaI, 26, 28, 30, 34, 39), Levinas uses the expressions "*se produire*," "*épiphanie*," and "*révélation*" to indicate the difference between the "invisible" face and the monstration or evidence of the phenomena.

14. AE, 7–8, 193–98; OB, 6, 151–56. *Dédire* is already mentioned at the end of the preface of TeI, xviii (TaI, 30).

Chapter 6, Through Being to the Anarchy of Transcendence

1. Cf. *To the Other*, 120–208.

2. In the main text, page numbers of *Autrement qu'être* are given first, separated by a dash from those of the English translation by Alphonso Lingis: *Otherwise than Being or Beyond Essence* (The Hague: M. Nijhoff, 1981). Where it seems appropriate, I have modified the translation. A revised text of the first chapter, with an introduction and explanatory notes, can be found in Adriaan T. Peperzak, Simon Critchley, and Robert Bernasconi, eds., *Emmanuel Levinas: Basic Philosophical Writings* (Bloomington: Indiana University Press, 1996), 109–27 and 185–88.

3. See chapters 4 and 5, above.

4. " . . . dans mon identité dépareillée" (x/xli). *Dépareillée* is not "unparalleled" but "made incomplete." The identity of the subject has a hole; it lacks the roundness of a complete return to itself.

5. "Vom Wesen und Begriff der Φύσις: Aristoteles' Physik B, 1," in *Weg-marken* (1967), 309–72.

6. It is not totally absent. Cf., for instance, 10/8: "it has known the meta-physical tearing off from Being" (*le métaphysique arrachement à l'être*).

7. In TH and TeI Levinas does stress the Other's height, and one cannot say that he drops it in AE/OB. In the latter, however, he shows that the beyond also implies the dimension of the low in the form of the sub-ject and the sub-stitution.

8. Cf. *To the Other*, 202–8.

9. Cf. the preface of TeI and my commentary in *To the Other*, 124–28.

10. Pascal, *Pensées et opuscules*, ed. Brunschvicq (Paris: Hachette, 1961), 468, n. 295.

11. Cf. E. Weil, *Philosophie Politique* (Paris: Vrin, 1956).

12. Pascal, *Pensées*, n. 451.

13. For more on Levinas's treatment of skepticism, see chapter 9.

14. The word *epos* ("epic"), which Levinas uses here to characterize the gathering, synchronical character of the modern practice and conception of history, might contain an allusion to Heidegger's use of the German word *Sage*, which can mean as well *saga*, as—in Heideggerian terminology—a rich "word" or *oracle* (cf. the beginning of section 3, 6/5). In any case, the contrast between Greek categories (*epos, ontology, kerygma,* etc.) and the language of the Other is obvious in these pages.

15. "Dieu et la Philosophie" was published first in 1975.

16. What is the meaning of "*par exemple*" in the seventh paragraph of section 6 (13/11)? "*Par exemple*" can be an exclamation of surprise or admiration. Here, it might also point at the exemplary character of the Good's goodness.

17. The "rays" of the Good which penetrate subjectivity (11/13) remind us of the "diffusive" essence of the Good in the Platonic and Neo-Platonic tradition.

18. In EDHH, 192, Levinas calls this service a "liturgy" and in 194–96 a "diacony."

19. Cf. Luke 17, 33: "Whoever seeks to gain his life will lose it, but whoever loses his life will preserve it."

20. First published in *Tijdschrift voor Filosofie* (1963), 605–23 (reprinted in EDHH, 187–202); English translation by Alphonso Lingis under the title *The Trace of the Other*, in *Deconstruction in Context*, ed. M. Taylor (Chicago: University of Chicago Press, 1986), 345–49. The quasitotality of this essay is integrated in HAH, 102ff.

21. EDHH, 201; TrO, 358. Levinas uses here and in HAH, 62 Bréhier's translation into French (Plotin, *Ennéades V* [Paris: Les Belles Lettres, 1931] 96–97). The English translation given in TrO, 358 and CP, 106 is very different. I translate here Bréhier's text into English.

22. Exodus 33, 21–23; cf. 34, 1–10.

23. AE, 14; OB, 12. However we read there also: "Trace qui luit comme visage du prochain."

24. AE, 11–12: "La subjectivité est le noeud et le dénouement—le noeud ou le dénouement de l'essence et de l'autre de l'essence." Lingis translates:

"Subjectivity is a node and a denouement—of essence and essence's other" (OB, 10).

25. Some important indications on the sense of "ethics" and "the ethical" and its relations to "the moral" and "the political" can be found in the interview by Richard Kearney in *Face to Face with Levinas*, ed. Richard A. Cohen (Albany: SUNY, 1986), 28–30.

26. "Ethique comme philosophie première," in *Justifications de l'éthique*, ed. G. Hottois (Editions Universitaires de Bruxelles, 1984), 41–51.

27. Cf. *To the Other*, 167–84.

28. AE, 24; OB, 19. "Starting from" translates here the expression "*à partir de*," which Levinas often uses to indicate the higher perspective from which the perspective of equality and general justice receive their meaning. See, e.g., AE, 19^{37}, 20^8, 23^{32}, 24^1; OB, $16^{19\ \&\ 29}$ (on the basis of), 19^{30} (from), 19^{38} (starting with). (Superscripts refer to lines of the pages.)

29. AE, 48; OB, 37–38. For the dependence of ontology on the Saying of responsibility, cf. also AE, 178; OB, 140; and AE, 9 n. 5; OB, 187 n. 6: "we will of course have to show that the necessity of thinking is inscribed in the sense of transcendence."

30. See note 28.

31. Heidegger, "Hegels Begriff der Erfahrung," in *Holzwege* (GA 5), 131.

32. DEE, 124–45; *Existence and Existents*, trans. Alphonso Lingis (Boston: M. Nijhoff, 1978), 72–85.

33. Cf. Plato, *Phaedo*, 114d6.

Chapter 7, The Other, Society, People of God

1. The "triangle" ipseity-alterity-sociality thematized by Paul Ricoeur in "Ipseité, Altérité, Socialité," in *Intersoggettivitá Socialità Religione* (Archivio di Filosofia 54, nos. 1–3 [1986]), 17–33, helped me to establish the perspective from which I examine the Levinasian work here.

2. Cf. E. Husserl, *Cartesianische Meditationen*, (HU 1), 124–35.

3. I have given some intimation of this in "Freedom," in *International Philosophy Quarterly* 11 (1971), 341–61, and in *Der heutige Mensch und die Heilsfrage* (Freiburg: Herder, 1972), 130–41.

4. I maintain the terms "experience," "phenomenon" and in certain contexts even "Being," because it seems to me that philosophy cannot do without them, although it can point beyond them. After *Totality and the Infinite*, Levinas avoided ontological language more and more. This is not because of any *Kehre*, however; the shift is rather a question of radicalization through hyperbole and emphasis.

5. Cf. TeI, 188; TaI, 213: "The third looks at me in the eyes of the other—language is justice. It is not that there first would be the face, and then the being it manifests or expresses would concern itself with justice; the epiphany of the face qua face opens humanity."

6. Cf. TeI, 188–89; TaI, 213–14; AE, 20; OB, 16; and AE, 200–5; OB, 157–61.

Chapter 8, Technology and Nature

1. M. Heidegger, "Die Frage nach der Technik," in *Vorträge und Aufsätze*, vol. 1 (Pfullingen: Neske, 1967), 5–36. Cf. *The Question Concerning Technology and Other Essays*, trans. with an introduction by William Lovitt (New York: Garland, 1977).

2. I borrow this expression from Professor John Caputo, who has used it to characterize the climate of Heidegger's thought.

3. M. Heidegger, "Bauen-Wohnen-Denken," in *Vorträge und Aufsätze*, vol. 2, 19–36.

4. Cf. *To the Other*, chapter 4.

Chapter 9, Presentation

1. Cf. "Langage et proximité," EDHH, 217–22 (CP, 109–13); and AE, 43–47; OB, 34–37. About the difference between writings and oral utterances, some hints can be found in AE, 217; OB, 170–71. See also TeI, 69, 150–53; TaI, 95, 175–78.

2. *Phaedrus* 275b–277a; "Seventh Letter," 341b–344d. Cf. TeI, 45, 69–71; TaI, 73, 95–98.

3. Cf. the analysis of desire at the beginning of TeI, 18–23; TaI, 33–36. If the later work does not often come back to the radical human desire for the absolute, this does not mean that Levinas rejects the analyses of TeI or deems them unimportant. His silence about desire may be explained by his emphasis on the "denucleation" of the subject and its extradition. Not only is there a danger of mistaking desire for a sort of *eros* that is our eminent *need*, but the subject (the I) does not have an interiority of its own that would be protected from its being delivered to the Other. In EDHH, 230; CP, 120, proximity is described as "a hunger, glorious in its insatiable desire." This desire is "hungry" from an absence that is the presence of the Infinite.

4. Cf. AE, 231: "A legitimate child of philosophical research" ("enfant légitime de la recherche philosophique"); cf. OB, 231, which reads "illégitime" ("bastard") instead of "légitime."

5. Cf. *Kritik der reinen Vernunft*, B 514, 785–86, 797.

6. AE, 214: "l'histoire de la philosophie occidentale n'a été que la réfutation du sceptisisme autant que la réfutation de la transcendence." OB, 169 has incorrectly: ". . . has not been the refutation . . ."

7. AE, 217; OB, 170–71. Cf. AE, 211; OB, 166: "the *simultaneity of writing, the eternal present* of a writing that records or presents results."

8. Compare what Levinas writes on the infinite regression as an expression of our finitude in EDHH, 224; CP, 115: "infinite regression—to the bad infinity—jeopardizes, all the more, the certitude of truth and is precisely for this reason also finite."

9. Cf. EDHH, 223–34; CP, 114–15; AE, 6–9; OB, 5–9; and AE, 43–65; OB, 34–51.

10. Cf. TeI, 45, 69–71; TaI, 73, 95–98, and Plato's *Phaedrus* 274b–277a.

11. The dimension of height (*hauteur*) is still very much present in *Totality and the Infinite*. Cf., e.g., TeI, 59; TaI, 86.

12. A similar conclusion imposes itself with regard to the relationship between the Other as *Thou* and the Other as the *third*. A further complication is that I experience myself, too, as an individual for whom I must care and as someone who is spoken to as well as one who is speaking to the Other who speaks to me.

Chapter 10, Transcendence

1. Cf. the beginning of "La philosophie et l'ideé de l'Infini" in EDHH, 165–67; and my commentary in *To the Other*, 89–90.

2. Cf. Arthur Rimbaud, *Une saison en enfer*, in *Oeuvres complètes* (Bibliothèque de la Pléiade) (Paris: Gallimard, 1963), 229.

3. Cf. the fourth and fifth quotes on the second page of AE, vi; OB, vii.

4. In this respect, the early essay *De l'évasion* already expresses a constant concern of Levinas's later work, notwithstanding the distance expressed in his letter of December 1981, which takes the place of a preface to the second edition of *De l'évasion*, with an introduction and notes by Jacques Rolland (Edition Fata Morgana, 1982).

5. Although Levinas insists on the nonreciprocity of the relationship between the Other and me, the asymmetry of this relation does not seem to exclude a double asymmetry in which I am "high" for the Other as the Other is for me. Cf. *To the Other*, 135–36, 171, 173–74.

Chapter 12, Becoming Other

1. I do not cite here all of Levinas's texts to which I allude. My debt is evident, however, in the fact that I borrow several of his thoughts and expressions which, by my attempt to make them mine, receive a sense more or less different from his. I hope that the difficulty of thinking for myself after, with, and between Hegel and Levinas does not obscure the profound recognition that I feel for all that Levinas's words and living presence have brought to me.

2. Cf. Hegel's "in den Bauch des Denkens hineinnehmen." Absorption by the stomach goes nicely together with the "bacchantische Taumel" in which the True is represented as a total intoxication.

3. The question is expressed in passages such as these:

> this still natural tension of being on itself that we have above called egoism, is not a wicked failing on the part of the subject, but is its ontology. We find it in the sixth proposition of the third part of Spinoza's Ethics: "every being makes every effort that it is capable of making to persevere in its being," and also in

the Heideggerian formula about the existence that exists in such a way that this existence is the issue for this same existence. (NP, 104)

We might ask if, to the authenticity for which Kierkegaard renewed our taste, there does not in a certain sense belong forgetfulness and suppression of this tension on the self that remains the Kierkegaardian subjectivity, and if a renouncing to self should not be the contemporary of this concern for salvation that philosophy takes too lightly. (NP, 105)

total altruism . . . that empties the Me of its imperialism and its egoism, even the egoism of salvation . . . (NP, 108)

The present study attempts to disengage this holiness, not in order to preach some way of salvation (which there would be no shame in seeking . . .). (AE, 76; OB, 59)

4. I use here the German translation by Josef Quint of *Meister Eckehart, Deutsche Predigten und Traktate*, 3d ed. (Hanser Verlag, 1969). On 170 of this volume, we read:

If you think of it correctly, love is rather a recompense than a commandment. . . . He who loves God in the way He must be loved and also is loved necessarily, whether we want it or not, and in the way all creatures love Him, must love his neighbor as himself and rejoice in her joys as in his own and desire her honor as his own honor, and he must love the stranger as much as his family. In this way, one is always in joy, honor and benefit; thus one is as if in the kingdom of heaven having joys more often than if he rejoiced only over his own good.

Heaven seems here to consist in a very human joy that ties living persons together by that which matters to them more than anything.

5. Matthew 5, 44–45, 48.

6. Luke 6, 35–36.

7. *Meister Eckhart, Deutsche Predigten und Traktate*, 189.

8. Ibid., 180.

9. Ibid., 186.

10. Ibid., 180.

11. Or "in the [quasi-mode of] beingness" or "in the essentiality" (*in der Seinsheit*) that God is in himself" (ibid., 214–15).

12. Ibid., 177.

13. Ibid., 184–85.

14. Ibid., 181.

Chapter 13, *Il y a* and the Other: Levinas vis-à-vis Hegel and Kant

1. DEE, 93–105; EE, 57–64; TeI, 116–17, 132–34, 137, 164–65; TaI, 142–44, 158–60, 163, 190–91; AE, 3–4, 207–10; OB, 3–4, 162–65.

2. Cf. E. Levinas, "Levy-Bruhl et la philosophie contemporaine," *Revue Philosophique* 147 (1957), 556–69; "Heidegger, Gagarine et nous" (DL, 255–59); TeI, 29–30, 49–50, 115–16, 121; TaI, 58–59, 77–78, 141–42, 148.

3. Cf. Plato, *Timaeus*, 30bff., 92c.

4. TeI, 187–91; TaI, 212–16; AE, 19–20, 84 n. 2, 103, 116 n. 33, 200–205; OB, 16, 191 n. 2, 81–82, 193 n. 33, 157–61; EN, 25–52; CP, 25–45. Cf. *To the Other*, 166–84, 229–30.

5. Cf. Aristotle, *De generatione animalium*, 736b28, cited by Levinas in EN, 44; CP, 40.

6. Cf. Adriaan Peperzak, "Hegel contra Hegel in His Philosophy of Right: The Contradictions of International Politics," *Journal of the History of Philosophy* 32 (1994), 241–64.

7. Among many places, one of the finest is the preface of TeI, ix–xviii; TaI, 21–30.

8. AE, 9, 17, 21, 148; OB, 8, 14, 17, 116: "null-site." The proper meaning of *non-lieu* is: withdrawal of a case by a judge.

Chapter 14, On Levinas's Criticism of Heidegger

1. Although I still have some reservations about my presentation of Heidegger's thought in this chapter, I have hardly altered its text, which first appeared in German in the collection *Heidegger und die praktische Philosophie*, ed. Annemarie Gethmann-Siefert and Otto Pöggeler (Frankfurt: Suhrkamp, 1988), because Emmanuel Levinas expressed his complete agreement with it when he called me after having received the volume from someone else.

2. "La pensée de l'être et la question de l'autre," in *Critique* 31 (1978), 187–97.

3. "Heidegger, Gagarine et nous," DL, 229–303. See also chapter 8.

4. Levinas's critique of Heidegger as expressed in this essay quotes many expressions and interpretations of the later Heidegger. Cf., e.g., "Die Frage nach der Technik" in *Vorträge und Aufsätze*, 13–44; "Bauen, Wohnen, Denken," ibid., 145–62; "Das Ding," ibid., 164–81; "Was heißt Denken?" ibid., 187–204; *Der Feldweg*; "Der Ursprung des Kunstwerks," in *Holzwege*, 18ff.; "Die Sprache," in *Unterwegs zur Sprache*, 32; "Der Weg zum Sprache," ibid., 246ff.

Chapter 15, Dialogue with Edith Wyschogrod

1. The first version of the following text was read in a session dedicated to the work of Edith Wyschogrod, held at the Convention of the Society for Phenomenology and Existential Philosophy in October 1992. From her numerous studies on Levinas I would like to quote here the following, on which my response is based: "Review of *Totality and Infinity*," *Human Inquiries* 10 (1971), 185–92; *Emmanuel Levinas: The Problem of Ethical Metaphysics* (The Hague: Nijhoff, 1974); "Emmanuel Levinas and the Problem of Religious Language," *The Thomist* 26

(1972), 1–38; "The Moral Self: Emmanuel Levinas and Hermann Cohen," *Daat: A Journal of Jewish Philosophy* 4 (1980), 35–58; "Doing before Hearing: On the Primacy of Touch," in *Textes pour Emmanuel Levinas*, ed. François Laruelle (Paris: Jean-Michel Place, 1980), 179–203; "God and 'Being's Move' in the Philosophy of Emmanuel Levinas," *The Journal of Religion* 62 (1982), 145–55; "Review of *De Dieu qui vient à l'idée*, *Review of Metaphysics* 36 (1983), 720–21; "Review of *Otherwise than Being or Beyond Essence*, *Review of Metaphysics* 36 (1983), 721–23; "Elementary Individuals: Toward a Phenomenological Ethics," *Philosophy and Theology* 1 (1986), 9–31; "From the Disaster to the Other: Tracing the Name of God in Levinas," in *Phenomenology and the Numinous*, ed. André Schuwer (Pittsburgh: Duquesne University Press, 1988), 67–86; "Derrida, Levinas and Violence," in *Derrida and Deconstruction*, ed. Hugh J. Silverman (London: Routledge, 1989), 182–200; "Does Continental Ethics Have a Future?" in *Ethics and Danger*, ed. Arleen B. Dallery and Charles Scott with P. Holley Roberts (Albany: SUNY Press, 1992), 229–41.

2. Only "Humanisme et an-archie," "La signification et le sens" and "La substitution" were available at that time; see Wyschogrod, *Emmanuel Levinas*, 219–20.

3. "Ethique comme philosophie première," in *Justifications de l'éthique*, ed. G. Hottois (Bruxelles: Editions de l'Université de Bruxelles, 1984), 41–51.

Index